State Capitalism

State Capitalism

How the Return of Statism Is Transforming the World

JOSHUA KURLANTZICK

A Council on Foreign Relations Book

OXFORD
UNIVERSITY PRESS

OXFORD
UNIVERSITY PRESS

Oxford University Press is a department of the University of Oxford. It furthers
the University's objective of excellence in research, scholarship, and education
by publishing worldwide. Oxford is a registered trade mark of Oxford University
Press in the UK and certain other countries.

Published in the United States of America by Oxford University Press
198 Madison Avenue, New York, NY 10016, United States of America.

Library of Congress Cataloging-in-Publication Data
Kurlantzick, Joshua, 1976– author. State Capitalism: How the Return of Statism is
Transforming the World / Joshua Kurlantzick. New York, NY: Oxford University Press,
[2016] LCCN 2015041700 (print) | LCCN 2015044813 (ebook)
ISBN 9780199385706 (hardcover: alk. paper)
ISBN 9780199385713 (E-book)
ISBN 9780199385720 (E-book)
LCSH: Government ownership—Developing countries. | Capitalism—Political aspects—
Developing countries. | Industrial policy—Developing countries. | International business
enterprises—Government policy—Developing countries. | Free trade. | Democracy—
Economic aspects. Classification: LCC HD4420.8 .K87 2016 (print) | LCC HD4420.8
(ebook) | DCC 338.6/2091724—dc23

9 8 7 6 5 4 3 2 1
Printed by Sheridan, USA

The Council on Foreign Relations (CFR) is an independent, nonpartisan membership
organization, think tank, and publisher dedicated to being a resource for its members,
government officials, business executives, journalists, educators and students, civic and religious
leaders, and other interested citizens in order to help them better understand the world and
the foreign policy choices facing the United States and other countries. Founded in 1921, CFR
carries out its mission by maintaining a diverse membership, with special programs to promote
interest and develop expertise in the next generation of foreign policy leaders; convening
meetings at its headquarters in New York and in Washington, DC, and other cities where senior
government officials, members of Congress, global leaders, and prominent thinkers come
together with CFR members to discuss and debate major international issues; supporting a
Studies Program that fosters independent research, enabling CFR scholars to produce articles,
reports, and books and hold roundtables that analyze foreign policy issues and make concrete
policy recommendations; publishing *Foreign Affairs*, the preeminent journal on international
affairs and US foreign policy; sponsoring Independent Task Forces that produce reports
with both findings and policy prescriptions on the most important foreign policy topics; and
providing up-to-date information and analysis about world events and American foreign policy
on its website, www.cfr.org.

The Council on Foreign Relations takes no institutional positions on policy issues and has
no affiliation with the US government. All views expressed in its publications and on its
website are the sole responsibility of the author or authors.

For Caleb and Jonah

Contents

1. The State Is Back in Business   1

2. The Types of State Capitalism   27

3. A Brief History of (State Intervention) Time   49

4. Why State Capitalism Has Re-Emerged   64

5. China's State Capitalism—A Closer Look   93

6. The Democratic State Capitalists—A Closer Look   115

7. The Lesser Threats: State Capitalism and Its
   Threat to Democracy   137

8. State Capitalism's Long-Term Economic Future:
   A Threat to Countries' Own Long-Term
   Development and to the World Economy?   157

9. A Greater Threat: State Capitalism's Long-Term
   Effectiveness and State Capitalism as a Model   175

10. The Greatest Threat: Resources, State Firms
    as Weapons, and the Two Big Authoritarians   203

11. Prescriptions for the Future   225

Acknowledgments   251

Notes   253

Index   277

1

The State Is Back in Business

In late 2013, in a highly publicized address to the Communist Party's plenum, new Chinese president Xi Jinping announced that the government would unleash the private sector, after decades of gradual economic reforms that left many of China's biggest industries in the hands of state-owned giants. Market forces, rather than the state, would now play a "decisive role" in the Chinese economy, Xi declared, a line touted by Chinese and foreign media. Many investors in China also interpreted the declaration as a sign of Xi's reformist plans. Some news stories compared Xi to sainted former leader Deng Xiaoping.

Xi, who had used his own political savvy to eliminate many rivals and make himself the most powerful Chinese leader within the Party since Deng Xiaoping, hardly shied away from comparisons to Deng, who oversaw the beginning of China's era of economic reform. Indeed, Xi portrayed himself to the Chinese public and foreign investors as a once-in-a-generation economic reformer who could streamline the Chinese economy, slashing waste and unleashing the private sector.

Clearly trying to emulate Deng, in 2014 Xi made a surprise high-profile trip to a new free-trade zone in Shanghai, the country's financial capital. The trip was designed to remind Chinese of Deng's early 1990s tour of southern China. Deng had used his southern trip to kick-start economic reform after the Tiananmen massacre paralyzed Chinese politics and China's economy as well.

In Shanghai, where media outlets favorably compared Xi's visit to Deng's "Southern Tour," Xi offered more promises that the private sector, not the state, would be empowered on his watch, praising the free-trade zone and urging local leaders to attract domestic and foreign private investment.

In late 2013 and early 2014, at the end of the eighteenth meeting of the Party's Central Committee, Xi and premier Li Keqiang announced more specifics of how they planned to help market forces play that "decisive role" in the Chinese economy. The Chinese leaders touted land reforms designed to make it easier for rural Chinese to sell their land, changes that would allow some state firms to go bankrupt and be liquidated, quicker approval processes for Chinese entrepreneurs and for potential foreign investors in China, an opening up of some energy projects to private companies, and an end to state-mandated prices in some sectors.[1] The two men promised that private companies would be treated equally, before the law, as state-owned Chinese firms, the first time any Chinese leaders had made such a promise. Premier Li also suggested that China could grow much more slowly than it had in years past—that Chinese people must accept slower growth as China kicks its addiction to cheap credit and cleans up bad debts in state-controlled banks, and as China makes the transition from an economy heavily dependent on manufacturing and state investment to one more reliant on services and consumer spending. In September 2015, Beijing announced more proposed reforms, including reforms designed to further liberalize state enterprises by pushing more state companies to sell public shares, giving boards of state enterprises more independence, and loosening restrictions on hiring and salary for state firms in order to attract better management talent from the private sector, among other changes.[2]

But Xi and Li's plans for economic reform, and a gradual economic slowdown that they called "the new normal," so far have amounted to little, and it is far too soon to see if the most recent announced reforms will have any impact. The sharp drop in China's stock markets during the summer of 2015, which stirred anger among Chinese investors and led some China observers to conclude that Beijing would respond by speeding up its economic liberalization, also has had little impact on the pace of reform. In fact, contrary to the impression perpetuated by top Chinese leaders that China continues to open its economy and reduce the power of the government over many sectors, over the past decade Beijing actually has taken back control of many parts of the economy, such as energy and commodities and information technology. The Xi administration also has clamped down on critics who question this continued state intervention or even argue that China's economy is slowing faster than the leadership desires. Indeed, state capitalism is, in many respects, on the rise in China— and all over the world.

STATE CAPITALISM SURVIVES IN CHINA

Since the mid-2000s, several generations of Chinese leaders actually have reversed economic reforms launched in the 1990s by former premier Zhu Rongji and pushed by admission to the World Trade Organization (WTO) in 2001. Zhu had forced many state-owned companies into bankruptcy, and made others privatize and sell off assets to survive. But since the mid-2000s, after Zhu Rongji retired, Beijing has been aggressively tightening government management of leading companies. Even under supposed reformist Xi Jinping, Beijing has been boosting state interventions in equity markets and increasing state subsidies to preferred firms in industries it considers critical, including energy, telecommunications, information technology, and most other areas that Beijing considers important to making the Chinese economy more modern, innovative, and globally competitive. One study showed that annually, Beijing and provincial governments set up eight thousand new state-owned investment companies to increase state control of industries in smaller cities and towns across the country.[3] China's State Assets Supervision and Administration Commission (SASAC), a kind of central administrator of state-owned companies, admitted in 2012 that state-owned enterprises (SOEs) now own 66 percent of all assets in China, an increase from 60 percent a decade ago.[4]

China's bank lending displays this trend toward greater state control of the economy's key sectors. Whereas in the 1980s and early 1990s, private enterprises in China had received increasing amounts of government loans, in 2009 and 2010, private small and medium sized enterprises got less than 9 percent of the US $1.1 trillion in loans handed out by government-controlled banks, according to economists Usha Haley and George Haley. Instead, state-controlled companies received nearly all of the $1.1 trillion in loans.

In many strategic sectors of the economy, the state companies are getting bigger and more dominant. Overall, reports GK Dragonomics, a leading consulting and research firm based in Beijing, the industrial output of China's SOEs has risen from six times as large as the median Chinese private company in 2004 to eleven times as large in 2010.[5] Today, of the forty-two biggest companies in China, only three are privately owned.[6] State enterprises account for about a third of all capital spending in China, according to a report by GK Dragonomics, whereas in most developed economies state companies account for no more than 5 percent of capital spending.[7]

Beijing now appoints senior directors of many of the largest companies, and they are expected to become Party members, if they are not already; the loosening of rules for hiring executives does not seem to apply to the biggest state enterprises. Working through these networks, the Beijing leadership sets state priorities, gives signals to companies, and determines corporate agendas, but does so without the direct hand of the state appearing in public. One study, by China scholar Minxin Pei of Claremont McKenna College, found that the Chinese Communist Party had appointed roughly 80 percent of all chief executives at state-owned companies, as well as half of all senior executives just below the rank of CEO.[8] And despite reforms announced in late 2015, Beijing still seems reluctant to let the largest state enterprises, in industries it considers strategic, go bust, a reform many economists have encouraged Beijing to allow. At the biggest state firms, reported *The Economist*, Beijing is "keeping party hacks in the most senior jobs . . . and cutting their salaries, a sure way to discourage top talent from the private sector."[9]

State-owned enterprises have become so resurgent in China over the past decade that their revival has created a common expression used among Chinese businesspeople, officials, journalists, and academics: *Guo Jin min tui*. In English, it means, "The state advances, the private sector retreats."[10] (Some businesspeople say *guo jin min tuia da chao*, which means a "tidal wave" of state advances.)[11] As GK Dragonomics found in its analysis of state firms, the strength of state companies also forces China's truly private companies into developing much closer relations with the Communist Party than they might otherwise like, in order to compete in many industries with state firms.[12]

Even former Chinese premier Wen Jiabao, who gave a series of speeches as he neared retirement that some observers interpreted as pushing for further reforms, actually publicly spoke out far more often about the benefits of China's centralized economic decision-making. "The socialist system's advantages enable us to make decisions efficiently, organize effectively, and concentrate resources to accomplish large undertakings," Wen told one group of top Chinese leaders.[13]

In the wake of the downturn in China's equity markets during the summer of 2015, Beijing's commitment to statist strategies was clearly evident. Some Chinese and foreign businesspeople hoped that the sharp slide of the Shanghai and Shenzhen exchanges might prompt the Xi Jinping administration to liberalize equity markets, and even the broader economy, since foreign investors worried about participating in equity markets that did not operate freely, and since Beijing would not be able to stabilize the stock exchanges without allowing a degree of market correction. The head of BlackRock, the giant money manager, and one of the few foreign companies with a license to trade shares on Chinese exchanges, warned that unless Beijing began to liberalize its equity markets, foreign capital investors were going to lose interest in putting money into China's exchanges.

Yet the reverse happened. During the markets' rise, Beijing had done little to discourage Chinese citizens from believing the government would ensure stocks rose and rose with no end in sight. In fact, Xi's administration utilized equity markets as a government tool to promote certain favored companies and types of innovation. State publications and prominent officials repeatedly praised equity markets, called on Chinese citizens to put their money in Chinese stock exchanges, and offered what were essentially promises that the markets were fail-safe forms of investing. In April of 2015, the state-owned *People's Daily* declared that China's bull market would continue surging, while in May it published an interview with an unnamed government insider—many China observers believe that the paper simply prints official government messages and attributes them to an insider's comments—who encouraged Chinese people to buy stocks, suggesting stock purchases were a kind of patriotic duty.

But many Chinese citizens had begun playing the markets with debt; margin lending in China had reached extreme highs by the spring of 2015. In contrast to most major markets, Chinese stock markets were powered by retail investors, not institutional investors, and so were subject to wild swings. A Goldman Sachs study of Chinese equity markets concluded that, as of early June, about 12 percent of the market capitalization of Chinese stocks had been purchased with debt, "easily the highest in the history of global equity markets." The study did not even take into account stocks bought with debt from China's shadowy networks of non-bank lenders.[14]

When the market turned bearish during early June 2015, this debt-fueled investing collapsed on itself. Chinese men and women sprinted to sell stocks to cover their debts, fueling a downward spiral. And there is no doubt that some Chinese investors—especially novices who had not previously witnessed a sell-off—felt betrayed by Beijing's past assurances that the markets were safe places where Chinese money would grow and grow. China's financial microblogs, where many ordinary investors chat, and which had previously often focused on market tips, filled up with broadsides against Beijing for "allowing" equity markets to fall throughout the summer of 2015. (By August 2015, the Shanghai exchange had fallen by over 40 percent from its highs earlier in the year.) In the wake of the market slump, few of the Chinese posting criticism on microblogs called for faster economic or political liberalization, of the kind some foreign investors and commentators suggested was necessary. Many Chinese investors demanded the government do *more* to "save" China's exchanges from the sell-off, even if doing more gave greater powers to the central government.

The government mostly attempted to "save" the Chinese exchanges rather than letting market forces play themselves out, even if they resulted in a major correction in the stock markets. Beijing launched several plans to reforms its exchanges over the long run, such as by curbing margin selling and linking mainland China's exchanges more closely with equity markets in more transparent and better-regulated Hong Kong. But these reforms were dwarfed by the government's efforts to control the market's trajectory. Starting in June 2015, Beijing poured state money into the market to stanch the bleeding, and is also believed to have been behind announcements by China's brokers association of a new target—4,500—for the Shanghai index. Beijing also halted IPOs, allowed for the suspension in trading in hundreds of companies that stood to be decimated by the rout, recruited state banks to funnel at least $200 billion to brokerages to help buy shares, and used official speeches and written commentary to assure ordinary Chinese that the market would stabilize.

Although the government eased up on its intervention in the late summer, by early September 2015, with equity markets falling again, Beijing started buying back shares on the markets once more. Some Chinese analysts and businesspeople speculated that the government propped up the markets again because it did not want them to be falling during a major parade held in Beijing in early September to mark the seventieth anniversary of the end of World War II. Beijing also launched highly public campaigns against Chinese financial journalists, short-sellers, and analysts who had dared question the fundamentals of China's equity markets or warned that they had farther to fall. Over the summer of 2015, the government detained over two hundred journalists, analysts, and other Chinese citizens who allegedly posted "rumors" online of problems in China's markets and accused Chinese officials of malfeasance in dealing with equity markets. In one prominent case, financial journalist Wang Xiaolu, of one of China's most respected financial publications, appeared on state television and "admitted" that his reporting had caused "panic and disorder." In his reporting, he had merely suggested that Beijing's intervention in the markets would not, in the long run, be successful in promoting stability.[15] Other prominent Chinese financial analysts also were hounded. As *The Economist* reported, "Police have also gone after executives with Citic Securities, the nation's top brokerage, eliciting confessions for insider trading in near record time. Then there is the mysterious case of Li Yifei, the head of China for Man Group, a leading hedge fund … She had been taken into custody, though subsequent reports said she had merely been summoned to a multi-day meeting with officials in an undisclosed location."[16]

BUT STATE CAPITALISM IS NOT JUST ABOUT CHINA

Although China's SOEs have received the most coverage of any state companies around the world, they are hardly alone. China is but one example of a new era of state capitalism born over the past decade, even though nearly all discussion in the West of the rise of state capitalism has focused on China alone. Throughout the developing world, many states are increasing their intervention in their economies. State capitalism today is hardly monolithic; instead, it is better understood as a continuum, just as free-market capitalism runs along a continuum from extreme laissez faire economics to a French or Scandinavian model of a highly regulated market economy.

Although some observers of state capitalism have suggested that only authoritarian states like China or Russia could be called state capitalists, in reality today's spectrum of state capitalists includes democratic states like Brazil and Indonesia; authoritarian states like China, Russia, Egypt, and Vietnam; and countries that lie somewhere on the continuum of political freedom, like Malaysia and Singapore. Modern-day state capitalism includes countries like the United Arab Emirates, Venezuela, and Russia, which have based their state intervention on government control of natural resources—often oil and gas but sometimes other resources—and state capitalists that are relatively poor in natural resources, like China and even India, have used government to build manufacturing and services sectors, encourage innovation, and create an economy based on far more than pulling resources out of the earth. It includes countries whose brands of state capitalism seems to have more staying power, precisely because they are not based on resource extraction, and those whose state intervention will fail—or, in the cases of Russia and Venezuela, already are failing. It includes a broad continuum of the types of intervention—countries whose governments control nearly all of the biggest companies in that nation, and countries whose governments control only a significant portion of the economy. It includes countries that are very open to trade, like Singapore, and those that are far less open to international trade. And it includes countries whose type of state capitalism could undermine the best aspects of free-market capitalism—innovation, entrepreneurship, individualism, and democracy—as well as those countries where state capitalism could coexist with individuals' economic and political freedoms.

Too often, Western policymakers and analysts have paid little attention to the rise of state capitalism, even as the number of state-capitalist economies has grown over the past two decades. Or, if policymakers and other opinion leaders have paid attention, they have focused only on China—they have not seen these distinctions within state capitalism, viewing state capitalism as either a threat to democracy and the free market or as a model destined to collapse on its own, and so not worth worrying about.

WHY THIS SHIFT MATTERS

But to understand this resurgence of state capitalism, and to more finely assess what is threatening or not about state capitalism, understanding these distinctions is critical. We first need to comprehend what is different about state capitalism today from previous eras of state intervention in economies, how we can better define state capitalism, and why the dramatic growth in state capitalism in recent years could potentially transform the international economy and international security.

Of course, almost every state intervenes in the economy to some extent. In fact, states have intervened in economies almost since the concept of a state emerged. But today's state capitalists are not like the statists of the last century, such as the Soviet Union or Mao's China; neither are they like the mercantilists of the seventeenth and eighteenth centuries, the European powers who practiced an extreme form of economic nationalism, including erecting high tariffs and other types of protection. The Soviet Union and Mao's China, of course, failed economically; after the collapse of the Eastern Bloc and the end of the Cold War, most developing countries embraced the idea of open economies and freer politics. In addition, no two state capitalists are alike, and this book will examine many different types of state capitalists.

Still, even accepting that there is no one definition of state capitalism, we need a more precise definition of who the modern state capitalists are, so we can understand how explosively state capitalism has grown, so we can weed out countries that do not belong in the category, and so we can better examine the successes and failures of state capitalists. No definition will ever capture this trend with complete precision, but for the purposes of this book, I identify state capitalists as countries whose government has a ownership stake in or significant influence over more than one-third of the five hundred largest companies, by revenue, in that country, a situation that gives these governments far greater control over the corporate sector than a government in a more free-market oriented nation like the United States or the United Kingdom. Generally, in these state-capitalist countries the government sees itself as having a direct role to play in managing the economy and guiding the corporate sector. I use the term "state capitalists" only to refer to countries and their governments (which I use interchangeably), not to any specific state-owned companies, although of course these state-owned companies are a central part of state capitalism. Below this one-third level of government ownership of companies by revenue, the economy is still determined primarily by the market, even though the state may play a significant role. In addition, setting the bar here disqualifies many developed economies, like France and Japan, whose governments are relatively interventionist but which do not micromanage the economy and the corporate sector to the extent of the modern state capitalists like China, Vietnam, India, Russia, Venezuela, or Singapore. These more developed economies, like France, may indeed use state funds to own large portions of some large French companies, but in these developed economies the government controls or has influence over less than one-third of the largest companies by revenue. Norway is an exception and qualifies as a state capitalist, although because this book focuses primarily on developing nations it will not discuss Norway in great detail, except as an example of some positive trends in state companies.

In many other nations, the government owns a majority stake in some companies but not as many as in the state capitalists; just having a state company or two does not make a country a state capitalist. Mexico's government owns the state oil giant, Pemex. Canadian provincial governments own energy companies HydroQuebec, BCHydro, and several others. Yet none of these countries have state-capitalist economies. Their governments may be more interventionist than those of, say, the United Kingdom, which has privatized nearly all its former state companies, but they are not state capitalists—the Mexican and Canadian governments own only a tiny portion of their countries' corporate sectors.

Governments' state spending also may account for more than one-third of an economy's total gross domestic product; government spending in the United States, supposedly a free-market bastion, now accounts for more than forty percent of GDP. But this government spending is primarily used for social welfare programs (particularly in Western Europe and Japan), as well as for defense; little of it is actually used to own and control corporations. Although social welfare programs, defense programs, and other types of state spending can give a government significant influence over the economy— higher defense spending sparks a range of flourishing defense-related industries that are highly dependent on government contracts, for example—these types of state influence are far more indirect than in the state capitalists, where the government simply owns controlling stakes of large companies.

In addition to the distinction between state ownership of companies and just state spending, and the distinction between state ownership of a handful of corporations below the one-third threshold, there is another important difference between the state capitalists and other countries. Most Western governments are willing, during times of severe economic crisis, to use government money to support and even wholly nationalize major companies—a strategy that could, in theory, lead to Western countries owning more than one-third of the corporate sector, although this has not happened in recent economic crises. But Western governments generally do not view such nationalist strategies as long-term policy solutions but rather as emergency measures. This was true even during the height of the 2008–2009 global financial and economic crisis, or even during the Great Depression of the 1930s. After an economic crisis passes, governments in most free-market-oriented nations usually withdraw state support for or outright ownership of troubled companies and banks, tighten up monetary policy, and again take a back seat to private industry.[17]

By contrast, in today's state capitalist economies, leaders usually view intervention in the economy and control of major companies not as temporary fixes but as central to long-term government policy and economic success. The 2008–2009 global economic crisis even sped up state intervention in many developing nations, but modern state capitalism was not born in the crisis. Its roots, as we will see, date back to the early 1990s.

Both the earlier mercantilists and the Soviet Union and Eastern Bloc states basically saw international trade and economic growth as zero-sum, and believed that the state had to control a country's economy completely, either through government directly or through the monarch's personal grants to trading companies. The new state capitalists are not returning their nations to the failures of autarky and communism; they have combined a high degree of state control of major companies with a degree of openness to global trade, as long as that trade does not threaten state control over certain key industries.

The new state capitalists have in fact opened their economies to some extent and generally embraced free trade, even allowing some of their state-controlled enterprises to trade some shares on domestic or international stock markets, though the shares are never enough to allow any outsiders to actually gain control of the companies. In general, the state capitalists today are far more integrated into the global economy than similarly interventionist states were during the Cold War or even the early post-Cold War period. Unlike previous state capitalists such as the Soviet Union or even the highly interventionist governments in postcolonial states like India, Indonesia, and Brazil during the Cold War, today's state capitalists generally accept that they cannot succeed by erecting such high barriers to trade that they isolate themselves. Some of the modern state capitalists, in fact—Singapore and Malaysia come to mind—are important pillars of the world

trading system, generally follow its rules, and—in the case of Singapore—
have been leading advocates for expanding free trade globally and in Asia.

Throughout this book, I also contrast state-owned companies with
private-sector companies. By private, I do not mean privately held—I simply
mean companies that are not owned by the state. The companies I call private throughout could be publicly traded companies, like technology giants
Apple or Microsoft, or they could not be publicly traded, like agricultural
giant Cargill Incorporated or many other smaller firms, which are normally
thought of as privately held entities. All these private-sector companies may
receive incentives from states, such as tax credits, loopholes in legislation
designed to benefit them, access to government contracts, and other incentives; they also may lobby governments to win business and alter legislation
tilted in their favor. However, unlike state-owned firms, these private-sector
firms are run by executives and boards that make decisions far less influenced by policymakers than state-controlled or state-linked companies. To
be sure, the state capitalists' SOEs resemble private multinationals in many
ways: they often use modern management techniques similar to any multinational giant, frequently have incentives to be as profitable as possible, and
sometimes fire managers who do not produce profitability.[18] But ultimately
the state companies are influenced by government far more directly, and
thoroughly, than any private multinational would be.

Although I define the state capitalists today by their ownership of such
a large percentages of their countries' corporate sectors, I also will briefly
examine some of the other ways in which state capitalists seek to control
and direct their economies. I will at times examine levers of economic control such as state spending on infrastructure, state social welfare spending,
and strategies to use state-owned banks to pursuing lending strategies
to companies in industries deemed strategic by the state. Sometimes the
companies receiving these loans are state companies; in some cases, they
are not state companies. Still, I only examine these other economic tools if
they are utilized to assist state companies, as in the case of much of the bank
lending and infrastructure spending designed to favor state companies, or
if they are utilized in a way that gives the government de facto control over
a technically private company. For example, as has happened many times
in Thailand or Brazil, that technically private company becomes so dependent on state lending or support that it winds up taking direction from
the government, such as allowing the government to pick the company

directors and other executive leadership, and to determine the company's long-term and short-term corporate strategies.

Of course, many countries spend money on social welfare or infrastructure or even on some incentives to promote strategic industries, to pick three examples. But not all states do so to foster state companies or to gain control of technically private companies. In state capitalists like China, the government views infrastructure investment as useful for two reasons—actually improving the quality of the country's physical infrastructure and bolstering state companies that are usually given infrastructure projects, often with little competition. So, I do not examine the many examples of governments spending money to promote industries or concepts but not to control companies—American or Canadian tax incentives for companies to invest in certain types of renewable energy these governments consider strategic, for instance.

Neither do I examine in great detail the sovereign wealth funds (SWFs)—state-owned investment vehicles like the Abu Dhabi Investment Authority or the China Investment Corporation—that have amassed some of the largest pools of capital of any funds in the world. Although these state-owned funds are important players in the modern international economy, and although I briefly discuss the funds, in the context of how they help support state-owned companies and work together with state development banks, I do not examine the SWFs in great detail in order to keep the scope of this book focused on state companies and the broader impact of state capitalism on global economics and security. The development of SWFs is the focus of many highly technical books that only examine the SWFs, and do so in much more detail than I could ever muster. Many SWFs also have been around for decades, giving scholars much more time to study them.

What's more, although the size and number of state funds has grown in the past decade, I do not believe their emergence poses the kind of challenge to liberal economics and politics that state capitalism, via state companies, could pose. There is less to distinguish SWFs from other types of investment vehicles—hedge funds, for example—than there is to distinguish state-owned companies from their free-market multinational competitors. Many of the SWFs have more transparency than state companies, and most of the SWFs operate within similar boundaries and norms as privately held investment vehicles like hedge funds.

Rank	Country	GDP (Millions of US Dollars)	Rank	Country	GDP (Millions of US Dollars)
1	United States	17,348,075	31	**United Arab Emirates**	399,451
2	**China**	10,356,508	32	Colombia	377,867
3	Japan	4,602,367	33	South Africa	350,082
4	Germany	3,874,437	34	Denmark	342,362
5	United Kingdom	2,950,039	35	**Malaysia**	338,108
6	France	2,833,687	36	**Singapore**	307,872
7	**Brazil**	2,346,583	37	Israel	305,673
8	Italy	2,147,744	38	Hong Kong	290,896
9	**India**	2,051,228	39	**Egypt**	286,435
10	**Russia**	1,860,598	40	Philippines	284,618
11	Canada	1,785,387	41	Finland	272,649
12	Australia	1,442,722	42	Chile	258,017
13	South Korea	1,410,383	43	Ireland	250,814
14	Spain	1,406,538	44	Pakistan	246,849
15	Mexico	1,291,062	45	Greece	237,970
16	**Indonesia**	888,648	46	Portugal	229,948
17	Netherlands	880,716	47	Iraq	223,508
18	Turkey	798,332	48	**Kazakhstan**	216,036
19	**Saudi Arabia**	746,248	49	**Algeria**	213,518
20	Switzerland	703,852	50	**Qatar**	210,109
21	Nigeria	573,999	51	**Venezuela**	206,252
22	Sweden	570,591	52	Czech Republic	205,270
23	Poland	547,894	53	Peru	202,642
24	**Argentina**	543,061	54	Romania	199,093
25	Belgium	534,230	55	New Zealand	197,502
26	Taiwan	529,597	56	**Vietnam**	185,897
27	**Norway**	499,817	57	Bangladesh	183,824
28	Austria	437,582	58	**Kuwait**	172,608
29	**Iran**	416,490	59	Hungary	136,989
30	**Thailand**	404,824	60	Ukraine	130,660

FIGURE 1.1. Biggest Economies in the World, with the State Capitalists in Bold.
Data: International Monetary Fund statistics, author's research.

STATE CAPITALISM IS GROWING

How do we know that state capitalism has expanded over the past two decades, and why does this growth in state capitalism matter so much—to the global economy, to global security, and to the United States itself? For one thing, the number of countries where the state controls more than one-third of the largest companies has steadily risen from its low point in the late 1990s—during the height of post-Cold War privatizations of former communist countries and other developing nations in Africa, Latin America, Asia, and Eastern Europe. In addition, global economic surveys show that state intervention in economies has increased over this time period, particularly among the countries above the one-third threshold. Several of the annual ratings surveys that analyze the state of economic freedom in the world agree that the growth of free-market capitalism has stalled and reversed since the mid-2000s, in part because of the rise of state capitalism. One of the two major international surveys of global economic freedom and the growth or decline of free-market policies, conducted by Canada's Fraser Institute, examines the policies and institutions in each nation to see how supportive they are of economic freedom and free markets—policies and institutions like legal systems that provide for voluntary exchange controlled by markets, property rights and protection from theft, freedom to enter and compete in markets, freedom to trade internationally, regulation, and government control of corporations. The Fraser Institute's research shows that average economic freedom has mostly stagnated since 2007, in part because of the growth of state capitalism.[19] Because of the rise of state capitalism, central planning "has made a comeback," particularly in developing regions of Asia and Latin America, the Fraser Institute notes.[20]

The second leading study of economic freedom and free markets in the world, produced annually by Washington think tank the Heritage Foundation, has had similar findings. The Heritage Foundation's annual Index of Economic Freedom uses categories like property rights, fiscal freedom, investment freedom, trade freedom, and business freedom to analyze the overall state of economic freedom in each nation and then compile regional and global averages of economic freedom and adherence to free-market economics. Although the Heritage Foundation is considered a relatively conservative and partisan organization in dealing with domestic US policy, its index is highly respected. In its most recent Index of Economic

Freedom, Heritage found that the global advance toward economic freedom, which had taken off in the late 1990s and early 2000s, has essentially stagnated.[21] Global economic freedom has stagnated for most of the past five years in the annual Index, in fact, in large part because of the growth of state capitalism in the developing world, and particularly in the group of countries identified here by the definition of state capitalism. Breaking the world down by regions, the most recent Index showed that in most developing regions of the world—Latin America, Asia, sub-Saharan Africa, the Middle East—economic freedom regressed or stagnated and state intervention increased the previous year, as it had, overall, since the latter half of the 2000s.[22] The ranking came out even before the Chinese government's massive intervention in China's equity markets during the summer of 2015. In regional giant Brazil, for example, the Index showed that economic freedom and free-market capitalism regressed the previous year, as it had for several prior years as well. "The state maintains an extensive presence in many sectors . . . [and] there is substantial tolerance [among the public] for state meddling in the economy," the Index's analysis of Brazil noted.[23] Similarly, the Index's scores of economic freedom and free-market capitalism for regional powers South Africa and Indonesia have slid year after year since the early 2000s, again largely because of growing state capitalism in these countries. In Indonesia, for instance, the Index noted that government spending has increased repeatedly over the past ten years. This spending is partly on new state outlays for stimulus measures and social welfare programs, and partly on nationalizing or subsidizing formerly private companies. The Indonesian government also is "introducing trade and investment barriers that include limits on ownership of banks and mines and export taxes," the Index's report on Indonesia noted.[24] Indeed, executives from several foreign resources companies operating in Indonesia said they found the business climate more challenging there in the mid-2010s than at any time in two decades, as the government erected new barriers to resource investment, tried to renegotiate tax deals with foreign investors who had already sunk capital into the country, and tore up bilateral investment treaties with a range of countries, among other decisions.[25]

One might think that statist economic strategies would always prove political winners, in any time period, since these policies could involve massive government spending on popular programs like job creation initiatives or handouts to small businesses and/or the poor. Yet fifteen years ago, politicians in large developing countries like Thailand and Brazil won major elections or led massive popular movements while advocating slashing the role of the state in the economy, cutting subsidies to state companies, balancing budgets so that the state did not run a primary deficit, and unleashing market forces in many sectors of the economy.[26]

In addition, polling across developing countries reveals deteriorating trust in free markets and free politics, and a growing interest in other, more interventionist models. In annual surveys conducted in 2011, 2012, 2013, and 2014, the polling firm GlobeScan and the *BBC World Service* together polled people in twenty-two nations, including many developing nations. In nearly every state polled, publics had deteriorating opinions of free-market capitalism, with significant pluralities believing that free-market capitalism was "fatally flawed and needed to be replaced" with some other kind of economic model.[27]

THE STATE CAPITALISTS COULD SUCCEED . . . OR THEY COULD BE ENORMOUS FAILURES

In some of the state capitalists, a combination of cheap state funding, political support for certain industries, and modern management techniques has proven successful, at least in the short term; the longer-term economic consequences, for these countries and for the world, could be significant. Since the early 2000s, for example, Chinese firms, many of them state controlled, have come to dominate global industries from high-end glass production to telecommunications infrastructure to paper manufacturing to cell phone chip production. China is projected to soon become the largest economy in the world in total GDP at purchasing power parity, surpassing the United States. (Purchasing power parity as a measure takes into account the strength of each country's currency.) As we will see, China's growth is not simply a result of a country with such a large population and entrepreneurial drive opening up to the world—China's growth is due in significant measure to its careful economic strategy, its relatively efficient state capitalism. This state capitalism poses significant possible long-term dangers— to China's ability to make further economic strides, to political reform in China, to Chinese innovation, and to the region's security. But China's economic strategy has played a role in its growth, though at the same time Beijing has amassed significant amounts of debt. Overall, by the summer of 2015, China's economy had the highest debt to GDP ratio of any of the world's ten largest economies. Although China has enormous cash reserves, eventually the Chinese government will have to grapple with the country's debt, moving China to an economic model somewhat less dependent on state spending and on exports. Still, even with this debt load, and with a severe downturn in China's stock markets, the country managed to grow by over 6 percent in 2015, a far higher figure than nearly every other major economy. Job growth, consumer spending, and other important indicators of economic health in China remained relatively robust. By the end of 2015, even China's stock exchanges were rallying once again.

Despite some scholars' arguments that no country's growth trajectory can compare to China's, China is not so unique, and the ability of some state capitalists to use state intervention to promote growth and innovation is another reason to examine modern state capitalism in detail. For example, in many industries controlled in part by Brasilia, Brazil now boasts world-beaters. Yet as we will see, at the same time, Brasilia's control has caused serious conflicts of interest and facilitated graft, and eventually led to a dramatic slowdown in the Brazilian economy and fears that Brazil might return to the cycles of recession and hyperinflation that it faced in previous decades. While China faced a near collapse in its equity markets in mid-2015, Brazil's government was rocked by a series of corruption scandals at some of the largest state enterprises; the chief of staff of Brazil's former president, Luiz Ignacio Lula da Silva, was charged with corruption, and the treasurer of Lula's party and a prominent senator from the ruling party were charged with corruption as well.[28] The chairman of Petrobras, the giant state oil company, stepped down in the midst of the corruption scandals. But the Brazilian government also has used its power to fund innovative companies that otherwise might have been unable to raise capital, and to nurture these firms until they grew large enough to compete domestically and internationally.

Three decades ago, the Brazilian government gave aircraft manufacturer Embraer lucrative contracts and other subsidies, seeing that it could potentially find a niche in smaller, regional aircraft that would not have to compete directly with giants Boeing and Airbus. Private investors were dubious, at first, of Embraer's chances, and with only private investment and a focus on short-term profits, the company probably would have failed, as did nearly every other regional jet maker in the world during the 1970s and 1980s. Instead, Embraer increasingly flourished, refining regional jet technology, and now is the world's biggest producer of regional jets.[29]

Although the Brazilian government still retains some control over Embraer by owning a percentage of Embraer shares, the company has now held several successful public share offerings.

WHY IS STATE CAPITALISM SPREADING TODAY?

There are several reasons why the world entered a new era of state capitalism, and we will discuss the reasons for state capitalism's emergence today at length in Chapter 4. For one, across the developing world over the past decade, the first and second generations of elected leaders have, with some exceptions, proven to be almost as autocratic as the autocrats they replaced. Elected leaders such as former president Hugo Chavez of Venezuela, President Jacob Zuma of South Africa, or Prime Minister Najib tun Razak of Malaysia, often have turned into a kind of elected autocrat, believing that one need only win elections, after which one can use power to destroy the rule of law, judiciary, loyal opposition, independent bureaucracy, and other checks and balances that comprise the constitutional elements of democracy. These elected autocrats have not taken their nations back to the harshest types of authoritarian rule, similar to the Soviet Union or Mao's China. And even in countries that have not made the transition to democracy, like China, new generations of leaders, unlike the totalitarian dictators of the twentieth century, cannot keep themselves in power only through repression. Instead, both the elected autocrats and even the leaders of modern authoritarian societies like China or Vietnam rely on mild (compared to the twentieth century's autocrats) repression combined with producing strong economic growth to retain their popularity and support their own legitimacy. Yet precisely because these new leaders—whether elected autocrats or actual autocrats (as in China) dependent to some degree on public support—are not true democrats, they desire growth that makes their nations internationally competitive but also buttresses their own legitimacy and political power. The ideal type of growth, then, for these leaders is modern state capitalism. When successful, this model is a type of capitalism that opens economies to the world enough to build trade surpluses, keeps growth high enough to absorb labor market entrants, strengthens leading industries, and promotes innovation, but simultaneously makes the government more dominant over the economy and, potentially, the political system.

At the same time as the rise of these elected autocrats and modern authoritarians, other international trends have combined to cause developing nations to question the wisdom of free-market, neoliberal economics, even after challenges to more statist economies like Brazil's and China's emerged in the middle of the 2010s. The Western financial crisis of the late 2000s dented the "Washington Consensus" idea that a combination of free-market economics and free politics is necessarily the wisest course for developing nations.

The failings of the Washington Consensus had many reverberations. In my previous book, *Democracy in Retreat: The Revolt of the Middle Class and the Worldwide Decline in Representative Government*, I chronicled how leaders in young post-Cold War democracies, and their advocates in the West, too often oversold democracy in the immediate post-Cold War period as an immediate panacea for the economy, suggesting that democratization also would bring rapid growth. When democratic change did not necessarily bring strong growth—economies in places like the Eastern Bloc, Africa, and Latin America struggled while democratizing in the 1990s— many publics soured on the notion of democracy itself. This souring had many effects: decreased public participation in politics; nostalgia for previous authoritarian eras; the rise of elected autocrats; increasingly poisoned, violent election campaigns; and sometimes an outright return to autocracy, whether through a coup or some other extra-constitutional means, like violent street protests that, as in Ukraine or Thailand, force leaders to give up office or even precipitate a military intervention in politics. In Thailand, for example, studies by researchers at the Johns Hopkins School of Advanced International Studies showed that over an eleven-year period between 2000 and 2011, Thais' support for democracy became noticeably weaker, while "authoritarian attitudes [i.e., support for authoritarian rule] became stronger."[30]

But the Washington Consensus's failings did not reverberate only in the ways I analyzed in *Democracy in Retreat*. Disillusionment with the Washington Consensus model goes back more than a decade in the developing world, as the first post-Cold War years did not produce the kind of growth and equality people in many developing nations had hoped for. In some countries, such as Kenya, Hungary, or Nigeria, publics soured on democracy, but they still generally held to a belief in free-market economics. In other places, like Russia, the West's economic failings inspired a desire for both more centralized, even authoritarian, politics and more centralized economics. And in still other countries like Brazil or Indonesia or South Africa, the holes in the Washington Consensus—and the continued strong growth of some countries that did not follow the Washington Consensus economic model—created a yearning for different economic paradigms even as publics remained strongly in favor of democratic political systems.

This yearning for different economic paradigms, and the state capitalism that has emerged in both democracies and autocracies, is now deep-rooted and not linked to any rise or plummet in the international financial system or global business cycles. In many developing countries, this shift toward state capitalism has become ingrained and will be difficult to roll back even if people in those nations want to. After all, globalization and new communications technology, which are only becoming more intrinsic to international economics and to people's daily lives, have also sparked skepticism of the free-market model. Indeed, the globalization and new communications technology that 1990s pundits like Thomas Friedman promised would create a more level international playing field, empowering small entrepreneurs anywhere on earth, has not had such an effect. To be sure, as technology writer Chris Anderson suggests in his seminal book *The Long Tail*, the Internet and some other new technologies like 3-D printing have allowed some new entrepreneurs to cater to increasingly segmented markets and to compete with larger firms. Anderson writes, "As the costs of production and distribution fall, especially online, there is now less need to lump products and consumers into one-size-fits-all containers. In an era without the constraints of physical shelf space and other bottlenecks of distribution, narrowly-targeted goods and services can be as economically attractive as mainstream fare."[31] In theory, he argues, this allows smaller companies to level the playing field with larger firms, catering to niche audiences and thereby reducing the power of giant global corporations.

But as we will see in much more detail, Anderson's theories, if they apply at all, only apply to a small subset of the retail industry. In many other important industries like telecommunications infrastructure, natural re-sources extraction, banking, aviation, automobile manufacturing, shipping, and others, globalization actually has had the opposite effect of Anderson's *Long Tail*. Globalization *has* affected these industries, but in a different way than Anderson or other techno-optimists imagined. Freer trade, better communications, and global economic integration theoretically have made it easier for a company from any country to explore natural resources in places around the world, or to compete in industries like aviation or auto manufacturing anywhere on the globe. But at the same time, globalization also has pitted more and more large firms against each other in these industries, with only the biggest and strongest surviving. Why? Because globalization in these industries has not opened up niches but instead has made economies of scale far more important to companies' survival.

THE CHALLENGE

Seeking to buttress their own control of political power, turning away from the Washington Consensus model, and developing larger and more powerful national champions in strategic sectors like telecoms and resources, many developing nations have abandoned primarily market capitalist approaches. Instead, they have created a new era of state capitalism. Although states have intervened in their economies for centuries, in the past two decades state capitalism has become far larger in scope, as many of the most powerful developing nations have increasingly turned to state intervention. In addition, state capitalism today is practiced differently than it was for the past century—it combines statist strategies with aspects of free-market multinationals in a far more sophisticated manner than the twentieth century's type of state capitalism. State capitalism today thus may have a better chance of surviving over the long term compared to strategies pursued by Maoist China, the Soviet Union, and even democratic state capitalists in the twentieth century like mid-century France. Modern state capitalism has genuine strengths that these earlier challenges to free-market economics did not contain. The modern state capitalists, drawing on the tools of powerful governments and the strategies of cutting-edge multinational businesses, may be able to adapt, innovate, endure competition with Western multinationals, and expand state-capitalist companies' growth around the globe.

As a result, this new type of state capitalism, though not without flaws, has proven more resilient, complex, and multifaceted than many previous challengers to the free-market economic model. State capitalism represents a serious challenge to free-market economics precisely because of its adaptability today, because it has combined traditional state economic planning with elements of free-market competition.

This challenge, then, is at the core of the analysis throughout this book; state capitalism today must be understood by Western policymakers and opinion leaders because it presents a real potential alternative to the free-market model, and as an alternative it presentsserious threats to political and economic stability around the world. Modern state capitalism, as an alternative to more free-market models, is not always a worry for the world; we will see that it can coexist with democracy and with stable, responsible government. But overall, state capitalism usually offers a vision of the future that is more protectionist, more dangerous to global security and global prosperity, and more threatening to political freedom than the alternative of free-market capitalism.

In addition, state capitalism has expanded dramatically among some of the most important developing nations in the world over the past two decades. Most of the countries with this level of state control of the economy are developing nations, although a few, like Singapore and Qatar, already have become rich—though Singapore and Qatar took very divergent paths to wealth. Under "developing nation," I include all countries listed in the World Bank's research reports as a "developing country," even though some of the developing countries, or emerging markets, are now as rich or richer than so-called developed nations.

The fact that most of them are developing nations, including many of the largest developing economies in the world, is important: these countries will provide much the world's growth over the coming decades, and so will command ever-larger power in international institutions. To be sure, over the course of months or even a few years, some of these nations' growth rates may fluctuate, or even shrink—this book was published just as China entered a significant economic slowdown and Brazil's economy fell into recession. But over decades, these countries will power the international economy, and many already have demonstrated impressive records of growth. Several of these nations—including China, Brazil, Russia, Indonesia, Thailand, the United Arab Emirates, South Africa, and India—are among the thirty biggest economies in the world, while others—like Singapore and Malaysia—are major economies within their regions. Indeed, Standard Chartered Bank estimates that most of the growth in the world economy between 2014 and 2030 will come from developing nations, and that the majority of this growth will come from a handful of the most populous and economically dynamic developing countries—Indonesia, China, India, Brazil, Vietnam, and several others.[32] Many of these developing nations qualify as state capitalists. How these emerging economies manage their development thus will be critical to the world's continued economic expansion, as well as to the health of international and regional institutions.

These emerging powers also increasingly are serving as models for other developing nations. Although many observers inside and outside of China now talk of a "China model" of development, China, with its decades of growth and extensive training programs for foreign officials, is not the only country that developing nations are looking to for economic and even political inspiration. Singapore, Brazil, Indonesia, and other democratic state capitalists increasingly are running training programs of their own for officials from other developing countries.[33]

ROADMAP FOR THE BOOK

The challenge of state capitalism may not always threaten freedom and international security. Brazil has become more statist economically over the past fifteen years while continuing to democratize and to play a positive role in regional and international affairs. But the rise of state capitalism presents five possible threats to the international system, to free-market economics, and to political stability in many important countries. We will first examine the history of state capitalism and then offer a more nuanced analysis of the state capitalists today, dividing them in ways that make it easier to understand their differences, and explaining in more detail why state capitalism has emerged and grown around the world in the past two decades.

In later chapters, we will examine these five potential threats in order from the least dangerous to the international system to those that are the most dangerous to global economics and security. The first challenge is that, in young democracies, state capitalism could potentially put too much power in the hands of a few leaders and help corrode democratic culture and institutions. The second challenge is that in state capitalists where political freedom has eroded, the breakdown in freedom can contribute to political instability. The third challenge is that in some of the most inefficient state capitalists, like Russia, these countries' economic weaknesses, exacerbated by state capitalism, will lead to economic collapses that could shock the entire global economy. Since many of the state capitalists also are the world's biggest emerging markets and are expected to be the main drivers of global economic expansion for the coming decades, a substantial slowing of their growth will slow down the entire world economy. The fourth challenge is the opposite of the third—that the most efficient and autocratic state capitalists, like China, will promote their own alternatives to international economic institutions and free-market economic models. Indeed, policymakers in the United States and other developed nations must struggle to understand when it might make sense, for the health of the global economy and for international security, to enact policies that prevent the economies of powerful state capitalists from collapsing, and when it might make sense to enact policies that facilitate the strangulation of the economies of powerful state capitalists.

Finally, we will examine the fifth challenge—that the most autocratic and powerful state capitalists will use their state companies as de facto weapons of war, creating serious conflict in some of the most strategically important places on earth. Western policymakers clearly should worry that state capitalism could lead to more countries using their natural resources firms and other state companies as weapons—a possibility that, given events in 2013, 2014, and 2015 in Southeast Asia and Eastern Europe, seems more and more like a probability. The Chinese government has publicly said that its state-owned companies will take the lead in Beijing's "going out policy" of increasing outward investment around the globe, particularly in areas like energy, natural resources, and telecommunications.[34] China's state-owned companies make up about 80 percent of China's outward direct investment today, and the biggest of these SOEs dominate Chinese outward investment.[35] Indeed, several Chinese state companies have, since the late 2000s, become enmeshed in China's disputes with other nations in East and South Asia. Meanwhile, under Vladimir Putin, Russia in the 2000s and 2010s already has developed a reputation for wielding its state-controlled natural gas giant Gazprom, which controls the largest gas reserves in the world, as a weapon against other states.[36] After the 2004 Orange Revolution in Ukraine, which helped bring opposition leader and vociferously anti-Kremlin politician Viktor Yushchenko into the presidency, the Kremlin warned Ukraine that it would cut gas deliveries.[37] For a time, Gazprom resumed normal commerce with Kiev. But in 2013 and 2014 and 2015, as the situation in Ukraine changed dramatically, Putin once again put Gazprom into play, with the Kremlin using it against Kiev and against Kiev's allies in Western Europe.

Finally, after chronicling and comparing the threats of state capitalism, we will examine how the United States and other countries have responded, thus far, to the rise of state capitalism, and how effective—or ineffective—that response has been. Then, we will offer some recommendations—for individuals, corporations, and governments—for understanding and effectively responding to the challenges posed by modern-day state capitalism.

2

The Types of
State Capitalism

China's brand of state capitalism is but one type of statist economics, even though it has received by far the most attention. To
understand state capitalism today, we must examine the different
types of state capitalists, the varying strategies they use, and the
impact of these strategies on their economies and political systems.
In addition, we must understand how the qualities of the various
state capitalists have helped them succeed or led to their failure. The
variety of state capitalists testifies to the model's adaptability, and
the economic success of several of the most prominent state capitalists demonstrates the model's strengths. Later, we will examine
the durability of that success.

AUTOCRATS VERSUS DEMOCRATS

There are many distinctions among state capitalists, but two distinctions are the most important, and they are closely linked. First, there
are autocratic and democratic state capitalists, as well as state capitalists whose governments fall somewhere in between on the political
spectrum (see figure 2.1). Second, there are state capitalists who are
more efficient economically and those who are less efficient economically (see figure 2.2). The state capitalists that could qualify as

Most Autocratic	Hybrid	Most Democratic
Saudi Arabia		
Kazakhstan		
Uzbekistan		
Egypt		
Algeria		
Iran		
Russia		
Qatar		
United Arab Emirates		
Vietnam		
China		
Venezuela		
Thailand		
	Malaysia	
	Singapore	
	Turkey	
	Argentina	
	South Africa	
	Indonesia	
		Norway
		Brazil
		India

FIGURE 2.1. Autocrats vs. Democrats in State Capitalism, with Countries Arrayed along This Spectrum the Major State Capitalists' Continuum.
Sources: Freedom House, Bertelsmann Foundation, Economist Intelligence Unit.

democratic state capitalists—or that are at least near the middle of the democratic/autocratic continuum—are relatively responsive to popular sentiment, even if they do not gauge this sentiment through elections. But being fully rather than partially democratic does not necessarily help foster higher efficiency. Essentially, the state capitalists that fall at least near the middle of the autocratic/democratic spectrum are the most economically successful over the long run. Those that are the most autocratic politically, having virtually no political freedom and no ability to respond to public sentiment, also tend to be the least efficient, or least successful, state capitalists. Although being the most democratic state capitalist does not necessarily make you the most efficient, countries need to achieve a minimum amount of political openness to make their state capitalism efficient. In later chapters, we will see in detail how the (relatively) more open state capitalists respond to public sentiment, monitor and potentially replace economic policymakers based on their success or failure, encourage entrepreneurship, and help fill gaps where the market fails to allocate capital efficiently. We will also see how the most autocratic state capitalists tend to eventually stifle entrepreneurship, prey on their own

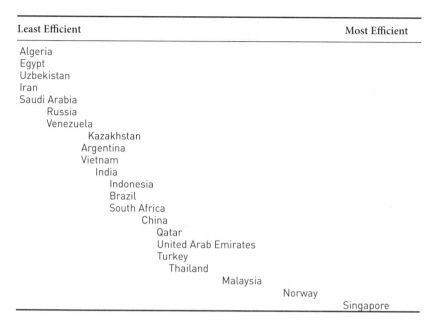

Least Efficient	Most Efficient
Algeria	
Egypt	
Uzbekistan	
Iran	
Saudi Arabia	
Russia	
Venezuela	
Kazakhstan	
Argentina	
Vietnam	
India	
Indonesia	
Brazil	
South Africa	
China	
Qatar	
United Arab Emirates	
Turkey	
Thailand	
Malaysia	
Norway	
Singapore	

FIGURE 2.2. Efficient vs. Inefficient in State Capitalism, with Countries Arrayed along This Spectrum.

Sources: Heritage Foundation Index of Economic Freedom, World Economic Forum, World Bank.

people simply to support a small group of leaders, fail to encourage effective management by economic policymakers, and undermine their own growth. And we will see that the most democratic state capitalists, though they may be only moderately efficient, pose little threat to the international economic system or to regional and international security.

In the most autocratic state capitalists, governments hold no truly contested elections for positions leading the country. Countries like Saudi Arabia do not really have elections at all; all of these states fall at or near the very bottom of Freedom House's annual index of political freedom, *Freedom in the World*, in the category of states defined as "unfree."[1] On the other end of the spectrum are the most democratic state capitalists, like Norway and India and Brazil, which are ranked among the politically freest countries in the world by rating organizations like Freedom House. They usually have free and (relatively) fair regular elections; protections for individual freedoms; free presses; solid checks and balances on their leaders, including independent judiciaries; and powerful anti-corruption investigators. Democratic state capitalists like Indonesia and South Africa, where democracy has emerged but still rests on weak foundations, are slightly closer to the middle of the scale between democracy and autocracy.

Somewhere in the middle of the continuum lie state capitalists that are hybrid regimes, combining some elements of democracy and some elements of authoritarianism—they hold regular elections that have some degree of competitiveness but are not fully free, or they at least have some degree of regime responsiveness to the public. These hybrid state capitalists include Malaysia, Thailand, Singapore, and Venezuela, among others. Indeed, these state capitalists lying on the middle of the autocratic/democratic continuum usually have copied some of the elements of democratic leadership, even if they are not actually democratic—and would probably deny that they had copied democracies. They tend to demonstrate a high degree of responsiveness to the domestic political and economic environment. China's political system, for example, generally rewards and promotes officials who govern capably and boost economic growth, and punishes those who do not. Other economically successful autocratic state capitalists, like Singapore during its most authoritarian periods, have utilized similar types of measures to make their governments relatively responsive.

Through this system in China, the Party gains a degree of public legitimacy and popular trust because of the Party's flexibility and responsiveness to public concerns or anger about certain officials. Though not as responsive as a democracy, the Party can be responsive to the political and economic environment in a way that more rigid or personality-driven authoritarian regimes, like Vladimir Putin's Russia or Robert Mugabe's Zimbabwe, cannot. And this level of responsiveness has, for now, convinced most urban Chinese that the central government—though not necessarily provincial governments—manages the economy and the country relatively well. In the most comprehensive recent face-to-face survey of Chinese opinion about the government, political scientists Wenfang Tung, Nicholas Martini, and Michael S. Lewis-Beck found that the average person's support for the government in Beijing was around 8.0 on a 10-point scale.[2] (Names of respondents to the surveys were kept necessarily confidential.) The three political scientists attributed this high level of support for the government to "political trust—a belief in the legitimacy of the government—[which] appears as the dominant reason for their broad support of the political system."[3] Most of the survey participants were urban, middle-class Chinese; rural, poor Chinese, who have not benefited as much from growth, might not say the same, but it is these urban middle classes who have the most political power and are critical to the Party's legitimacy.

Some of the state capitalists in the middle of the autocracy/democracy spectrum also use specific performance targets for officials and managers of SOEs; these governments often fire officials and SOE executives who do not meet targets.[4] In particular, President Xi Jinping, Premier Li Keqiang, and the current generation of Chinese leaders have become used to performance targeting and to the idea that the Party must maintain legitimacy with the public by defusing popular anger about corrupt, rich, and poorly performing officials. The targets set in these countries usually include a combination of quantifiable factors, including growth rates, fiscal revenue, numbers of industrial parks started, average income per head in the areas that an official is responsible for, profitability (for SOE heads), reduction of waste in government or corporate spending, amount of investment attracted to a province or subprovincial level, perceived amounts of corruption, and other factors. Officials and leaders of SOEs who meet the targets are rewarded financially by the central government; those who do not can be fired. Notable for an authoritarian state, in China the targets focus more on results than on process, according to a detailed study of China's nationwide performance targeting by Lynette Ong of the University of Toronto.[5] In other words, the performance targeting is flexible and pragmatic enough to absorb new ideas and not become too focused on ideology.

Over time, Singapore's performance targeting, instituted when Singapore was clearly an authoritarian state in the 1960s and 1970s, has helped make its economy one of the world's star performers. Targeting and punishment for ineffective officials and corporate leaders have created an environment that carves out political freedoms from economic freedoms and otherwise upholds a strong rule of law, which has made Singapore, already a major port and trading center during its colonial period, extremely attractive to foreign investors since it gained independence. Indeed, Transparency International, the global organization that analyzes corruption in each country, consistently ranks Singapore as one of the least corrupt nations in the world—usually less corrupt than the United States.[6] One comprehensive study of Singapore's government-linked companies compared them to a group of the most profitable private companies in the city-state, and found that the government-linked companies had better corporate governance and higher valuations than the private firms.[7]

In the most autocratic state capitalists—Saudi Arabia, Algeria, Iran—there is, by contrast, an almost total lack of responsiveness to the public. Besides a lack of truly contested elections, most of these countries lack other basic mechanisms to monitor and potentially respond to public sentiment. These highly autocratic states also have minimal rotation among their leaders, who tend to be highly insulated from the general public and much of the business community, compared to countries on the middle of the autocratic/democratic scale, like Singapore, where the government is in close contact with a wide range of business leaders.

As a result of this insulation, effective apparatuses of repression, and total lack of responsiveness, in the most autocratic state capitalists, small groups of leaders easily prey on the state. They turn the economies into vehicles for self-enrichment, driving out entrepreneurs. Many of these autocratic predators also are rich in natural resources, which is not surprising; natural resources can keep their economies growing for a time, as in Saudi Arabia, but vast corruption and poor environments for business creation eventually lead to slowing growth and uneven development. As many experts have shown, economies based on extraction of natural resources almost always have high levels of corruption and fail to achieve broad-based development. (Norway, which found oil after it had already become rich and a vibrant democracy, is a notable exception.) Natural resource riches often insulate the government from pressure for political reform and create easy avenues for graft.[8] However, as we will see, the most autocratic state capitalists also tend to make the worst use of natural resources, making their economies the least efficient.

EFFICIENT VERSUS INEFFICIENT

In addition to the autocratic/democratic divide, the state capitalists listed on our chart of the world's biggest economies in Chapter 1 can be divided into those whose economies are more or less efficient—most simply, economies that maximize their potential and those that, at least to some extent, squander their potential growth. The most efficient state capitalists, like Singapore and Norway, are some of the more efficient economies in the world. More specifically, in these countries, companies boast high productivity, capital and labor inputs are utilized well in both state and private companies, financial markets allocate capital productively, infrastructure and other government projects are completed in the most cost-effective way possible for quality work, and the country gets the economic maximum out of the natural resources it possesses, among other positive attributes.

Yet these economies, though efficient, still meet the definition of state capitalism, so it is not fair to say that they are efficient simply since they are, at their core, free-market economies. Singapore, despite being open to trade, is not Hong Kong, where the market rules and the state plays a minimal role in the corporate sector other than controlling the property market. If these economies were achieving efficiency simply by pursuing free-market strategies there would be little new to say about them. As we will see, these countries' state companies may copy—or even improve—some techniques of private companies, and their economic policymakers may blend some tools of state intervention with some laissez-faire strategies, but they still meet the definition of state capitalists we have established.

And as we will see, it is not true that all the efficient state capitalists are achieving efficiency in spite of their state capitalism—that they would have grown even faster if they had liberalized their economies faster, or that they have grown rapidly because of some inherent advantages over less successful developing nations.

It is true that in most of the state capitalists, support for state companies and state banks requires at least some degree of what economists call financial repression. Economists Carmen M. Reinhart and M. Belen Sbrancia define financial repression as limits on interest rates and the direction of lending by a captive domestic audience; states can set such limits by owning banks, by capping commercial banks' interest rates, or by imposing restrictions on financial markets in other ways.[9] Some economists believe that without this financial repression, countries like China and Malaysia would have grown faster over the past four decades.

In China, for example, the Chinese government restricts the ways in which Chinese savers can deposit their money, leaving them little alternative but to put their savings into state banks and get low interest rates on their money or to put their money into real estate or the stock market. The government also essentially caps the interest rates commercial banks can offer to savers. Since these Chinese deposits then go into state banks, and the state banks don't have to pay Chinese savers much for their money, state banks—and thus the government itself—are awash in cash that they can then use to buy assets in China and around the world, and to make loans to state companies that are, to some extent, thus subsidized by Chinese savers.

Because the Chinese government has not freed up deposit rates, foreign lenders are basically prohibited from competing for Chinese savers, and capital controls keep Chinese citizens from legally moving their savings off-shore. State banks have little competition to attract savers, except from what is called the "shadow banking system," that is, non-bank lenders who operate without government approval throughout the country.[10] Many years, the rate of interest that Chinese savers get from Chinese banks, about 1 percent, is lower than the annual inflation rate, meaning that Chinese people are effectively losing money by keeping their money in state banks.

Skeptics of China's state capitalism, and of state capitalism in general, argue that this financial repression badly skews economies. They contend that whatever efficiencies China and other state capitalists are achieving, they are achieving these efficiencies in spite of, not because of, the state's policies. For instance, the state's policies have helped build China's mountain of debt, they argue, and contributed to bubbles both in the real economy and in China's equity markets, where retail investors became convinced that the state would always try to ensure stocks went up. Without financial repression and other types of state control, they argue these countries would grow faster and would create healthier banks, stronger companies, and broad-based development. Financial repression in China, they argue, leads to banks prioritizing giving credit to state companies, making it hard for private Chinese firms to get bank loans and to grow.[11] Critics also say China's policies create a self-reinforcing cycle, in which Chinese men and women come to expect the state to prop up both the real economy and equity markets, creating popular pressure on Beijing to do so during times of crisis.

This skepticism about the long-term success of state capitalism, and the economic distortions it can create, is reasonable, but it is not necessarily correct. For one, even more free-market economies often employ some degree of financial repression. Many developed, and relatively free, market economies have banks partly or completely owned by the state—a form of financial repression. In fact, many free-market economies' central banks have, at times, intervened in the economy to keep commercial interest rates artificially low—another type of financial repression. Even in the United States, the Federal Reserve's post-2008 economic crisis policy of quantitative easing—a policy of forcing long-term interest rates to remain artificially low by buying up assets from financial institutions such as bank debt and Treasury notes—is in itself a form of financial repression, though hardly as severe as the type practiced in China.

What's more, throughout the 1960s, 1970s, 1980s, and early 1990s, several of the high-growth Asian economies that set the standard for development—Japan, South Korea, and others—also used many different tools of financial repression to keep interest rates low and to direct flows of capital into projects favored by the state, such as certain industrial and manufacturing sectors. Sometimes, these countries used these tools of financial repression to direct capital right into SOEs in sectors that Tokyo, Seoul, Singapore, Taipei, and others wanted to build up. In other cases, these Asian tigers used tools of financial repression to keep interest rates low and channel capital into technically privately owned companies in industries the government wanted to support. By keeping rates low and giving these privately owned companies, like Korea's giant *chaebol* conglomerates, artificially cheap capital, the state was playing a major role in boosting the prospects of these private firms. The tigers' use of financial repression to channel capital to favored industries helped these countries develop strong manufacturing and industrial bases, and—along with other factors like an embrace of free trade and the growing American consumer market—made them into some of the world's export powerhouses. Even the World Bank, which for decades had argued that tools of financial repression like capital controls, interest rate ceilings, and directing credit to certain companies would not be successful development strategies, admitted, by the end of the 1990s, that it had been wrong—a degree of financial repression had been partly responsible for the tigers' development and their creation of strong industrial and manufacturing bases.

In addition, it remains unclear whether China's financial repression—though it lowers households' savings and, in general, produces lower returns on capital nationwide than might be possible—actually is worse for growth and development than a less financially repressive economic policy would be in a developing nation. Although Chinese savers could get more return on their money in a more open economy, Chinese savers are more satisfied with the Chinese system, even with all its financial repression, than many Western economists believe. This satisfaction stems from the fact that although returns on savers' capital are low in Chinese banks, this capital has been used to raise standards of living and promote growth effectively over the past thirty years.

As James White, a prominent analyst of China's economy notes, this bargain that Chinese savers have struck with the state—low returns on capital if the state uses the money it collects to promote high growth and development—makes sense, even though it is possible that in a freer financial system Chinese people would be getting higher interest rates on their deposits. He notes:

> At the heart of growth [in China] is a focus on capital investment in infrastructure, designed to create more productive lives, funded by a government which may bear losses but is capable of capturing the still positive side-effects (externalities) from rising tax revenues . . . The Chinese are comfortable with low capital returns [i.e., not getting much from their savings] if the pay-off is a stronger economy [overall]. This has been the case . . . The aim is to raise living standards of all households. As a result, capital is used and treated remarkably differently [than in the West,] often to the consternation of external observers and investors . . . At a macro-level, the higher allocation of capital in China has led to falling profit growth and lower returns for capital [i.e., stocks, savings accounts, real estate, and other investments in China give poor returns compared to those in other countries]. . . . [But the state has used the capital it amasses to create] an economy that has achieved an unparalleled balance of growth and low inflation. China's economic performance in the last 20 years has been remarkable; very strong growth and low inflation.[12]

More generally, the argument that all of these state capitalists would have grown faster if they had pursued more rapid economic liberalization assumes that the market is always the most efficient allocator of capital, even in countries where stock exchanges are small and illiquid and it is very hard for businesses to raise capital in any other way. It also assumes that economic liberalization always fosters long-term economic competitiveness, when it remains unclear whether executives of private-sector multinationals always pursue strategies based on maximizing long-term competitiveness rather than short-term profits and/or gains in share prices. A recent study by Aldo Musacchio and Francisco Flores-Macias of Harvard Business School comparing the performance of Brazil's state companies and private-sector multinationals found that the most efficient state companies were competitive, in a range of sectors, with leading private multinationals.[13] Yet at the same time, lending by Brazil's massive state development bank may have pushed some private lenders out of the lending landscape, since the state bank offers government-subsidized interest rates that are hard for private banks to match. Some critics charge that Brazil's state bank may have made loans to certain larger companies favored by the ruling Workers Party, although it remains unclear whether these charges are true.

What's more, many of the relatively efficient state capitalists, like Singapore and Thailand, would have made only minimal gains in efficiency over the past forty years by lowering their barriers to trade, one of the aspects of economic liberalization, since they had very low trade barriers at the onset of their phases of high growth. Indeed, countries like Thailand, Malaysia, and Singapore have for decades already been relatively open to trade—sometimes, as in the case of Thailand, having as low tariff barriers as developed nations in many sectors.

Of course, freeing trade is not the only component of economic liberalization. But if the state capitalists had allowed faster liberalization in other aspects of their economies, they would have given up several advantages enjoyed by state planning and a slow process of economic liberalization. If the state capitalists we examine had embarked upon a process more similar to the shock therapy liberalization the economies in eastern Europe underwent in the 1990s, they would have had to give up the protections for state companies that, in some countries like Thailand and Brazil, have helped nurture nascent industries into achieving economies of scale and competitiveness. In addition, they might have given up the currency controls and other tools used to restrict currency exchange and speculation that in many of the state capitalists, have helped protect their still-developing economies from currency speculation and short-selling. Indeed, we will see how China's gradual liberalization of the renminbi has allowed it to keep some degree of control over speculation in the currency as the renminbi gradually becomes unpegged and floating and becomes used in foreign trade by Chinese firms and other companies. During the Asian financial crisis of the late 1990s, Malaysia also used capital controls to put a halt to speculation and rapid capital outflows. The International Monetary Fund (IMF) now accepts that capital controls often have some utility in developing economies.

Overall, many of the state capitalists already have demonstrated relatively impressive efficiency, at least for now; in the long term, state capitalism's efficiency remains unclear. Although there is no one all-encompassing annual study of economies' efficiency, one comparable to Freedom House's annual survey of political freedom around the globe, the World Economic Forum's yearly index of economic competitiveness is at least a well-researched attempt to rank countries by economic efficiency. The index, called the *Global Competitiveness Report*, analyzes each country's labor market efficiency, financial market efficiency, macroeconomic environment and overall economic policymaking, goods market efficiency, economic institutions, infrastructure, and several other factors—all to produce a composite score that basically demonstrates which economies are most efficient. Annually, efficient state capitalists like Singapore, China, Norway, Qatar, and Malaysia rank in the top tier of the World Economic Forum's *Global Competitiveness Report*.[14] Singapore has for many years either topped the report or come in second.

By contrast, the most inefficient state capitalists are, simply, economic nightmares and usually rank at or near the bottom of the *Global Competitiveness Report*. Among the lower-rated large economies are Iran, Russia, most of the Central Asian state capitalists, and Egypt, among others. These inefficient state capitalists actively hinder entrepreneurship, have major companies that are enormously wasteful of capital and labor, possess financial markets that allocate capital inefficiently and operate opaquely, rarely seek to produce infrastructure or any other state goods and services at low costs (since higher costs often mean more opportunities to steal from public projects), and suffer from many other hindrances to efficiency.

By analyzing where these Freedom House and World Economic Forum rankings overlap, we can see that most of the efficient state capitalists also are at least moderately democratic, on the autocratic/democratic spectrum. Why are the more efficient state capitalists normally those that rank as at least moderately democratic on the autocratic/democratic spectrum? (Qatar, an exception, has such a tiny native population and such massive natural gas wealth—it has the highest GDP per capita of any country in the world—that its leadership has to do little to foster innovation, efficiency, or broad-based development, since it has so much money and so few people to take care of.) In state-capitalist countries with a higher degree of responsiveness, governments have been forced by the public, at least to some extent, to use their power to promote innovation and broad-based development. These efficient state capitalists also have been better able to co-opt leading talent from the private sector. In large part, this is because entrepreneurs in these countries have a higher degree of trust—compared to entrepreneurs in predatory and autocratic state capitalists like Russia—that working with the government will not lead to their ideas and capital being seized, that the government is not only interested in grabbing for now but in investing for the future. The Chinese, Singaporean, and Thai governments, for example, have at times been able to co-opt some of the best talent in the country into state enterprises or into private-sector partnerships with state enterprises. Yet at the same time, these countries like China are not full democracies and so are not subject to the kinds of popular pressure on governments to spend state money on certain state companies and other outlays that win votes but are highly inefficient economically.

To be sure, Chinese and Thai state capitalism, to take two examples, have created their fair share of predatory elites. Thailand has more generals than the United States, with a far smaller army, and most of these Thai generals do little actual combat commanding. Instead, the generals sit on the boards of many leading Thai state enterprises, serve little useful function, and frequently try to overthrow the government, as they did in May 2014. But for now, predation in Thailand and China has not overwhelmed a legacy of solid and constructive policymaking.

It is impossible to know how much faster China and Thailand could grow if not for official corruption, but graft in these countries has not reached the tipping point common in some autocratic regimes, like Russia today or Myanmar during the decades under army rule, in which elite enrichment becomes the primary, rather than the secondary or tertiary, purpose of state enterprises. In places like Russia or Myanmar during the long era of army rule, the fact that state enterprises' primary function is self-enrichment becomes clear if one looks into how these state firms operate, as I had the chance to do several times researching Myanmar's state oil and gas company during the period of military rule. Past the point where corruption completely undermines growth, state enterprise managers do not make investments for the future, preferring to repeatedly strip assets from state companies for their own gain; Myanmar's state oil and gas company was, under military rule, letting critical petroleum infrastructure rust and decay, since the company's managers spent their time focused on how to move money into offshore accounts for the ruling generals. Past this point, state enterprises become so graft-ridden that absent regular state subsidies and book-cooking, they cannot be profitable.

Bringing the best talent into the government does not necessarily guarantee the regime's survival, which is why only more open state capitalists, those confident in their government's legitimacy, are willing to even attempt to bring new, fresh-thinking talent into government—the regime runs the risk that this new talent will push to further open up politics and even topple the country's entire leadership. Indeed, Singapore has for years co-opted many of its most talented young people into government and the ruling People's Action Party (PAP), yet eventually some of those talents tired of the constraints of what was still basically a one-party system. They left government and have helped build up the Workers Party, the first viable opposition party that Singapore has had in decades. In the past decade, the Workers Party has become a voice for change, but it also has been able to reassure the public that its leaders are not firebrand radicals, in part because its leaders formerly worked for the PAP or worked in public-private partnerships with state enterprises. The Workers Party in 2011 captured one of Singapore's multi-person group constituencies for the first time, paving the way toward a more competitive political system in the city-state. Although the opposition party did not make gains in the 2015 election, it maintained its control of the multi-person group constituency.

In the more efficient state capitalists, the government also promotes scaling up innovation by acting in some ways as a kind of venture capitalist, supporting nascent industries that do not yet attract significant private capital. These initial investments often allow small companies with ideas to build their businesses into larger and profitable companies.

Many of the more efficient state-capitalist economies also have achieved a degree of long-term macroeconomic stability, which multiple studies have shown was critical to East Asian economies' growth during the Cold War. Brazil, which suffered from hyperinflation in the 1970s, 1980s, and 1990s, has achieved this macroeconomic stability since the early 1990s by introducing a new currency (partly linked in value to that of the dollar) and maintaining a primary budget surplus every year. China has achieved it by maintaining a relatively stable currency peg, although Beijing has begun to loosen the peg and allow China's currency to float somewhat.

Again, having some degree of openness is important to maintaining macroeconomic stability. In more open state capitalists, the outside world has at least some expectations regarding these states' economic policymaking plans, and international investors are able to gain some insight into the people running economic policy. In Brazil, state policies are laid out in the normal budgetary process, which is similar to the process of passing a budget in the United States or other established democracies; Brazil's state bank now publishes its lending portfolio for the public. In China, while policymaking is still not transparent enough, the government has achieved a degree of macroeconomic stability in part by rotating leaders of the People's Bank of China and providing some transparency about its macroeconomic policymaking through announcements of five-year economic plans, press conferences with senior economic officials, and regular interaction with economic policymakers from many other countries. Still, as President Xi Jinping and Premier Li Keqiang have admitted, for China to maintain stability and ensure the continued confidence of global markets and investors, the government will eventually have to become even more transparent about debts within Chinese banks, reduce easy credit, and pursue other tough fiscal reforms.[15] Whether the Chinese leadership will actually undertake these reforms remains an open question.

The inefficient state capitalists, which often have oil, gas, or other resources, almost always fail to utilize these resources to create foundations for prolonged growth—or at least to build globally competitive resources companies in areas that would be naturally related to resources like natural gas storage and shipping, petrochemicals, diamond cutting, fertilizer production, and others. Qatar, again, is an exception; its autocratic government has used its resource wealth to build internationally competitive companies in gas-related industries like petrochemicals and fertilizer, as well as to help create other globally competitive firms, like media giant *Al Jazeera*. Still, even in Qatar the competitive companies that have been created depend heavily on expatriate management and expertise.

Free-market oriented nations can fall prey to the resource curse. Nigeria is a perfect example of the problem. The country squandered hundreds of billions of dollars in oil wealth on various types of official corruption, never built any of its own successful companies in industries related to oil extraction, and used little of its oil money to foster Nigerian entrepreneurship. But the highly autocratic state capitalists are even more vulnerable to the resource curse than Nigeria, where after years of wasteful spending, increasingly open politics has created a new generation of Nigerian politicians willing to criticize an official culture of corruption, crack down on graft, and attempt to invest oil wealth more effectively.

No such new generation of politicians has emerged in the most autocratic state capitalists, like Russia and the Central Asian nations. With resources concentrated in state-owned companies like Russian gas giant Gazprom—which has little of the oversight created for state companies in more open political systems—the government in autocratic state capitalists has even greater control of natural resources than in a more free-market economy. Political leaders in these countries have carte blanche to select the leaders of major resources companies. Resources companies thus are more likely to be turned into political piggy banks while simultaneously crushing smaller entrepreneurs and driving away business talent.

Indeed, unlike Brazil or China or Singapore, Vladimir Putin's Kremlin has not used the state's sizable currency reserves to invest in young Russian companies, promote new industries, or even make new investments in oil and gas extraction technology. Neither has Russia forced state firms to compete with each other and with foreign firms operating in their domestic markets, as Singapore and many of the other most efficient state capitalists have done. Instead, in Russia, state companies throttle any potential private-sector competitors. Under Putin, the Kremlin has allowed just one or two state firms to dominate nearly every leading industry, with each company staffed by Putin loyalists. Companies that have resisted state takeover have been sacked with enormous tax bills until they sell out. Many of the most promising young entrepreneurs in Russia simply have fled the country to launch their companies in London, San Francisco, New York, Berlin, or other places.

The combination of state firms quashing private competitors, vast forests of regulation and red tape, minimal competition between state companies themselves, and barriers to foreign firms entering Russia's domestic market has dramatically stifled entrepreneurship and the efficiency and creative destruction created by the free market. Russia today has almost no viable start-ups in industries like clean energy, nanotechnology, social media, pharmaceuticals, or other industries that have been expanding and likely will have a long life in the twenty-first century, even though expatriate Russians have been central players in Silicon Valley, the high-tech clusters in London and Cambridge, and many other cutting-edge companies outside of Russia. Even in industries where Russia has powerful large companies, like oil and gas—industries that will be less important as substitutes for fossil fuels emerge—Russia lacks a network of small, entrepreneurial oil and gas companies that could be developing new exploration or refining technologies and, in the future, adding value to Russian oil and gas.

As Russia economist Anders Aslund noted, in a study of Russian start-ups, "from December 2012 to April 2013, the number of individual entrepreneurs [in Russia] slumped by 367,000 because of an increasingly hostile business environment."[16] The crush of the state hand on the economy combined with the need to pay off many officials to launch companies also has fostered an enormous illegal, or gray, economy, in which Russians try to avoid dealing with the state at all by hiding their businesses as much as possible. The existence of a huge gray economy is common in inefficient state capitalists, since the formal economy is so difficult for entrepreneurs. Russia's underground economy annually produces goods and services worth more than 40 percent of the country's official GDP, according to a study by Global Financial Integrity, a nonprofit that tracks underground economies.[17]

Like other inefficient state capitalists, in the regular, or non-gray economy, much of Russia's economic production is consumed, locust-like, by the corruption, cronyism, and rent-seeking of the circle of officials and bureaucrats close to the Kremlin. Unlike in China, Singapore, or Brazil, where governments set the general direction for state companies and leave everyday decision-making to the heads of these companies, the Russian government frequently directs state companies' everyday decision-making, crippling and paralyzing management, and deterring private investment in these companies. Many of the Russian state companies channel a sizable percentage of their earnings back to executives and to a small circle of government officials, according to investigative reports on the Russian economy by the *Financial Times*.[18] In perhaps the most infamous case, after Russia won the rights to host the 2014 Winter Olympics at the Black Sea town of Sochi (a subtropical town that is one of the few places in Russia that actually has little snow, and which has long been one of Putin's favorite places), Russia spent over $50 billion constructing the Olympic site, roads, housing, hotels, and other facilities—by far the largest amount ever spent on an Olympics.[19] Russia spent all this money even though the Winter Games have fewer sports and a smaller international television audience than the Summer Games. Nearly all of the Sochi money came from state banks and the state budget itself. By contrast, Britain spent around $19 billion on the 2012 London Summer Games.[20]

Where did all that state money go? "The Sochi Olympics are an unprecedented thieves' caper," wrote Boris Nemtsov, a former deputy prime minister under Putin who has authored several papers on self-dealing and cronyism at the Olympics site.[21] Arkady Rotenberg, an old friend of Putin's who now runs an infrastructure company that has made billions providing pipes to state giant Gazprom, was granted over $7 billion in mostly no-bid Sochi Olympics contracts for building Olympic infrastructure; another state company run by a close Putin friend, Russian Railways, got around $9 billion in Olympic contracts.[22] Focused primarily on enriching themselves, the state firms bungled Sochi's construction, and many parts of the site, like the pipes, ski jumps, and coastal barriers, needed to be rebuilt.[23]

The self-dealing infects nearly all of Russia's biggest state companies. In one of the most infamous cases, that of state-linked pipeline owner Transneft, an internal report on corruption inside the firm was leaked to shareholder activist and blogger Alexei Navalny. The internal audit documents, which Navalny posted online, alleged that some $4 billion in Transneft funds had been siphoned out of the company and into the pockets of insiders during the construction of a pipeline traveling across Siberia to the Russian Far East.[24]

Meanwhile, predation at the biggest state companies and among the highest officials in Russia, as in other inefficient state capitalists, trickles down. Corruption undermines the rule of law and solidifies the perception, among average Russians and officials all over the country, that government predation is the norm, an accepted, unavoidable part of doing business. As corruption has become more entrenched, the Kremlin has only taken superficial measures to stop it. These superficial measures offer a contrast to those taken by more efficient—though still graft-challenged—state capitalists like China or Vietnam. These economies operate relatively efficiently, because the country is run (at least in part) in order to promote growth, not just to enrich a small handful of elites. Both China and Vietnam suffer from corruption, but that corruption has not overwhelmed their economic systems as it has in Russia, and the governments in Beijing and Hanoi are responsive enough to the public that Beijing and Hanoi must take actions against the most inefficient, extreme types of graft.

WHY THESE DISTINCTIONS MATTER

The overlap between these two charts, then, offers important lessons that will help guide our understanding of what we should worry about with state capitalism—and also guide our policies for addressing the rise of state capitalism. The overlap helps debunk the myth, common among Western policymakers, that state capitalism today is inherently linked to autocratic government. Indeed, as we see from these rankings—which are supported by other analyses of democracy around the world like the Bertelsmann Foundation's Transformation Index and the Economist Intelligence Unit's annual analysis of democracy around the world—democracies like South Africa, Brazil, Indonesia, and Singapore have adopted state interventionist strategies to support industries and individual companies their governments consider most important to development. Economic freedom in these nations has eroded even as political freedom has remained relatively vibrant or even expanded, as in Indonesia and Brazil. Since these are electoral democracies, albeit with many imperfections—they may use a variety of tactics to make it challenging for opposition parties to win elections—we can more easily assess the popularity of state economic intervention than in an authoritarian state. In general, publics in these democracies have supported this growing interventionism over the past decade. Politicians who adopted these types of interventions have been highly successful in parliamentary and presidential elections; politicians who have attempted to reduce state economic intervention have not, in Indonesia, Brazil, Malaysia, and other more democratic state capitalists. Polling data further demonstrates the popularity of state economic intervention in these nations; publics from Indonesia to Brazil, when polled, support growing state economic intervention.

Indeed, the democratic state capitalists further muddy the question of whether economic growth leads to greater political freedom (a theory that is no longer without doubters) or whether political freedom promotes greater economic growth. Or, perhaps, political openness and *some* degree of economic openness are self-reinforcing, but only some degree. After all, in some of the more open state capitalists, economic efficiency has not necessarily lead to a further embrace of free-market reforms, or to complete democratization.

For sixty years, policymakers and political scientists have believed in the long-standing idea, traced back to the modernization theories of political scientists Seymour Martin Lipset and Samuel Huntington, that as countries reach a certain average standard of living—around $7,000 per capita[25]—the population increasingly puts pressure on the government to reform and prompts democracy to emerge.[26] Despite challenges over the past decade, this modernization theory remains accepted wisdom among most policymakers in the West and continues to dominate thinking about democracy promotion and, more broadly, about a wide range of economic policymaking.

As I examined in *Democracy in Retreat*, this link between economic freedom and political freedom already is fraying in other ways. Middle classes in countries from Egypt to Thailand to Ukraine to the Philippines, frustrated by the graft and poor leadership of the men and women elected in their countries' initial democratic elections, and desiring to hold onto certain political privileges that would be undermined by democracy, often have turned against democratic practices and institutions, supporting coups or violent street protests or judicial interventions to take down elected governments.[27] These middle classes did not necessarily sour on economic freedom, but they did sour on political freedom. Since the publication of that book, other reports, books, and studies have further demonstrated the idea that middle classes in many developing countries are becoming increasingly conservative, turning against political freedom and often trying to install authoritarian governments in place of democratically elected leaders. In a 2014 study by the Bertelsmann Foundation, author Serhat Unaldi, examining a range of nations in Asia, showed that the size of each country's middle class had little correlation to that nation's score on the Foundation's Transformation Index, one measure of nations' democratization. Unaldi found that, in fact, many nations in Asia saw their index score—in other words, their political openness—decline as the size of their middle class increased in recent years. He notes that throughout the region, "the established middle class [has] grown more defensive. Its members had simply not learned how to share [political freedoms.] These middle-class reactionaries [have] supported authoritarian." Even in Indonesia, Unaldi notes, a country that clearly is progressing toward solid, consolidated democracy, middle-class men and women have been the least willing to embrace that democratic change.[28] The Indonesian middle classes heavily supported the 2014 presidential campaign of Prabowo Subianto, a former Suharto-era general who, during the election campaign, had raised doubts about the viability of Indonesian democracy, suggested that he wanted to return Indonesia to centralized, strongman rule, and proposed abrogating the current Indonesian constitution and returning to an earlier version that had few protections for democratic freedoms or civil liberties.

The efficiency and the annual growth figures of such a broad range of state capitalists, from democratic to somewhere between democratic and autocratic, further undermines modernization theory. And if we question the basis of modernization theory, we must rethink the decades-old assumption that Western nations should simultaneously promote political and economic freedom through their aid programs and broader foreign policies. We will explore further whether and how we can rethink democracy promotion. Perhaps democracy promotion can occur, successfully, in even some of the most state-dominated economic environments, as long as these states are politically responsive to their publics to some degree.

Still, we must wonder whether political openness, economic efficiency, and state control of large segments of the economy can coexist over the long term, without undermining innovation or, possibly, consolidating too much power in a small group of politicians' hands, making it hard to be both democratic and state capitalist in the long run. We will explore whether it is possible for countries to maintain this balance.

THREATS

As we will see, the variety of state capitalists' political systems, and the wide variety of how state capitalists act in international affairs, also will show that it is not simply economic centralization that should inherently worry citizens in state-capitalist nations, and leaders of countries like the United States. There are democratic state capitalists, like Indonesia, that have become increasingly responsible and effective leaders, on issues ranging from economic integration to peacekeeping to democracy promotion, even as they have become more economically centralized. We will more closely examine what factors in state-capitalist nations make each nation either a potential worry to the world or a benign actor.

In general, state capitalism offers a future that is less desirable than the one offered by democracy and free-market economics, despite the fact that markets can be unstable and crisis prone. Indeed, in some cases, state capitalism poses a potential challenge to the dominance of free-market economics and, to some extent, to democracy. But not always. Only three types of state-capitalist countries should be worrying—potential threats to their own people, to neighboring nations, to foreign companies, and to the international economic system and international security: efficient and relatively autocratic state capitalists, like China, that could pose a real challenge to fundamental assumptions about free markets and free politics that have undergirded the international system for decades; state capitalists that are autocratic but inefficient and which could suffer economic meltdowns that could spark global economic crises; and autocratic state capitalists that, through accidents of history, maintain sizable economies and globally powerful state companies yet are so repressive that authority is concentrated in the hands of one or two leaders. In this third group of state capitalists, these countries have both the wherewithal and the concentrated, controlled power to use their state companies, like Gazprom, as weapons. Of course, some state capitalists fit into more than one of these categories of threatening countries.

In addition to understanding the three types of countries that pose threats, we should comprehend the five discrete challenges from state capitalism, which we introduced earlier and will examine in detail in later chapters: state capitalism's impact on political freedom within countries; its impact on countries' political stability and, possibly, the stability of entire regions of the world; its effect on the global economy; its challenge to international institutions and the model of free-market economics; and its potential to facilitate the use of state companies as de facto weapons of war. But first, we must step back and examine the history of state capitalism, in order to understand more clearly what makes today's state capitalism unique.

3

A Brief History of (State Intervention) Time

Since the beginning of the modern nation-state era, dating from the Peace of Westphalia in the seventeenth century, states have been intervening in their economies, even in the most supposedly free-market societies. During the colonial era, governments in Europe usually practiced some form of mercantilism, which prioritized building up a state's assets, primarily natural resources and precious metals. Mercantilism included high protectionist barriers and a suspicion of free trade; mercantilists believed that the global economy was a zero-sum game and that free trade would not enlarge the economies of trading partners. The mercantilists created national champion companies and used high barriers to trade to protect domestic innovation and resources. Of course, today's state capitalists are far more nuanced in their protectionist measures and do not disdain free trade; they embrace the international economy in a way that seventeenth- and eighteenth-century mercantilists did not.

Even as the theory of mercantilism began to decline in popularity among the European powers, due to criticism by leading economists of the Adam Smith school, most of the European powers of the eighteenth and nineteenth centuries still funded explorers to new territories and determined which trading companies or individual entrepreneurs would obtain control of potentially prosperous colonies. Reigning monarchs in Europe retained the power to grant patents to entrepreneurs for new technologies, or to issue stock offerings. They also continued to prioritize the amassing of precious metals. When these trading companies needed to fight off potential rivals from other European powers or from native groups already living in the colonized areas, European governments often would use their navies and marine forces to protect the favored trading companies' assets. In some cases, as in the infamous Opium Wars in China in the nineteenth century, European powers even used their military might to help government-supported trading companies consolidate their ability to sell dangerous and addictive products to weaker nations.

Though the United States was founded, in part, on a notion of establishing a different type of economy and political system from the European powers, from the early days of independence, the US federal government played a significant role in the economy. During the early years of its existence, the United States, for example, used high tariffs and other import restrictions to protect many of the young country's industries from competition with European firms. The government drove Native Americans out of regions that were then allocated to certain companies, and it played a central role in the creation of the first transcontinental rail line, which opened up the West to commerce. After the Civil War, however, and particularly beginning in the early twentieth century, the US government began to play a far more central role in the economy's development, providing tax incentives for cutting-edge manufacturing and sponsoring some of the largest and most productive laboratories and research institutes in the country, many of which ultimately were spun off into companies. This support continued even after the end of the Keynesian stimulus programs of the Great Depression.

Other leading industrialized economies became even more state directed in the early and mid-twentieth centuries, partly as a response to the Depression and partly, after World War II, as a legacy of the politico-economic nexus created by fighting wars. Still, all of the industrialized economies usually viewed state intervention either as a temporary fix to short-term economic problems (as in the United States during the Great Depression) or confined state intervention to a handful of industries, usually involved with national security, energy, and agriculture. Few Western states utilized state intervention in as many sectors as modern state capitalists like China or even Brazil today. In post-World War II France, the most *dirigiste* of the major powers, the government took back control of parts of the economy, which had been far more open in the interwar period. The post-WWII French government controlled most major utilities, the burgeoning nuclear power industry (which would become the world leader in cutting-edge nuclear power plants), and some sectors related to national security like steel and aviation. Still, France played a major role in multilateral trade negotiations and, later in the Cold War, reduced state control over many sectors of the economy.

Japan, which between the nineteenth-century Meiji Restoration and World War II had already developed a range of state strategies designed to create a group of internationally competitive enterprises called *keiretsu*, continued its state support of some leading industries in its postwar rebuilding period. With the powerful Ministry of International Trade and Industry (MITI) leading Japan's postwar rebuilding, MITI's bureaucrats and other Japanese officials pushed some smaller Japanese manufacturers to merge and encouraged state-linked banks to offer manufacturers soft loans and other types of cheap credit. In addition, MITI and other government agencies offered significant subsidies to support innovation in automaking, electronics, heavy industry, shipbuilding, and other industries. The Japanese government required companies in certain industries to reinvest a share of profits into innovation or into creating economies of scale, according to a study by the World Bank. The Japanese government also instituted tariffs and other protectionist measures that insulated many Japanese automakers, electronics manufacturers, and other industries. By the early 1980s, the Japanese system had become so successful that Japan was running massive trade surpluses.

Outside of the industrialized powers, state intervention in the economy was common in the twentieth century, but it rarely worked, for most developing nations embraced an autarkic, uninnovative, and unnuanced form of state intervention different from today's version of state capitalism. For much of the twentieth century the Soviet Union and Maoist China, as well as smaller communist states like North Korea and Yugoslavia and many others, used state intervention to speed up industrialization in attempts to catch up to the capitalist Western nations. However, despite some initial successes in industrialization, neither the Soviet Union, China, nor North Korea ever allowed independent, critical outsiders to examine their economic models, as state capitalists like China and Singapore do today. In addition, unlike most of today's state capitalists, the economies of the USSR and communist China were not really intertwined with the global economy or participating in multilateral free-trade regimes; Soviet and Chinese industries rarely competed directly with the most technologically advanced Western and Japanese multinationals. And by the 1970s, as the USSR, other Eastern Bloc nations, and China began to allow in independent observers and some journalists, it was already becoming clear that the communist model was failing. The decline of the Soviet Union, Mao's death, the ascendance of Deng Xiaoping to the top of the Chinese leadership, and Deng's injunctions to begin opening up the Chinese economy seemed to seal the USSR/Chinese model of state capitalism as an utter failure.

In the early 1980s, in fact, China unleashed a wave of economic and political reforms that, in many ways, were more far-reaching than any reforms Beijing has tried since. The government allowed the creation of new private village and township enterprises; broke up communal farming plots; and tolerated a wide range of public dissent in print, public spaces, and even in some Party publications. Intellectuals voiced much of this dissent, a sharp contrast to today, when the majority of public protests in China occur in rural areas.[1] In the mid and late 1980s, large public protests took place for days, or even weeks, in major Chinese cities without being stopped; today, the paramilitary People's Armed Police would crush any such protest within hours.

Indeed, middle-class anger in China during the 1970s and 1980s over corruption, inflation, and the destructive legacies of the Cultural Revolution on Chinese culture and society led to the massive urban protests that ultimately sparked the Tiananmen Spring of 1989. China's educated urban middle classes—students, academics, professionals, early private businesspeople—were in the center of these 1980s protests. Following 1989, as we will see, the Party put into place a wide range of measures designed to ensure that the urban middle classes would no longer oppose Communist Party rule but instead would support the authoritarian, state-capitalist system. These measures have worked, at least for now: polling data reveals that urban middle classes are the most supportive of the status quo of any groups within Chinese society.[2] The majority of protests that do erupt in China now take place among poor migrants to cities or in rural areas, which tend to be poorer than cities and have enjoyed few of the state-provided advantages urban areas have received during China's boom.

During the post–World War II period, many other postcolonial states also tried varieties of state intervention in their economies. Though these interventions were not as extreme as those of the USSR or Maoist China, they still required heavy government subsidies of industry, high tariffs, and significant centralized state planning—and these interventions also failed miserably. Many leaders in decolonizing parts of Africa, Latin America, the Middle East, and South Asia had embraced socialism or quasi-communism during their battle against colonial rule. They embraced these models in part because of their studies in left-leaning universities, in part because they could reap aid from the Soviet Union, and in part because of their desire to take a different path than the colonial-style capitalism they had personally witnessed. Socialism, or at least quasi-socialism, could be advertised as a clean break from colonial times, and the postcolonial leaders who did not embrace socialism, such as Ivory Coast's Félix Houphouët-Boigny, often were portrayed by the majority of independence leaders as lackeys of the West. Leaders like India's Jawaharlal Nehru, Indonesia's Sukarno, and many others launched import substitution economic plans. Import substitution strategies relied on central planning to direct the economy and used high tariffs and other protectionist measures to, in theory, support the development of local industry and agriculture, which would grow and "substitute" for imports from richer countries. State-dominated import substitution plans also concentrated great power in the hands of the ruler, a fact that did not go unnoticed by autocratic postcolonial leaders like Nasser or Sukarno, who built cults of personaly around themselves.

Almost universally, these newly independent nations failed to produce much growth. In the early post-independence period, India struggled along at growth rates of 3 to 4 percent annually, which were mocked by outsiders as the "Hindu rate of growth" and which were barely enough to keep pace with India's expanding population.[3] The Indian state created an enormous bureaucracy to manage the economy, which came to be known by businesspeople, unhappily, as the "License Raj," the successor to the British Raj. India's statist economics also allowed the prime minister, if he or she wanted, to use vast economic powers to entrench their political power. Jawaharlal Nehru, who had a strong commitment to democratic politics, was relatively reluctant to use this economic power to crush political opponents, but his daughter, Indira Gandhi, was not.

India was hardly unique. Under independence hero and first president Sukarno, Indonesia's economy nearly collapsed, leading to nationwide famines in the early 1950s and political ferment that ultimately resulted in the military deposing Sukarno in the mid-1960s. Before that coup, Sukarno, too, used Indonesia's state capitalism as a tool to build up his personal power base and punish any political opponents. In sub-Saharan Africa, meanwhile, postcolonial import substitution strategies failed to produce competitive domestic manufacturing in nearly every nation; countries remained dependent on commodity exports; and as the price of commodities plummeted in the 1980s, the continent's economies drifted. Indeed, the 1980s and early 1990s in Africa became known as the "lost decades."

In the postcolonial period, import substitution did not produce strong growth in Latin America or the Middle East either. Countries like Argentina, which had been among the richest in the world in the early twentieth century, fell far behind the industrialized West. Like most countries in sub-Saharan Africa, many Latin American nations also ended the 1980s poorer than they'd begun the decade.[4] By the early 1990s, most African and Latin leaders were looking for any solutions that would halt a death spiral of underdevelopment and isolation from the global economy.

Of course, there were many reasons for the weak growth rates in these postcolonial societies, including the colonists' failure to leave behind a strong rule of law in many places; vicious internal strife in many newly independent nations like Burma, Indonesia, or Nigeria; a global glut in many commodities; and many other factors. But the fact that so many postcolonial economies barely grew at all during the import substitution period seemed the death knell for this model and fostered the post-1989 triumphalist mentality of advocates of the free markets, free politics Washington Consensus model. The West's triumph over communism was proof, as Francis Fukuyama famously argued in his landmark 1990 essay "The End of History," that liberal democracy combined with market economics represented the direction in which the world would inevitably evolve.[5]

The term "Washington Consensus" was originally intended by its author, economist John Williamson, to mean a discrete and limited set of economic initiatives particularly developed to address many of the economic problems facing Latin American nations in the late 1980s and 1990s. The initiatives included fiscal discipline, tax reform, liberalizing exchange rates, privatization, and trade liberalization, among other changes.[6] But the term soon took on a far broader meaning among many development experts and world leaders. It came to signify broad reforms, promoted not only for Latin America but for the entire developing world, and designed to open markets, increase financial transparency, and reduce government intervention in the economy. Political reforms that would also foster freedom by shrinking the role of the state also fell under the term's umbrella.[7] Proponents of the Washington Consensus boasted about the potential results and brooked little criticism of their proposals. In perhaps the most famous example, World Bank officials throughout the 1990s promised that these policy reforms, if implemented throughout the developing world, would slash global poverty in half.[8] Later, in an internal assessment of its policies during this decade, the Bank admitted that it still didn't know "how to improve institutional performance [i.e., how to promote economic growth]" and that the Washington Consensus had been "the dominant view, making it difficult for others to be heard," even though these proposed reforms actually had had a mixed impact on growth and political change.[9] Another retrospective comprehensive analysis of the Washington Consensus, by former World Bank chief economist Joseph Stiglitz, found that proponents of its reforms made little effort to tailor its prescriptions to individual countries and actually paid little attention to whether the growth, if produced, alleviated poverty or really addressed inequality at all. Worse, Stiglitz also concluded that the Washington Consensus failed to even promote significant growth in most of the nations where it was applied, even as it ignored the balanced, important role that a state can play in development.[10]

The lack of an obvious alternative model in the late 1990s and early 2000s only emboldened advocates of free markets linked with free politics. Compared to the Cold War, no major powers now dissented loudly from this new orthodoxy. After the 1989 Tiananmen crackdown, China adopted a more modest public approach to foreign policy and spent most of the 1990s and early 2000s wooing foreign investment and refusing to publicly offer any alternative to the Washington Consensus. Under then-premier Zhu Rongji, China also seemed to be slowly heading toward a free-market economy, breaking up some SOEs and publicly vowing to reduce state influence over its banks. Russia, decimated economically by the fall of the Soviet Union, and nearly bankrupt in the mid-1990s, also was in no position to offer any alternative to the Washington Consensus.

At the same time as the Eastern Bloc was collapsing, Africa and Latin America were suffering lost decades, and the West was winning the Cold War, the most state-directed Western economies suddenly stumbled as well, making the Washington Consensus appear even more dominant. Though countries like Japan and France, the most important Western economies with a heavy state hand, had not controlled as much of their economies as China or Brazil today, they had employed more state intervention than the United States or most other industrialized states. Yet Japan's 1980s dominance collapsed in a frothy real-estate and stock-market bubble—even though, throughout the 1990s and 2000s, when Japan supposedly entered its own "lost decades," the country still maintained low unemployment, rising life expectancy, and a growing current account surplus, which means that Japan was still building a massive trade surplus with most of its major trading partners. The very idea of the "lost decades" indeed may be a fiction, yet in the early 1990s, as the Washington Consensus concept grew more powerful, Japan's supposed downfall added fuel to the advocates of a more free-market capitalism.[11] The most state-centered European economies, like France and several Nordic states, also were struggling in the early 1990s, and responded by privatizing many state companies. The early 1990s Swedish debt crisis shocked Scandinavia into reform and the creation of the European Union opened up borders and forced reforms onto large state enterprises throughout Western Europe.

The United States had never had as interventionist a government as France or Japan, although the US government did play a major role in protecting nascent American manufacturing from European competitors, and in the mid-twentieth century Washington amassed enormous power over the economy through stimulus and wartime spending. After World War II, the federal government's share of American GDP dropped and then slowly increased again due to social welfare programs launched in the 1960s. But even as the government's share of GDP grew, Washington did not control a large portion of American companies, and so the government still had only modest control over the corporate sector, compared to countries like Japan or France—and certainly compared to the state capitalists today. In the 1990s, the US government reduced the defense budget, cut some entitlement programs, and saw government spending as a percentage of GDP fall slightly.

After the financial crisis of 2008, the federal government spending's share of GDP grew slightly, as the Obama administration bailed out several large financial institutions and tried to reverse a severe economic downturn. Still, by the late 2000s, according to studies like the Heritage Foundation's *Index of Economic Freedom*, the US economy was far more open to multilateral free trade than any of its large peers in the developed world. Even during Obama's first term, when the federal government intervened heavily in the economy, Washington's influence over American corporations remained largely indirect, other than with General Motors, which was briefly owned by the government, and with a select number of financial companies that received government bailouts. By Obama's second term, the federal government had divested itself of its entire stake in GM, ended its bailouts of financial institutions, and drastically cut the federal budget as well. Overall, the Obama administration's second-term budget cuts known as sequestration brought the total amount of federal spending down significantly from its first-term highs. In addition, the government slashed federal expenditures on the types of public-private basic science partnerships that had helped build Bell Labs and other giants of an earlier American era. In its second term, the Obama administration also cut the defense budget, shrinking the US Army to its smallest size since before the Second World War. The defense budget had been a major source of funding for basic science and technology research and a link between government and industry.

THE EAST ASIAN ECONOMIES

Of all the developing nations that experimented with highly state interventionist economic policies during the Cold War, only a small number of East Asian economies prospered. These countries, which became known as the "tigers" or "tiger cubs" or, in World-Bankese, the "High-Growth Asian Economies," included South Korea, Taiwan, Singapore, Thailand, Indonesia, Malaysia, and Hong Kong. Although Japan had developed into an industrialized state before the Cold War, it boomed during the Cold War and sometimes is grouped into these high-growth economies. Overall, the twenty-three economies in East Asia posted the fastest growth of any region of the world between 1965 and 1990, according to the World Bank's statistics. All but Hong Kong were known, at least at some point during that period, as "developmental states," ones in which the government played a central role in economic planning during the high-growth period.

The tigers and tiger cubs were successful. The Korean War leveled Seoul twice and left South Korea with a GDP per capita roughly equal to that of Congo, but South Korea transformed itself into one of the largest economies in the world in 2013. Japan rebuilt its economy after the Second World War, and Taiwan and Singapore joined the list of the world's richest countries as well. Thailand in the 1970s and 1980s consistently posted some of the highest annual growth rates of any country in the world. Indonesia and

Malaysia grew from poor, largely agricultural countries in 1960 where more than 20 percent of the people lived in poverty and did not have enough to eat into middle-income nations whose larger cities increasingly resembled rich metropolises like Tokyo or New York rather than impoverished metropolises in other developing regions like Africa and Latin America.

The tigers and the tiger cubs were so successful, in fact, that some observers today see the strategies of modern state capitalists like China and Brazil and South Africa as simply an updating of the tigers' and tiger cubs' models from the Cold War era. Like the tigers, China in its reform era has devoted significant resources to primary education, resulting in youth literacy rates of nearly 98 percent; in many other developing nations, the youth literacy rate is less than 70 percent.[12] Like other high-growth Asian economies, China also has created some favorable environments for foreign investment, particularly in the special economic zones along the country's coast; many years over the past two decades, China has been the world's top recipient of foreign direct investment. Randall Peerenboom, a leading China scholar at La Trobe University in Australia, calls China's state capitalism "déjà vu all over again," since he believes it so resembles the strategies of the high-growth Asian economies.[13]

Of all of the tigers and tiger cubs, South Korea and Cold War-era Singapore came closest to the modern state capitalists. Their Cold War-era governments, led by autocrats until the late 1980s, made clear, conscious decisions to use state resources and protectionism to create powerful corporations in industries considered vital to the countries' growth and strategic interests, like shipping, steel, automaking, and electronics. Under successive autocratic regimes, South Korea's Economic Planning Board determined the economy's every shift, setting export targets for each industry that it treated like national missions. South Korea maintained some of the highest tariff barriers in Asia, while forcing manufacturers in industries like shipbuilding, car-making, and electronics to consolidate into conglomerates called *chaebols*. The *chaebols* then were given almost exclusive control of certain industries, as well as the authoritarian government's assistance in repressing unions and keeping wages artificially low.[14] Yet by the 1980s, the ties between state and *chaebols* were loosening. South Korea was becoming wealthier and politically freer, and the sense of a national mission shaped by the Korean War and Korea's subsequent poverty had begun to fade. The *chaebols* became international companies, came under many foreign jurisdictions, and became far less willing to simply take direction from Seoul.[15]

As Korea entered a period of democratization, the *chaebols* also became less fearful of labor unrest or political change, and so less indebted to the government and its security forces.

Other tigers also employed statist strategies, though they were usually less state dominated than South Korea. After separating from Malaysia in 1965, Singapore's government, run by technocrats loyal to Singaporean founding father Lee Kuan Yew, created a master plan for decades of development, including using government-controlled banks to build up Singapore's port, its financial sector, its electronics manufacturing, and other industries. The Singaporean government also enacted a broad range of coercive socioeconomic policies designed to help promote growth, including mandating the use of English as a first language, and demanding that Singaporeans commit a high percentage of their income to a national pension plan, among other strategies. Tough penalties for corruption, combined with highly competitive salaries for government officials—Singapore's prime minister, who runs a country of just over five million people, earns around US $1.7 million per year, compared to around $250,000 for the US president—helped make the city-state one of the least corrupt places in the world.[16]

To be sure, today's state capitalists have learned some lessons from the tigers and tiger cubs, and there are some similarities between modern state capitalists and the tigers' models. China clearly looks to Singapore's past successes as an example for the People's Republic, and senior Chinese leaders also have studied South Korea's experience in using protections and subsidies to create giant national champion companies in industries like shipbuilding, auto manufacturing, and telecommunications. Chinese officials have set up regular visitor programs to study Singapore's political and economic models, and the Central Party School in Beijing, the institution that trains senior Chinese leaders, has run several articles in its internal publications on the "Singapore model" and invited a range of senior Singaporean ministers and civil servants to come lecture at the Central Party School.[17] In addition, several leading Singaporean universities now have extensive training programs for officials from across China, including Nanyang Technological University, the Lee Kuan Yew School of Public Policy, and other Singaporean schools of higher education. Most of the Chinese officials who come to study Singaporean political and economic management are chosen by the Party, according to several Singaporean academics who have worked closely with Chinese officials.[18] China's state television broadcaster even in 2012 filmed a ten-part series on Singapore, according to Singaporean media, a project reportedly endorsed by President Xi Jinping.[19] The series got extensive play on Chinese television. Singapore's *Straits Times* newspaper reported:

> The series . . . is believed to be a blueprint of sorts for the new administration [in China.] It aims to showcase Singapore as a model for China as it charts a fresh path after the 18th Party Congress . . . The production team said Singapore has created a "unique miracle in the world" and it would like to find out how to adapt this for China's "further reforms and sustainable development." The Chinese Communist Party has been eager to learn how Singapore maintains a one-party dominant system in a prosperous and stable society. But while the city-state has been an exemplar for China since the 1980s, Mr Xi [Jinping], according to several sources, is keen to reaffirm the Singapore model for China's reforms.[20]

But there are significant differences between the tigers of the Cold War and today's state capitalists; today's state capitalism, whether in China, Brazil, or South Africa, is not simply an updating of the East Asian growth model. For one, unlike South Korea, most of the tigers and tiger cubs relied on the free market as much as on state intervention. None of the tigers or tiger cubs had state companies that dominated as large a percentage of the economy, either in terms of assets, capitalization, or percentage of GDP, as state companies do in Russia, China, or other state capitalists today.

In fact, compared to other developing nations during the Cold War, many of the tigers actually had economies that were relatively open to trade and investment, and that allowed the domestic private sector considerable freedom. Hong Kong, one of the fastest-growing Asian tigers, had some of the lowest tariffs in the world—lower than mother country Britain—while by 1975, less than two decades after gaining independence, Singapore was ranked by Canada's Fraser Institute as one of the ten freest economies in the world, in part because of its openness to trade and in part because of its willingness to leave the private sector alone in many parts of the economy. Japan, Indonesia, and Malaysia all were ranked throughout the Cold War as among the freest economies in the world by the Fraser Institute. Of the fastest-growing Asian economies, only South Korea routinely was ranked as having high tariffs, compared to the global average, during the Cold War period. Several of the high-growth Asian economies also were among the biggest advocates of multilateral free-trade negotiations in the world. Taiwan and Hong Kong, among other tigers, were early advocates of multilateral free trade, were relatively open to foreign investment in most industries, and generally did not seek to create state-controlled or state-linked national champion companies. According to the most comprehensive study of East Asian growth, produced by the World Bank in the early 1990s, the region's economic success was due less to South Korea-style centralized planning or state control of industries than to governments getting other fundamentals right, including creating a strong rule of law and property protections, helping reduce fertility rates, investing in primary education, fostering a stable macroeconomic environment with low inflation, and using government incentives to promote high rates of individual savings. Only on a few selected occasions, and only in Northeast Asia, the study concluded, did state intervention significantly help the tigers and tiger cubs grow.

In addition, over the course of the Cold War, nearly all the tigers became more and more open economically. Their growth, in fact, helped spark more independent companies, ones less dependent on the state; this is the opposite of the trend occurring today in many state capitalists, in which countries like Indonesia are becoming more economically closed. "Intervention declined [in the high-growth Asian economies]," the World Bank study noted.[21] Even the most state-controlled tigers, like South Korea, gradually opened their economies to more foreign investment; dropped protections for many domestic industries; reduced government control of leading banks and financial institutions; and joined regional, bilateral, and multilateral trade agreements. The Asian financial crisis of the late 1990s further fueled this trend. It led to the privatization or bankruptcy of many state-linked banks and state-controlled large industrial corporations in the tiger economies.

Nearly every high-growth Asian economy has also become politically freer over time. South Korea, Indonesia, and Taiwan have shed their autocratic pasts to become nations ranked "free" by Freedom House; Japan is of course a democracy as well. Even Malaysia, Singapore, and Thailand, which have maintained state control of some parts of their economies, are freer politically today than they were in the 1950s or 1960s. Though Malaysia is not a truly free democracy—in its 2013 national elections, the long-ruling Barisan Nasional coalition used massive gerrymandering and alleged widespread fraud to win a majority in parliament—it has a real, vibrant parliamentary opposition that potentially could win a national election the next time one is held.[22] Singapore, which like Malaysia also has been ruled since independence by basically the same ruling coalition, called the People's Action Party (PAP), also now has a legitimate opposition party in parliament that aggressively scrutinizes and condemns many government policies. In the most recent Singaporean national elections, held in 2011, the PAP gained its lowest share of the popular vote in its history.[23] Even Thailand, which has regressed politically over the past decade, with both royalist elites and authoritarian populist parties subverting democratic institutions, and a military junta taking power in 2014, is freer politically than it was fifty years ago.

In addition, other than Japan, which long has been a major military power but was emasculated in the international political and military arena by the post-World War II American-written constitution, none of the tigers or tiger cubs were large enough or powerful enough to dominate their neighbors in Asia. The tigers and tiger cubs thus were not in a position to use their state-controlled companies as weapons on the international stage, and risk the possible security consequences of such actions. But the most powerful state capitalists today, like China, Russia, and Brazil, wield far more strategic influence regionally and internationally than any of the high-growth Asian economies did during the Cold War. All the tigers other than Japan were relatively small states, in population and in area, and all accepted the post–World War II Bretton Woods international institutions, which were dominated by developed Western nations and Japan. Having lost the Second World War, Japan accepted a demilitarization in exchange for a guarantee of American protection. The tigers and tiger cubs focused primarily on their own development and survival, rather than projecting force elsewhere or trying to remake larger international institutions. By and large, they accepted the international status quo, a contrast from modern-day Russia and China.

Other than ultra-successful Singapore, none of the tigers or tiger cubs tried to suggest that they had economic models to impart to other nations, either. In the early 1990s, some Singaporean elites tried to suggest that Singaporean economic and political strategies could serve as examples to other developing nations—the "Asian Values" debate of that decade originated in large part from ideas put forth by Lee Kuan Yew and Singaporean intellectual and bureaucrat Kishore Mahbubani.[24] But at the time, the idea of Asian Values did not really catch on, even in other Southeast Asian nations—although, in recent years, a growing number of developing countries have sent officials to Singapore to study Singaporean economic strategies. And none of the other tigers or tiger cubs promoted their own concept of a developmental model during the height of their Cold War-era growth.

During the Cold War, the tigers and tiger cubs generally did not try to promote themselves as models, but as state capitalism has re-emerged today, the leaders of state-capitalist nations, we will see, have publicly modeled their strategies on the tigers and tiger cubs. They have done so even if their brand of modern state capitalism actually has relatively little in common with the economic policies utilized by Japan, Taiwan, or South Korea during the Cold War. One of the most popular and polarizing brands of state capitalism has been pursued in Thailand, where over a decade of statist economics has helped fuel a political conflict that has destroyed the kingdom's social and political fabric.

4

Why State Capitalism Has Re-Emerged

The village of Mae On, a twenty-minute drive from the northern Thailand city of Chiang Mai, looks like it could be an advertisement for tourism to the kingdom. Mist-covered hills, cousins of a larger mountain chain that extends north into Myanmar and eventually China and the Himalayas, are dotted with terraced, emerald-green farms of cucumbers, okra, rice, and even coffee, an increasingly popular crop in the north. Winding and narrow roads meander up the mountains, passing waterfalls, limestone cliffs, and groups of Western tourists in Lycra shirts breathlessly pumping their bikes up the steep terrain. In Mae On village itself, a central market covering one square block is surrounded by stalls selling thick pork curries, wide *sen yai* noodles, and slices of pineapple and papaya kept cold on chunks of ice. As night falls in January, a cooling breeze arrives from the north, bringing temperatures down to an almost chilly (for Thailand) sixty degrees Fahrenheit, and local residents puttering around on motorcycles wrap themselves in two windbreakers and wool hats, as if they were in the Alps.

The Mae On area attracts tourists to its coffee plantations, mountain bike trails, and scenic views, but it remains relatively poor and isolated compared to thriving Chiang Mai just a few miles away, where massive malls sell the latest American and Chinese DVDs and the newest iPhone updates, and Mercedes idle in the parking lots, their liveried drivers waiting for passengers to come out of the supermarkets. Few residents in Mae On (other than a couple of expatriates) own cars. But residents of the village say that compared to two decades ago, Mae On has gotten much wealthier, and they credit their success to one man: the most controversial, and popular, Thai politician, former prime minister Thaksin Shinawatra. Thaksin, a telecommunications billionaire turned populist politician, served as prime minister between 2001 and 2006, when he was ousted by a military coup. Still, his influence remained as he controlled a series of successor parties that won elections after the 2006 coup government handed power back to the Thai voters. Ultimately, Thaksin and his allies got his younger sister Yingluck elected prime minister in 2011, as a pro-Thaksin party, Puea Thai, dominated parliamentary elections that year.

Puea Thai remained a party directed by Thaksin's missives from abroad; he regularly called in to party meetings to dictate strategy and traveled the globe as a kind of informal ambassador for his sister once she became prime minister. Many Thais wondered whether Yingluck was making any decisions at all. At one point in the 2011 campaign, Thaksin referred to Yingluck as his "clone." He also helped come up with a campaign slogan for that election that clearly indicated who was really still in charge of the party: "Thaksin thinks, Puea Thai does."[1]

Though Thaksin, whose family originally came from the northern suburbs of Chiang Mai, has not actually lived in Thailand for nearly a decade (he lives in exile today in Dubai and other places), in the Chiang Mai area it was, until the spring of 2014, almost as if he never left. Cab drivers displayed his photo on their dashboard right next to Buddha images and pictures of ancient Thai royals, as if he was an idol or could provide them protection from harrowing road trips. Community radio stations broadcast his speeches from exile, and vendors in nearby villages sold posters of the politician grinning and T-shirts bearing his image. Billboards featuring Thaksin and other local politicians from his party dominated the landscape on the sides of roads. "Thaksin was the first politician who listened to poor people," said one store owner in the Chiang Mai suburbs. "He came here and he heard our problems and he didn't just tell us what to do, like the Democrats [the other main political party in Thailand, which has less support among the poor] . . . No one from Bangkok was like that before."[2]

Thaksin clearly was—and is—a masterful politician, one capable of that Clinton-esque skill of appearing intensely and genuinely interested in every person he speaks with. Working with foreign consultants during his first prime minister campaign in 2000–2001, he also developed some of the most sophisticated political advertising Thailand had ever seen, as even many leaders of the Democrat Party admitted at the time.[3]

But it was not only Thaksin's slick advertising and willingness to appear to be listening to poorer rural Thais that won him office in 2001 and made his organization the most powerful political party (until a 2014 military coup essentially banned Thai political parties in another attempt to defang Thaksin's political machine—an attempt that most Thai political analysts, and even many junta members, believed ultimately would fail). Thaksin's state capitalist policies were enormously popular with the majority of poor and working-class Thais. Even in Thaksin's 2000–2001 campaign, he was the first Thai politician to really promise a platform of policies to voters, including many types of state intervention in the economy such as new state credits for microenterprises, a new state-funded universal health-care scheme, and many others. The platform was credited by many Thai voters and political scientists as the most important reason for his smashing 2001 win.

Almost immediately after he became prime minister in 2001, Thaksin followed through on his promises of far-reaching intervention in the economy. His government launched a series of interventionist economic policies that became known colloquially as "Thaksinomics." After the 1997 Asian financial crisis, which began in Thailand that summer with the devaluation of the Thai baht and quickly spread across developing Asia, the Democrat Party, ruling Thailand at that time, followed orthodox, neoliberal economic prescriptions to right the economy. The Democrats relied on the help of an IMF rescue package and advice from a range of Western consultancies and lenders. The Democrat government tried to force failing Thai banks and companies into bankruptcy, clean up non-performing loans, cut excessive state spending, and reduce state involvement in banks and major companies. It seized the assets of fifty-six indebted finance companies, many of which were little more than Madoff-style pyramid schemes or boiler-room operations with minimal reserve capital. It launched a fast-track plan to privatize some sixty state companies and allow foreign investors to take stakes in them, although the unpopularity of the plan led the Democrats to backtrack somewhat.[4]

Many of the Democrats' reforms made sense in a country where poorly regulated finance companies had run wild, taking huge credit risks with minimal capital reserves, creating an enormous real estate bubble in Bangkok, and bidding up a frothy Thai stock market to heights that did not reflect the real value of most listed companies. And prodded by these reforms, external aid, and the broader recovery in Asia, the Thai economy began to slowly recover in the late 1990s. But unemployment remained stubbornly high. The Thai state, which had not even had the currency reserves in 1997 to defend Thailand against attacks by speculators on the Thai baht, did little to assuage laid-off Thais' pain. The Democrats' reform and privatization strategies resulted in the downsizing of many banks and other bloated companies that, though inefficient and sometimes outright criminal, nonetheless had employed large numbers of Thais or had indirectly created jobs for construction laborers, food vendors, maids, and other working-class Thais. The Democrat Party was portrayed in the 2000–2001 election campaign by Thaksin and his allies as uncaring elites, pursuing policies dictated by the West and harmful to ordinary Thais. It was a brutal, and successful, portrayal, not helped by the fact that some Democrat leaders—like urbane Stanford- and Harvard-educated finance minister Tarrin Nimmanhaeminda—let themselves be caught smoking fat cigars with Western bankers at the skyscraper penthouse of the Foreign Correspondents Club of Thailand.[5]

The Thai Democrats had pursued political reforms as well as their economic reforms, though the Democrats assumed that even as more Thais became politically active, the market-oriented, pro-Democrat Bangkok elites who had run the country for centuries would still dominate Thai politics. The Bangkok elites believed they would continue to dominate politics even as the system changed to empower and enfranchise all Thai adults, including the rural poor, who still made up the majority of Thais and had never had a real alternative to the Bangkok-dominated Democrats. It was, for the Democrat Party, a badly mistaken assumption.

Still Thailand as a whole seemed clearly on the democratic path, in part because of reforms pushed by Democrats. In fact, throughout the 1990s, Thailand was considered by much of the world a model of democratic transition. Thailand held a series of free elections in the 1990s and early 2000s. In 1997, amid the Asian financial crisis, Thais passed a constitution that was among the most progressive in Asia and was called the "People's Constitution" because it was so popular. It laid out broad protections for human rights and, by making it harder for small parties to get into parliament, helped consolidate Thai politics into a seemingly stable two-party system.

Foreign officials took note as well, regularly praising Thailand for its openness and democratic values during the 1990s and early 2000s. "Thailand's freedom, openness, strength, and relative prosperity make it a role model in the region for what people can achieve when they are allowed to," US assistant secretary of state James Kelly declared in 2002.[6]

Yet while the Democrats opened up politics—which they would later regret, once the rural poor had another party to vote for—they had done little to reduce economic inequality. When the Asian financial crisis hit Thailand in the late 1990s, Bangkok certainly was hurt: real estate prices collapsed, and many projects in the capital were left unfinished, their concrete skeletons dotting the skyline like some kind of Blade Runneresque scene. The crisis hit the rural poor even harder than it hit Bangkok natives. Many of the rural poor, originally from the populous, impoverished, and drought-hit northeast, had come to Bangkok to work in construction, taxi-driving, housecleaning, and other types of manual labor. These poor migrants were the first to lose their jobs in the crisis. They often returned to the northeast to find no work there either due to falling prices for rice or to a series of droughts. Indeed, income per capita in the poorer Thai provinces decreased more sharply during the crisis than in the capital.[7] Protestors from the rural northeast camped out for weeks at a time just outside the Democrat prime minister's residence, setting up huts and cooking fires along a polluted canal less than two hundred meters from the ornate official home, with its domes and soaring white pillars.[8] At the same time, Thailand's deteriorating currency made it harder for farmers to buy critical machinery that might help them survive the droughts, and farmers got little help from the Democrat Party's IMF-backed rescue program.

After sweeping the elections in 2001, Thaksin partly abandoned the neoliberal economics of his Democrat predecessors. He overrode the formerly independent Bank of Thailand, the equivalent of the US Federal Reserve, until it went along with his plans to plow large amounts of state money into the economy and buy up formerly private companies. Bank governors who did not go along with Thaksin's ideas were forced out of their jobs, even though the Bank of Thailand, like the Federal Reserve, was supposed to be immune from pressure from elected politicians.[9] Thaksin simultaneously increased state decision-making over what he considered

Thailand's strategic sectors, assuming control over many important industries like rubber, aviation, and rice, among others. Under Thaksin, the Thai government created new mechanisms for state loans to microenterprises and cut interest rates to their lowest in the country's modern history. The low rates and state loans to microenterprises, primarily in poorer parts of Thailand's north and northeast, unleashed a flood of cheap credit that stimulated consumer demand for new cars, houses, mobile phones, trucks, and other purchases.

This use of expansive money supply in itself was hardly unusual; in a way, it could seem like a typical Keynesian response to an economic crisis, little different from the stimulus plan enacted by the Obama administration in its first term or from other Keynesian stimulus plans utilized in Western countries in the wake of the global economic slowdown of 2008–2009. Yet Thaksin took the Thai economy in directions far beyond typical Keynesian strategies. In addition to mandating cheap credit, he used the power of his office to push—indeed, force—many Thai banks to offer extremely cheap loans not only to village microenterprises but also to firms in bigger industries Thaksin considered strategic. He pushed the national electricity provider to lower electricity rates for strategic industries—aviation, oil and gas production, cement making. These "strategic" industries included many companies that Thaksin's government would then take de facto control of by dominating board appointments. Under Thaksin the state also took direct control of several of Thailand's largest and most prominent companies.

Openly admiring authoritarian, statist former prime ministers Lee Kuan Yew of Singapore and Mahathir Mohamad of Malaysia, Thaksin also launched a range of what he called new "megaprojects" designed to improve Thailand's physical infrastructure. Thailand needed better physical infrastructure, but the projects were primarily planned to plow money into leading Thai construction and transportation firms, helping them to consolidate under state direction, like the giant South Korean *chaebol* of the past. (By this point, the *chaebol* had become independent, massive multinational corporations, but that distinction seemed to make little difference to Thaksin, who idealized the *chaebol* of the past.) Thaksin also pressured Thai producers in certain sectors, like rubber production, to form cartels designed to raise the price of exports on the global market and simultaneously increase the power of Southeast Asian governments over commodities markets.

Although a 2006 coup removed Thaksin from office and, through post-coup changes in the Thai constitution, attempted to reduce the power of Thaksin's party, it failed to stem Thaksin's appeal to the rural poor. Thaksin remained influential in exile, and his party quickly morphed into successors with different names but similar policies. A transitional coup-appointed government held elections in 2007, expecting to have diluted the popularity of Thaksin's statist strategies and helped the Democrats gain office. But Thaksin's party, with a puppet leader standing in for the exiled Thaksin, dominated the vote again, in part with promises to continue state intervention in the economy. Eventually, Thaksin maneuvered to have his sister installed as party leader, and she won an overwhelming mandate in the 2011 national elections.

Yingluck continued many of Thaksin's statist policies. She continued his policies of amassing control of companies, of offering cheap credit, and of expanding social welfare programs. She created a new scheme designed to create a floor under the price paid for Thai farmers' rice. The rice project became such an enormous state subsidy that, when grilled in parliament in 2013 about its total costs, the commerce minister could not even give a figure of the total price of the scheme.[10]

Yingluck also initiated multiple megaprojects, which were designed in part to upgrade needed physical infrastructure but also to promote state companies. She launched a massive, $70 billion infrastructure project funded by state borrowing and designed to improve Thailand's rail, road, and other transit systems.[11] Domestic construction and infrastructure companies were given priority over foreign firms in the infrastructure bidding, but domestic firms that would bid for the projects also found that to win their bids, they had to agree to much greater government influence over their corporate decision-making. Overall, under Yingluck, Thailand's public debt continued to balloon, while the idea that the government should take a more active role in directing bank lending, managing companies in key industries, and controlling many other aspects of the economy became more and more entrenched among top policymakers.[12]

Despite spiraling public debt, many Thai and foreign economists credit Thaksinomics with helping restore Thailand's economic growth by stimulating consumer demand, focusing on key strategic industries, and effectively using the power of the state to rebuild these industries after the Asian financial crisis.[13] The Thaksin government's universal health-care scheme has saved at least eighty thousand Thai families from bankruptcy, according to a study by the World Health Organization. Income inequality in Thailand has shrunk since the advent of the Thaksin era in 2001—a major success—although the country still suffers from some of the worst economic inequality in Asia. But the verdict on Thaksin's economic and social policies is hardly unanimous: many economists and Thai policy analysts argue that while achieving some goals, Thaksinomics has left Thailand with a crushing debt burden to be borne by future generations. Some economists further argue that Thaksinomics failed to encourage the kind of innovation that often comes from truly private companies, who are forced to compete with—and usually lose to—Thai national champions in many industries. Thailand still applies for far fewer patents annually than neighboring nations like China or Singapore. Thailand under Thaksin witnessed few examples of entrepreneurial Thai private companies growing up into profitable and mature corporations.

THE RISE OF ELECTED AUTOCRATS

Thaksin was emblematic of a new type of leader who has emerged in the developing world over the past decade—an elected autocrat. The rise of elected autocrats is one of several reasons why modern state capitalism has emerged and grown over the past two decades. By examining the reasons behind the rise of modern state capitalism, we can better understand how quickly state capitalism has spread throughout the developing world.

The elected autocrats include men and women like Thaksin, Cambodia's prime minister, Hun Sen; Malaysia's prime minister, Najib Razak; or Venezuela's former president, Hugo Chavez. These leaders actually did win relatively free national elections, and then used their power to crush all of their opposition. There are others, like Russian president Vladimir Putin, who did not take office via truly competitive elections but nonetheless have some means of public consultation and are far more beholden to public opinion than the dictators of the twentieth century. These "elected autocrats" thus uphold the electoral components of democracy (at least in a facile way) while ignoring, or actually undermining, the constitutional, legal aspects of democracy.

In many young democracies, or states falling somewhere between democracy and autocracy (e.g., Venezuela and Thailand), weak new institutions have been unable to constrain these elected autocrats, and regular elections are the only aspect of democracy that has survived, if it has survived at all. Indeed, as I chronicled in *Democracy in Retreat: The Revolt of the Middle Class and the Worldwide Decline of Representative Government*, since the early 2000s, the height of the post–Cold War global wave of democratization in the developing world, democracy's worldwide progress has stalled and gone into reverse.[14] This democratic regression has been chronicled by Freedom House, the Bertelsmann Foundation, and many other organizations, as well as by my own research at the Council on Foreign Relations.[15] The number of truly free electoral democracies has dipped since the early 2000s. According to Freedom House, democracy's "forward march" actually peaked around the beginning of the 2000s.[16] A mountain of evidence supports that gloomy conclusion. One of the most comprehensive studies of global democracy, the Bertelsmann Foundation's Transformation Index, declared in its 2014 version that democracy is in a state of "stagnation" throughout the developing world. The few countries that have made significant progress toward democracy in recent years are canceled out by those that are regressing, the index found.[17] The previous version of the index, released in 2012, also found that democracy was stagnating or regressing around the world.

State capitalism, in many of these regressing countries, has been both a cause and an effect of this political backsliding. In some of the cases of political regression, like Egypt or Russia, the countries already had histories of state control of many companies, though the degree of that control varied. Many of these nations went through political and economic reforms at the same time in the post–Cold War period, and, like Thailand, no longer would have qualified as state capitalists by the early 2000s. But an initial generation of elected leaders, like Thaksin, had little commitment to democracy, rolling back democratic institutions and damaging democratic culture. Nearly all of this first generation of elected leaders also deepened state control of the economy as they were chewing up democratic institutions. Sometimes, they made places like Venezuela or Thailand that had not been state capitalists in the past—they had relatively open economies—into state capitalists. In other cases, like Russia, they vastly expanded the state capitalism that had existed before. We will see later on how many of these leaders were wise enough to realize that while developing state capitalism, they should not cut themselves off from the world; several of these countries, including Thailand, remained relatively efficient economies.

In some of these countries, the tradition of state involvement in the economy allowed leaders like Vladimir Putin to expand that control further; state capitalism thus can be an effect of the rollback of political reform combined with a history of statism. In other places, leaders like Thaksin expanded the state's control of the economy, and state capitalism then further weakened democracy by providing leaders powerful tools to use to favor political allies and destroy opposing politicians. Thaksin, Hugo Chavez, Malaysia's Najib tun Razak, and similar leaders in this era of democratic regression have wielded these tools to decimate political opposition. Thus, state capitalism in these regressing nations has been a cause of the rollback of democracy.

Sometimes, when the first generations of elected leaders in developing nations failed to embrace democratic institutions, people in these nations embraced undemocratic political answers to the challenge of elected autocrats. In particular, elites and middle classes, who had lost political power at the hands of populist elected autocrats, have turned against democracy. At times, as in Ukraine, Thailand, or Egypt, these elites and urban middle classes have held large, violent protests against elected—if indeed highly flawed—leaders. In some cases, as in Thailand and Egypt, middle classes and elites have openly called for the armed forces to intervene and end elected democracy and have held demonstrations designed to create pretexts for army interventions. In 2006, the Thai armed forces responded to protests paralyzing Bangkok and calling for military intervention with a coup, and in 2009 army leaders—and, allegedly, the royal palace—helped broker defections in parliament to topple an elected government. In 2014, Thailand's military, again responding to political unrest precipitated by middle classes protesting in Bangkok, ousted the elected government in a coup and promised to return the country to a more managed and less democratic type of rule. Between late 2013 and the middle of 2014, demonstrations in Bangkok shut down parts of the city for extended periods, blocked voting for a replacement government, and forcefully shuttered government ministries.[18] After the May 2014 coup, the army leader-turned-prime-minister, Prayuth Chan-ocha, left open the possibility that Thailand would not hold elections again for some time. The junta suggested that even when Thailand did return to electoral democracy, it would not resemble electoral democracy as defined by any standard definition. Thailand's parliament could become an institution with some members appointed (probably by the military and the royal family) and many members selected by educated groups of people—coded language for saying that most of the parliament would essentially be chosen by Bangkok elites, in the same way that Hong Kong's legislature is mostly chosen by Beijing and a small handful of pro-Beijing Hong Kong elites.[19] In addition, the 2014 junta repressed civil liberties extensively, detaining hundreds of activists, academics, journalists, and opposition politicians for reeducation sessions that allegedly included various types of torture.[20]

Yet even when middle classes and elites in these countries helped engineer the overthrow of elected autocrats like Thaksin or Egypt's Mohamed Morsi, the authoritarian successor governments rarely jettisoned state control of large segments of the economy. In Thailand, junta head Prayuth Chan-ocha continued most of Thaksin and Yingluck's state capitalist policies, in part because he needed to prevent the poor and lower middle classes, who had been the biggest backers of the deposed Yingluck, from rising up against army rule. In fact, Prayuth proposed several policies, such as new legislation that would erect higher barriers to foreign investment in the kingdom, that were even more interventionist than those of the Yingluck government. Similarly, Abdel Fattah al-Sisi, the head of the junta that overthrew and jailed Egypt's Morsi, quickly vowed to put into place statist economic policies like grand new infrastructure projects that would benefit Egyptian companies.[21]

GROWING WEAKNESSES IN OTHER MODELS

Leaders from Thailand to China to Brazil have found it far easier to make the case for state capitalism over the past decade, as many Western economies have still not recovered from the economic crises of 2008–2009. Indeed, the weaknesses in free-market models of capitalism are a second major reason why state capitalism has caught on in developing nations. Growth in developing Africa, Latin America, and South Asia remained weak in the 1990s and early 2000s, even as it boomed in some more statist economies like China, Vietnam, Malaysia, and Singapore. Indeed, as economist Dani Rodrik notes, even as Western nations advocated for the Washington Consensus, developing world leaders saw that, in Rodrik's words, "one of the paradoxes of the last two decades of globalization is that its biggest beneficiaries [China, Vietnam, Brazil, India] have been the countries that have flouted its [the Washington Consensus'] rules."[22]

Meanwhile, the late 1990s Asian financial crisis left a legacy in the minds of many Asian policymakers and publics that actually fostered greater post-crisis state intervention, even though statist policies were partly to blame for the graft and massive debts in state banks that had helped cause the crisis. During the crisis, several of the countries like Thailand, that had adopted orthodox, IMF-promoted reforms designed to open their economies, reduce state control over major companies, root out cronyism, and shutter failing banks, faced years of severe economic downturns. Both Thailand and Indonesia began to recover by the early 2000s, and probably would have continued to recover if they had maintained more liberal economic policies; even the initial attempts at reforms promoted in Thailand and Indonesia at the height of the crisis helped make the countries' banks and finance companies more efficient and more profitable. Asian countries like South Korea that pursued liberalizing reforms during the crisis and continued those reforms for the next decade saw significant effects—South Korea's economy became far more dynamic, a dynamism that ultimately paid off in more globally competitive and innovative South Korean companies.

But the effects of these reforms took years, and in the meantime, the publics in these countries faced spiraling unemployment, which they blamed on the reforms. In South Korea, a far richer country than Thailand or Indonesia, the public was better able to handle the initial shock of liberalizing reforms, but in Thailand and Indonesia, the damage of the economic crisis in 1997, combined with the initial impact of IMF-prescribed reforms in 1998, pushed many people into poverty. In Indonesia, more than 20 percent of the population had fallen below the poverty line by the end of 1998. The fact that these reforms were seen as being demanded by foreigners, and implemented with little heed paid to local sensitivities, angered Thais and Indonesians even more and paved the way for renewed state capitalism. In one now-famous photo from early 1998, then-IMF head Michel Camdessus towered, arms folded, over Indonesian leader Suharto during the signing of an agreement for an IMF bailout package. Camdessus apparently did not realize that in most countries in Southeast Asia it is considered a major insult to keep your head above that of your host.

By contrast, Malaysia and China, which shunned IMF advice and kept their currencies pegged and protected and many of their banks and large companies in state hands, survived the crisis far stronger initially than Thailand or Indonesia had. China and Malaysia did not face the upsurge of poverty during the crisis that battered neighboring Indonesia. After the crisis, both foreign and Malaysian economists agreed that Malaysia's capital controls and currency peg helped it, at the time, protect itself from some of the worst capital flight and speculation in Southeast Asia, speculation that had undermined the Thai currency and worsened the crisis.

Thais and Indonesians and people from other crisis-hit nations saw how Malaysia and China continued to prosper, relatively, during the region-wide downturn. Beijing and Kuala Lumpur did not implement reforms to their state-owned financial sectors, and within their banks debts continue to pile up, but Malaysia grew by 6.1 percent in 1999, only one year after the height of the Asian financial crisis—a time when most of the rest of Southeast Asia was still struggling.[23] Malaysia's autocratic and charismatic prime minister, Mahathir Mohamad, toured the region in the wake of the crisis constantly touting his state interventionist approach, portraying it almost as an anticolonial effort—the colonists being Western investors and the IMF. The moral of the Asian financial crisis spread beyond Southeast Asia as well. Officials and leaders visiting Southeast Asia at the time from many developing nations got the impression that only countries that had not given in to liberal economic reforms had survived without a heavy dose of pain. It was an impression that Thaksin, among other incoming leaders in the 2000s, would play upon.

During the Asian financial crisis, Western governments and the international financial institutions remained highly confident in the Washington Consensus model, even as leaders from developing nations began to question it. Yet later, the 2008–2009 economic and financial crisis dented Western governments' confidence as well. Western, free-market economies suffered so badly in the late 2000s and early 2010s that other models looked potentially attractive by comparison, even if in the long run the state capitalist model's durability remains unproven. Even by 2014, when this book was finished, many European economies had not recovered from the shocks of 2008–2009: Spain, the thirteenth-largest economy in the world, had an unemployment rate of 27 percent for the general population and a staggering 57 percent for Spaniards under 25 years old.[24] Italy, the ninth-largest economy in the world, by 2014 was running an unemployment rate of nearly 12 percent, a twenty-year high, and for many months following chaotic parliamentary elections could not even form a government.

Not only critics in the developing world but also many Western observers now openly wonder whether a more centralized model, as practiced in China or Singapore, might avoid the short-term profit orientation that created the maze of gambling-type derivatives and mortgage investments that sparked the 2008–2009 financial crisis. With a more centralized model, less dependent on (or, one might say, less accountable to) shareholders, governments could in theory make economic decisions for the longer term, instead of focusing on short-term profits. The 2008–2009 crisis, argued former US deputy Treasury secretary Roger Altman, has left "the American model . . . under a cloud."[25] "This relatively unscathed position gives China the opportunity to solidify its strategic advantages as the United States and Europe struggle to recover," Altman noted.

These seeming flaws in the West appeared especially notable when compared with what seemed like the streamlined, rapid economic decision-making of the Chinese leadership, which did not have to deal with such "obstacles" as a legislature or judiciary or free media that actually could question or block its actions. "One-party autocracy certainly has its drawbacks. But when it is led by a reasonably enlightened group of people, as in China today, it can also have great advantages," wrote the influential *New York Times* foreign affairs columnist Thomas Friedman. "One party can just impose the politically difficult but critically important policies needed to move a society forward."[26] Even John Williamson, the author of the original economics paper that had coined the term "Washington Consensus," started to question his own views, authoring a paper in 2012 titled "Is the Beijing Consensus Now Dominant?" The paper admitted that, over the past two decades, many aspects of China's economic strategy had proven far more effective than free-market economists like Williamson originally had imagined.[27]

The West's own embrace of intervention in the economy during the 2008–2009 crisis further dulled the shine of the free-market model, though this intervention was temporary and did not reach the level of the state capitalists. In the late 2000s, many Western countries nationalized portions of their own economies, from the US's Troubled Asset Recovery Program (TARP) to the European Union's (EU) bailout of Greece to the nationalizing of major banks in several EU countries. These temporary measures often had defined end points—in contrast to interventions in states like Russia, China, Thailand, or Brazil that had no clear end point. Still, programs like TARP or the EU bailouts undermined the rhetorical authority of Western nations to push free-market capitalism on developing states.

STATE CAPITALISTS PROMOTE THEIR MODELS

Since the 2008–2009 crisis, China and several smaller countries that have created relatively efficient state capitalism like Singapore have become more vocal about advocating their models of development. As we will see in more detail in examining China's model, the efficient state capitalists have promoted their models through training programs for visiting economic officials, through media outlets, and through other avenues.

As leaders of major emerging markets, whether democracies like Brazil or autocracies like China, meet more regularly, economists, businesspeople, and journalists from these countries interact more too, leading to further organic cross-fertilization of ideas about state capitalism. Major emerging economies have increasingly invested in other emerging economies, as well as becoming markets for other emerging economies' products. The emerging powers increasingly have worked together to reshape institutions like the IMF and the G-8, now expanded to the G-20. At summits of the so-called BRICS nations (Brazil, Russia, India, China, and South Africa), these emerging powers have challenged many established international institutions, including the makeup of the UN Security Council and the use of the dollar as the world's reserve currency.[28] They have proposed creating a BRICS development bank financed by the largest developing nations, and a $100 billion BRICS reserves fund to be used to help stabilize other developing countries hit by financial crisis, the kind of stabilization that used to be provided solely by the World Bank and IMF.[29] With the support of many developing nations, China has created a new infrastructure bank for Asia as well. Opinion leaders from developing nations have used these summits, as well as bilateral meetings and more regular academic exchanges, to study the economic models of places like Brazil and China and Singapore.

THE EMERGENCE OF NEW CRITICS

Many of these developing nations also contain growing segments of opinion leaders who have become harsh critics of market reforms and proponents of state control of companies. The emergence of these critics has added intellectual fuel to the push for state capitalism in countries from China to Brazil. Some of this criticism is founded in historical traditions.

In India, a strong statist, anti-Western strand of economics and politics has been part of the country's identity since independence. And, despite economic reforms in the 1990s that liberalized some of the economy, "the internal anticolonial strain in the newly independent India morphed into sustained anti-imperialist posturing within the political discourse on world affairs [during the Cold War]," notes India specialist C. Raja Mohan.[30] India had maintained friendly relations with the Soviet Union during the Cold War, while the United States tilted toward Pakistan. Though the end of the Soviet empire and the bankruptcy of India's completely state-dominated economic model in the early 1990s would undermine some Indians' faith in non-alignment and socialism, this antipathy toward the Western model and this belief in the power of state intervention would remain potent among many Indian opinion leaders.

Years of socialist economics and state control of large companies and massive tariffs and domestic regulations—the so-called License Raj that empowered bureaucrats and terrified businesspeople—collapsed in the early 1990s, as India faced a balance of payments crisis that threatened to bring the economy crashing down. Then-finance minister (and later prime minister) Manmohan Singh saw the crisis as an opportunity, and pushed through reforms designed to slash red tape, make Indian manufacturing and services globally competitive, and lure investment comparable to that attracted by powerhouse neighboring economies like Thailand and China. India's growth rate picked up, to over 7 percent for much of the 2000s, with services growing particularly quickly. But it did not reach the pace of the Chinese economy, and by the late 2000s the Indian economy was slowing again, partly because Singh's initial reforms had not been fully implemented, with many sectors of the economy still overburdened with red tape or dominated by monopolists, and partly because Indian politics had become even more fragmented, with the Congress Party having trouble putting together coalitions to pass legislation.

As India's economy faltered in the late 2000s and early 2010s, particularly in comparison to a still-thriving Chinese economy—India's press constantly featured columns and stories comparing India to China—many left-leaning intellectuals pushed for renewed state influence in sectors of the Indian economy. In 2012, the country's growth rate dropped to just over 5 percent year-on-year, not enough to absorb the massive numbers of Indians entering the job market as the country hit a demographic bulge. Private investment dropped. Singh, aging and at the head of the Congress

Party's unwieldy coalition, which included quite a few leading politicians who still believed in traditional Indian statist economics, seemed to have little appetite for another go at serious economic reforms, like opening up new sectors or slashing corporate taxes and fuel subsidies. In 2011, the government under Singh abruptly shifted course, drawing up a new National Manufacturing Plan that would reinstitute significant state involvement in many sectors and reverse some of the reforms of the 1990s and early 2000s. Singh's government then imposed new conditions on foreign investors in retail in India, dramatically restricting their opportunities to sell goods in India.[31]

Singh's shift in course was not enough to save the Congress Party, which was swamped in 2014 parliamentary elections by the Bharatiya Janata Party (BJP) and its leader, Narendra Modi. But it was hardly clear that Indians wanted a drastic reduction of state capitalism, though Modi and the BJP historically had pursued more right-leaning and market-oriented policies. Modi had made Gujarat, the state he had run, one of the most business friendly in all of India by opening up labor markets and launching incentives to attract foreign and domestic investors. Yet the normal tendency of Indian voters to toss out incumbents, and the Congress Party's weak leadership in the election campaign, highlighted by feeble party head Rahul Gandhi, was largely to blame for the massive 2014 defeat. What's more, in the aftermath of the BJP's huge win, it became apparent, in post-vote questionnaires, that many Indians had simply voted for Modi, and not his party, since they viewed him as a decisive leader and a self-made man, a sharp break from dynastic Congress Party rule.

CHINESE CRITICS

In China, critics of the economic reforms launched in the 1990s and early 2000s have become known as the "New Left," although "left" and "right" bear little resemblance to what these terms mean on the American political spectrum.[32] The New Left includes several prominent academics and writers. Several of the New Leftists' books have become enormous hits, such as the bestseller *China is Not Happy*, which was published in 2009 and advocated continued state control of many sectors of the economy. Though there are many strands of the New Left, most of the New Leftists call for the state to support indigenous innovation, protect and consolidate companies in some of the largest industries, reduce reliance on foreign investment and exports as drivers of the economy, and create a broader social security net to reduce income inequality and provide programs for the poor. Many also argue—with some reason—that Western nations, particularly those in continental Western Europe, used subsidies to prop up domestic manufacturing and agriculture and high tariffs to support their own nascent industries and farmers in the early and mid-twentieth century, or simply controlled major companies outright, so why shouldn't developing countries do the same now? China's state enterprises must remain "pillars of the economy," wrote one famous New Left economist, Lang Xianping.[33] By contrast, more right-leaning intellectuals and Party leaders mostly advocated market-oriented reforms similar to the free-market, neoliberal policies advocated today by the IMF and World Bank and most developed economies.[34]

China's New Left, like Indian statists, draws on some historical foundations within China. Unlike leftist intellectuals in the West, where criticizing Western society was almost required to prove one's left-wing bona fides, most of the Chinese New Leftists also are extremely nationalistic, arguing that right-leaning Chinese intellectuals who promote market reforms and privatizing state companies have been co-opted by selfishly individualistic Western ideas and have become un-Chinese. Some of the New Left's writing has verged on conspiratorial paranoia, suggesting that American companies are trying to destroy the Chinese economy and accusing foreign multinationals of trying to introduce genetically modified crops that will ruin all of China's native species, for example. (These critiques form an interesting counterpoint to the frequent criticism, voiced in the American press and in Congress, that American multinationals are not doing enough to assist American workers, and instead are selling out to China.)

Some of the New Left books, like *China is Not Happy*, have become so popular that their ideas have filtered down to the general public in urban areas, forcing Party leaders to pay attention to New Left intellectuals. In urban China, nationalism already had become a potent force in the 2000s, partly because of the ways in which the Party, which could no longer rely on communism as a unifying ideology, had inculcated nationalism in younger Chinese through school history textbooks portraying China as a power that had been emasculated for centuries by Western countries and then Japan, but would rise again—under the Party's leadership, of course.

Rising income inequality in China, which skyrocketed during the reform period of the 1990s and 2000s, has helped provide ammunition for the New Leftists. As Charles Freeman, a China specialist who has studied the New Leftists extensively, notes, the Party recognized, as the 2000s wore on, that income inequality was driving many protests in China, and would have to be addressed to keep the Party in power. This recognition, along with the public popularity of some New Left ideas, gave several New Left writers and intellectuals entrée to the highest levels of the Party. Bo Xilai, the popular governor of Chongqing province, openly embraced many of the New Left ideas, calling for a return of massive state intervention in the economy, particularly in controlling companies in many sectors. Bo also increased Chongqing province's spending on social welfare programs such as subsidized housing and even held mass mobilization campaigns designed to resemble those of the Maoist era, which was remembered with a rosy glow, the purges and mass murders and famines going unmentioned.[35] (Bo also aggressively wooed foreign investment by cutting corporate tax rates, though he tended to play down that part of his economic policymaking when talking to the public or to Chinese opinion leaders.[36])

Though Chinese Party leaders would disassociate themselves from Bo following his arrest in 2011 on murder charges—allegedly after he failed in his aggressive tactics to win a top position within the senior Party leadership—all of the members of future president Xi Jinping's leadership circle paid visits to Chongqing while Bo was still governor.[37] They came to Chongqing to bask in Bo's popularity and to study his ideas.

The broader popularity of New Left books, the popularity (for a time) of Bo, and the New Left's tinges of nationalism, which jibed with the nationalist mood in urban China, gave the New Left a strong swath of public support by the late 2000s. By 2013 and 2014, several New Left intellectuals had positioned themselves as allies of new president Xi Jinping, even though Xi had publicly called for some of the most sweeping, pro-market reforms in China in two decades.[38]

Many of the New Leftists wound up pleased with Xi, as the Chinese leader adopted a more assertive foreign policy than his predecessors, centralized political control more than any leader since Deng Xiaoping, and did not open the economy in the ways he had promised.

In addition, promises of serious economic liberalization remained just promises. Xi launched a real fight against corruption, jailing several high-level officials in state companies, including a senior executive at state oil giant PetroChina. These arrests emboldened Chinese reformists who believed that Xi's government was serious not only about fighting graft but also about cutting down the power of state firms and unleashing market forces. But the corruption campaign did not extend into other types of economic reforms; it was designed in large part to remove potential enemies of the president, who was consolidating his personal political power.[39] By the end of 2014, prominent China specialists such as the Council on Foreign Relations' Elizabeth Economy were calling Xi "an imperial president" who had amassed enormous personal political power.[40] And only a few months after becoming president, Xi launched an almost Maoist-style ideological campaign against "Western influences."[41] In a document leaked to the *New York Times*, Communist Party leaders under Xi circulated a memorandum outlining several supposedly subversive "Western" concepts that could bring down the Party and the government; prominent officials and public intellectuals were warned not to speak openly about these concepts.[42] The memo, called "Document No. 9" and written as a kind of warning to top Party members, listed the seven threats barred from public discourse. On the list, alongside democracy, was "neo-liberal" economics.[43] Although the memo might seem laughable to an outsider in its apocalyptic *Dr. Strangelove* tone—"Western forces hostile to China and dissidents within the country are still constantly infiltrating the ideological sphere"—it was consistent with Xi's repeated warnings in 2013 to other top officials that China should not copy Western models of free-market economics and democracy, according to several Chinese academics.[44]

We will see in much greater detail how state capitalism continues to thrive under Xi and Li. State companies certainly know how to make their case to senior Communist Party leaders. Several executives from SOEs have lobbied government officials heavily during major Party meetings in Beijing. Some SOEs' chiefs argued that the state companies were actually even more profitable than they had been a decade ago, noting that in the first half of 2013, the largest state companies, which come under the direction of the central body called the State-owned Assets Supervision and Administration Commission (SASAC,) saw their profits increase by over 18 percent year-on-year, a very impressive figure.[45] Other executives from state firms stressed that in an increasingly hostile Asia where China was involved in low-level conflict with Japan, Vietnam, and other countries over disputed territory, state firms were critical to maintaining government dominance of important resources and of many industries essential to national security.

Some academics and leaders of state firms played on Xi's nationalist leanings to suggest that state capitalism remained an important part of China's overall power. Entering office, Xi appeared far more nationalistic than predecessors Hu Jintao and Jiang Zemin; before becoming president, Xi had slammed foreign countries that criticized China's style of development and rights abuses, and he had called for China to return to its central role on the world stage. Assuming the top job, Xi soon offered other suggestions that he would be a more assertive nationalist than either Hu or Jiang. In his first notable speech as party chief, Xi called for a "Chinese Dream," a concept left intentionally vague but one that could be read as calling for China to return to its status as one of the biggest powers, if not the dominant power, in the world, or at least in East Asia.[46] Xi also spoke out more publicly for an assertive Chinese army and navy, calling on the military to get ready to "fight and win [wars]."[47] During his first year as president, Xi also sent signals that China would take an increasingly hard line with foreign investors in industries where Chinese state companies were powerful, or if foreign investors complained about Chinese competitors' tactics. The *Financial Times* reported, "Since he [Xi] came to power . . . foreign companies have been targeted by corruption investigations, price-fixing accusations and state media-led smear campaigns."[48] In the spring of 2014, Xi's government also reportedly demanded that all Chinese SOEs end any contracts with Western consulting firms, like McKinsey and Company and Bain Consulting. "The top leadership has proposed setting up a team of Chinese domestic consultants who are particularly focused on information systems in order to seize back this power from the foreign companies," the *Financial Times* reported.[49] Although China is a World Trade Organization (WTO) member, Beijing has never signed WTO agreements that commit signers to treating all bidders equally in procurement of government contracts or in dealing with state firms. The consulting companies thus had little immediate recourse after being sacked. (China has signed other WTO protocols that appear to outlaw this kind of sacking of consultants simply because they are foreign, but these protocols are almost impossible to enforce.)

Criticism in Democracies

In Brazil, Turkey, and Indonesia, similar critics of orthodox economics as in China emerged in the late 2000s, as Western economies imploded, the Washington Consensus sprang leaks, and politics in these countries opened up, making it easier for opponents of any government policies—including privatizations—to garner support. As in China, the critics in other developing nations called on their governments to reverse privatizations and roll back reforms instituted in the 1990s and early 2000s. Under the presidency of Fernando Henrique Cardoso between 1995 and 2003, Brazil had privatized nearly all of the largest state-owned manufacturing companies, slashed the inflation that had dogged the country, and stopped the tap of state spending that had repeatedly scared off investors and devalued the currency.

In some ways, critics of the periods of privatization actually were able to have more influence in Brazil, India, Turkey, and other democratic nations than in autocratic states like China. They could rally the public and vote in leaders, like Lula, who shared their beliefs—a luxury the New Left in China did not enjoy. And even between elections, advocates of state intervention in democracies like Brazil or India had far more influence than peers in places like China because it is easier to organize and influence policymakers in an emerging democracy than in a place like Beijing or Moscow, where any open dissent could be punished by jail time.

In South Africa, Brazil, Turkey, and Indonesia, among other countries, more vocal, vibrant democracy has sparked public support for intervention in many sectors of the economy. In South Africa, the post-apartheid economic policies of the 1990s and early 2000s had created macroeconomic stability and a clutch of powerful, private South African companies, like supermarket giant Shop Rite. But growth only put a small dent in the inequality created by decades of apartheid. Nelson Mandela, with his enormous popularity and credibility among South Africans, was able to essentially go against public opinion calling for greater wealth transfer to the poor and more state intervention in sectors like mining and energy. Mandela used his time as president to promote moderately market-oriented economic policies, as well as to prevent more radical ANC members from pushing legislation to seize white farmers' land. His successor, the urbane, anglophile Thabo Mbeki, pursued even more orthodox free-market policies, using tax reforms to encourage foreign investment and adopting a policy called "Black Economic Empowerment" that helped ensconce some of the most educated and politically savvy black leaders at the tops of many South African corporations but did little for any black South Africans below the elite. Today, South Africa's economy is one of the most unequal in the world.[50]

But as in Brazil, as South Africa's democracy has come of age and public opinion has played a larger role in shaping government policies, that public voice actually has pushed for greater state economic intervention to combat inequality and to create national champion state companies. Younger leaders of the ANC, dissenting economists like prominent critic Moletsi Mbeki (brother of former president Thabo Mbeki), and leading breakaway unions representing mineworkers recoiled from the policies of the 1990s and 2000s. These critics argued that these Black Economic Empowerment policies, while diversifying the highest levels of South Africa's biggest companies, had only created a new class of ANC-connected black tycoons, such as former head of the National Union of Mineworkers—an ANC ally—Cyril Ramaphosa, who became a wealthy mining executive. As Ramaphosa and a small circle of ANC colleagues got rich, South Africa still had enormous wealth gaps. (By 2013, Ramaphosa was worth more than $700 million, according to *Forbes'* ranking of the richest Africans, and also had returned to government service to become deputy president.[51]) And like Ramaphosa, many former ANC anti-apartheid lions appeared comfortable with the mostly white elite and no longer interested in promoting social equity. Before stepping in as deputy president, Ramaphosa even adopted the pastimes of the old apartheid elite, like breeding expensive game for high-end hunts.[52] When mineworkers struck in 2012 for better benefits at a large mine outside Johannesburg owned by a company whose board Ramaphosa sat on, he sent emails to company heads castigating the strikers and calling for a harsh crackdown on them.[53]

DEVELOPING NATIONS LOCKED OUT OF GLOBAL CAPITAL

Many developing nations also found out, in 2008 and afterwards, that it had become far harder for companies from their countries to access international capital markets. This sudden drop in international capital flows to developing nations also helped foster the growth of state capitalism, particularly the creation of state banks and other state-dominated financial institutions in developing nations.

In the decade before 2008–09, foreign banks, particularly from Europe, had increasingly concentrated their lending on large emerging markets, where global growth was concentrated and where there was, initially, less competition in the banking sector. But in 2008 and 2009, foreign banks suddenly stopped lending in many emerging markets, at the same time as the economies of Europe, the United States, and Japan—the primary markets for goods produced by most developing nations in East Asia and Latin America—slowed or went into recession, leading to reductions in consumption in the rich world. Many developing nations had very shallow domestic capital markets, with small stock exchanges, few locally owned banks, and little of the type of venture capital industries common in the United States, Europe, and wealthy Asian nations like Singapore. In Brazil, for example, a study by economists Aldo Musacchio and Sergio Lazarrini found that between 1995 and 2009 the country's average stock-market capitalization to GDP was only 43.1 percent, compared to 129.7 percent in the United States.[54] In other words, companies in Brazil were able to raise a relatively small percentage of their working capital from the country's stock markets, because these stock exchanges were dwarfed by those in the rich world. And Brazil actually has some of the larger stock markets in the developing world; in other emerging markets like Thailand, Vietnam, Malaysia, South Africa, and India, the stock markets have even smaller capitalizations than in Brazil, making it even harder for local companies to raise capital through public offerings.

With weak, shallow domestic capital markets, both large and small companies in developing nations are far more dependent on global capital than rich countries in the West or Asia. And in 2008–2009, this sudden drying up of global capital for emerging markets, on a scale not seen in decades, further helped convince leaders in nations like South Africa, Brazil, Thailand, India, and China that the state needed to take back some control—or more control—of banks, to ensure consistent lending to domestic companies and to prevent domestic companies from being completely at the mercy of international capital markets. Greater state control of banks, they believed, would help remedy market failures and keep indebted domestic state and private companies alive. As one Thai politician said, "We allowed the international banks to take over too much [of the Thai banking sector] the last crisis, in the 1990s . . . We won't make the mistake again . . . We need stronger local capital markets."[55]

The Thai government and Thai companies were not the only ones either considering renationalizing banks or looking to state banks from countries like Qatar, China, and Brazil for loans at a time when they could no longer get them from European lenders like HSBC or BNP Paribas. During the

2000s boom, capital had poured into emerging markets, primarily from European banks, which far outstripped banks from the United States, Japan, or other developed economies in emerging market lending.

But during this time period, few developing nations built strong domestic capital markets, instead relying on cheap loans from developed-world banks. As crisis-hit European nations like France have passed legislation forcing banks to maintain higher capital requirements and to invest more within their own borders, these European institutions, which had been the major sources of emerging world investments, have started a process of massive deleveraging. Until 2011, European banks accounted for about 90 percent of all foreign bank lending in Africa, Eastern Europe, and the Middle East, for example. In 2012, an analysis from consulting firm Deloitte estimated that 71 percent of European financial institutions would reduce their lending abroad for five years or more.[56] That same year, Credit Suisse estimated that European banks' returning to lending in their home markets would strip as much as $1 trillion in funding from foreign markets over the coming decades.[57]

Vowing never to be so dependent on global capital markets, many developing nations either expanded their state development banks, launched new state-controlled banks, or nationalized commercial banks. Brazil's development bank increased its lending by over 700 percent from 2000 to 2010; as economists Musacchio and Lazzarini found, companies that "borrow from Brazil's development bank pay less in interest payments overall [than those borrowing from private banks.]"[58] Even as pro-free-market a publication as *The Economist* admitted in an article that Brazil had survived the 2008–2009 global economic slowdown better than some other developing nations in part because "it was useful to have state-controlled lenders when credit from abroad dried up."[59] State-owned China Development Bank also dramatically increased its lending after 2008.

A growing number of developing nations also decided to create or enlarge state-controlled SWFs and/or to use these funds to bolster state control of companies in many sectors of their economies. In many state capitalist nations, the funds invest as much as 30 or 40 percent of their total assets domestically, whether or not these domestic investments deliver the highest possible returns. In Singapore, for example, SWF Temasek Holdings invests around 31 percent of its assets domestically.[60] Between the early 2000s and 2010, the total combined assets of the ten largest SWFs in the world grew from around $1 trillion to more than $4 trillion.[61] By 2017, according to several forecasts, SWFs will control as much as $17 trillion in assets.[62]

Of course, in the long term, these state development banks and SWFs' dual bottom lines—trying to make the most profitable investments while also assisting companies from their home countries, even if those companies are poorly run—could be recipes for wasteful lending. Already, by 2008–2009, many Chinese and Vietnamese state banks, which had to fulfill this dual function, had as high or higher amounts of non-performing loans as some of the Western banks that sparked the economic crisis—but the Chinese and Vietnamese banks, in opaque political and business climates, did not always have to reveal their losses. Still, in the wake of the 2008–2009 crisis, and watching the examples of Brazil, China, and others, many developing nations ignored the potential long-term implications of greater state capitalism in the banking sector.

ECONOMIES OF SCALE

Finally, within many individual industries, shifts in the global economy also seem to have propelled the rise of state capitalism. Because these industries do not generally involve selling directly to consumers, smaller companies within these industries do not benefit from online marketplaces that attract individual buyers and find niches—they are not the kinds of industries that might benefit from the "Long Tail" of the Internet proposed by Chris Anderson and other techno-optimistic writers.[63]

In the natural resources extraction industry, one can see how globalization over the past two decades actually has worked against smaller companies. As globalization creates greater global consumption of resources, since hundreds of millions of people from developing nations are lifting themselves from poverty and using more and more energy, the most easily accessible resources in the world are quickly being depleted. Now, promising deposits of oil, natural gas, copper, and other minerals are in places that are harder and harder to access, due to physical remoteness or political instability. In addition, safely and cost-effectively extracting these new deposits requires massive investments in research and development. These resources might be in the uppermost reaches of the northern Arctic, such as in Siberia. Or they could be found in southeastern Congo, a virtually ungoverned region of what is probably the largest failed state in the world, but which has vast troves of minerals. Or they could be buried in shale, rock that is much harder to drill gas out of than older deposits of petroleum in places like the Middle East. As one *Associated Press* article examining the low profitability of the biggest oil multinationals in the mid-2010s noted:

> Profit and production at the world's largest oil companies are slumping badly. Exxon Mobil, Shell and BP all posted disappointing earnings this week. Chevron is expected to post a profit decline. All of them face the same problem: The cost to get newfound oil from remote locations and tightly packed rock is high and rising. And it takes years and billions of dollars to get big new production projects up and running. . . . The new oil being found and produced is in ultra-deep ocean waters, in sands that must be heated to release the hydrocarbons or trapped in shale or other tight rock that requires constant drilling to keep production steady. That makes this new oil far more expensive to get out of the ground than what's known as conventional oil—large pools of oil and gas in relatively easy-to-drill locations. Those reserves have always been hard to find, but now they are all but gone outside of the Middle East.[64]

Given the challenges of bringing oil and gas to market, many Western energy companies have gone out of business in the past two decades or been forced to consolidate into multinational supermajors like ExxonMobil to achieve the economies of scale needed to survive. To be sure, a few smaller oil companies, like Houston-based EOG Resources, have been able to make money from the shale gas boom in the United States. But smaller companies usually must partner with the oil and gas giants to bring this harder-to-find oil and gas to market today. Meanwhile, the bigger players continue to struggle with the high costs of getting oil and gas to market. Even with industry consolidation, the largest Western energy companies now are smaller than the biggest state capitalist energy companies, like China's oil and gas firms or Russia's state giants or Brazil's state energy giant Petrobras. These state giants are able to utilize government subsidies, soft loans, protections against foreign competitors, and other incentives to achieve enormous economies of scale that make them feared competitors and allow them to make the vast capital outlays needed to get oil and gas out of the earth in the increasingly challenging locales where petroleum companies search.

A 2014 article by the *Wall Street Journal* summarized Big Oil's growing challenges, the same challenges that have forced consolidation and have made multinationals like ExxonMobil weaker competitors compared to state oil giants. "Chevron Corp., Exxon Mobil Corp. and Royal Dutch Shell

PLC spent more than $120 billion in 2013 to boost their oil and gas output—about the same cost in today's dollars as putting a man on the moon," the *Journal* article noted. "But the three oil giants have little to show for all their big spending. Oil and gas production are down despite combined capital expenses of a half-trillion dollars in the past five years."[65]

In industries like telecommunications infrastructure, automobiles and automobile parts, aviation, and shipping, similar economies of scale have become essential to making ever more complicated planes, boats, cars, or telecoms. The growing expense of research and development and of developing technologies that function and can be sold across a vast range of international markets has created high barriers to entry and survival. Even large private multinationals, seeing the need for economies of scale to survive, have been consolidating into ever larger giants such as wireless company SprintNextel. But as in resources extraction, these private giants are finding it increasingly difficult to compete with state-linked firms that have the enormous assets of their governments behind them and that benefit from significant subsidies for research and development. Huawei, China's global telecom giant, has received low-interest loans worth some $30 billion from state-controlled China Development Bank to foster the company's overseas expansion.[66] Indeed, while many Western telecommunications infrastructure firms have shrunk over the past decade, Huawei has expanded rapidly and now supplies every major European telecommunications carrier.[67] In 2012, for example, Huawei's global sales revenues increased by more than 8 percent year-on-year, with net profits of nearly $2 billion, a 33 percent increase in profits from the previous year—stunning growth at a time when the telecommunications infrastructure business has become intensely competitive, with nearly impossibly thin profit margins.[68] In 2013, Huawei's global revenues again increased by roughly 8 percent year-on-year, and the company recorded operating profits of over $4.5 billion.[69]

The more powerful developing nations embracing state capitalism in industries from energy to banking to telecommunications are putting pressure on other nations to create or expand state-controlled companies as well, in order to possess competing economies of scale. This pressure is particularly intense in regions where state companies are not only big players in industries like energy or telecommunications but also potential weapons in disputes with other nations. In Southeast Asia, for example, the Vietnamese government has expanded the capital, workforce, and exploratory activities of PetroVietnam, the state petroleum company, even though many Vietnamese state companies are sinking in debt and holding back the entire Vietnamese economy. (The bookkeeping of Vietnamese state companies is extremely obscure, and their true debt burdens can be difficult to pin down.) Hanoi has done this, according to several senior Vietnamese officials, since China increasingly has used state-owned China National Petroleum Corporation, accompanied by Chinese paramilitary vessels, to sink exploratory rigs in areas of the South China Sea also claimed by Vietnam. In response, Hanoi has expanded PetroVietnam's abilities to explore in the South China Sea, in order to potentially make its own claims to areas of the sea, while also beefing up Vietnam's naval and coast guard forces. As both China and Vietnam expand their explorations in the South China Sea and their naval exercises in disputed waters, the possibility of a military clash between the two countries is increasing.

The pressure put on Vietnam and other countries by Chinese state companies in industries like energy or construction is unlikely to abate. The Chinese government has decided that state-owned companies should lead China's outward investment, particularly in emerging markets. According to data compiled regularly by the Heritage Foundation, SOEs comprise more than 90 percent of Chinese outward investment, even since the launch of Xi and Li's supposed economic reforms. The four Chinese companies with the largest outward investments all are state firms.[70] And as the next chapter shows, despite the current Chinese leadership's promises that they will enact sweeping programs of economic liberalization, there is little reason to think that, when Xi and Li step down after two five-year terms, China's state companies will be weaker than they are today.

5

China's State Capitalism—A Closer Look

Beginning in the middle of June 2013, global financial markets tumbled down a whiplashing roller coaster. Emerging markets, particularly in Asia, witnessed massive sell-offs of their bonds, enormous slides in their stock markets, and investors dumping their currencies as fast as they could. India's rupee fell to historic lows against the US dollar, and other Asian currencies plummeted by as much as 20 percent against the dollar. Meanwhile, investors furiously sold off their holdings of Thai, Malaysian, Indonesian, Indian, Chinese, and other Asian bonds. Alex Feldman of the United States-ASEAN Business Council, a trade organization based in Washington and focused on Southeast Asia, said, "It's chaos in the region now, every day the [region's] stock markets open and as soon as the bell goes it's a frenzy of selling, selling, selling."[1]

At the beginning of the sell-off, the markets were roiled by Federal Reserve chairman Ben Bernanke's public comments that, by 2014, the Federal Reserve might stop its policy of quantitative easing and start raising interest rates again. But as the summer and fall wore on, and the Fed did not immediately halt quantitative easing, it became clear that traders frantically selling off Asian stocks, currencies, and bonds had another, seemingly more terrifying nightmare: they were worried about the prospect of an economic collapse in China, the world's second-largest economy. By the summer of 2013, the interbank lending rate in China—the rate at which banks lend to each other, which rises when there are fears that the banks being lent to cannot pay back their debts—had jumped precipitously. Financial columnists, economists, and many traders warned that Chinese banks, which for years have been piling up debt lending to SOEs and building infrastructure, would now be facing a severe credit crunch. China's money markets slowed to a near halt, China's own stock markets recorded several of their largest one-day drops, and the Chinese central bank revealed that Chinese savers had taken out as much as $40 billion from Chinese banks in May alone. Many Western fund managers began reducing their funds' exposure to the Chinese market. *Forbes* columnist and longtime China analyst Gordon Chang, who had worked for years in China and had long predicted China's economic demise, wrote during the June 2013 credit crunch, "Each crisis is getting worse than the previous one ... Essentially what you're going to have is catastrophe [economic] failure."[2]

Outside the country, short-sellers and virtually anyone who doubted that China could continue to post the sizzling growth rates it had been recording for three decades started a familiar echo: Chinese banks' debt loads signaled the arrival of an event doomsayers have been predicting for thirty years—not a slowdown but a meltdown of China's economy. A Chinese meltdown, of course, would be catastrophic for the international economy, since nearly every other country in Asia is dependent on trade with China—as are, increasingly, most Western multinationals. In addition, China's years of growth had helped it to buy up over $1.2 trillion in US debt, allowing the US government to finance its own massive stimulus spending and years of housing bubbles.[3]

These concerns were not new. Almost since Beijing began reforming in the late 1970s, as Deng Xiaoping consolidated his control over the Party, China's economy has attracted naysayers. Doubters have focused on many aspects of Chinese state capitalism. By only partially privatizing massive state companies, and then reassuming control of many of the largest companies, the government, they argued, was creating enormous economic inefficiencies; by continuing to intervene heavily both in the real economy and equity markets, it was inflating bubbles and making many Chinese people think the government would never let important economic sectors fail. Beijing, critics maintained, was building up national champion companies that would be made too large to fail in industries like energy, telecommunications infrastructure, and automaking. China was using cheap credit from state banks to help these indigenous companies grow, while amassing excessive amounts of government debt and impeding the economy from becoming less dependent on state spending and more dependent on consumer spending. China's state-controlled banking sector has made it hard for outsiders to estimate the total amount of nonperforming loans in China's four biggest banks—adding further fuel to the argument that, one day, the China model's opacity, cheap credit, and overall state meddling will cause the economy, and China's political system, to implode.[4]

In part, these predictions have seemed almost wishful—perhaps if the Chinese economy collapsed, its authoritarian political system might come undone as well, creating the possibility of democratization and advances in human rights for over a billion people. Over a decade ago, Gordon Chang, then a lawyer with years of experience in Shanghai, already was touting China's meltdown. In fact, he had crystallized these hopes in his bestselling 2001 book *The Coming Collapse of China*, which based its collapse scenario on an economic crisis, fueled by the failure of state economic policies and corruption within the Party, snowballing into the collapse of the Communist Party and then broader political change that would bring democracy to China.[5] More recently, even as poll after poll has shown that the Chinese urban middle classes who would be key to any democratization generally support the government, the wish that economic collapse would produce political change has emerged again—only this time, collapse theorists are careful not to set a specific time frame in which an economic meltdown would lead to political change. In the spring of 2012, Larry Lang, a prominent Hong Kong-based economist who for years has been predicting the demise of China's economy and its political system, announced during a lecture in Kunming, in mainland China's Yunnan province, that China's manufacturing industry will "completely collapse" by 2015 and that the economy quickly will collapse as well.[6] Andrew Nathan, an expert on China at Columbia University, and a far more temperate and reasoned analyst than Lang, also in 2012 and 2013 predicted that China was on the verge of great change, a prediction echoed by the *Financial Times*.[7] "The resilience of the authoritarian regime in the People's Republic of China is approaching its limits," Nathan argued. "Deep changes have been taking place that eventually will have major consequences."[8]

In June 2013, the collapse theorists quickly emerged. But this time—as in so many previous cases with China—they were wrong. The Chinese economy did not melt down; in fact, it grew more strongly in 2013 than every other large economy in the world at a similar level of economic development. China's growth rate up was up alongside countries like Libya and Afghanistan, countries recovering from war or other disasters, whose growth rates in 2013 were so high because they had nowhere to go but up.

The Chinese rebound in 2013 illustrated several important points. For one, China's state and private companies may be getting too easy credit from state banks, but that does not mean these firms are necessarily unproductive zombies like some of the Thai and Indonesian construction and finance firms that were caught up in the 1997 Asian finance crisis. In 2000, Gordon Chang predicted that most of China's SOEs would not "see the second decade of the new millennium," that they could not remain state linked, reform, and become competitive with foreign businesses and in foreign countries.[9] He was wrong. Many of the Chinese state enterprises are productive enough to become serious international competitors. Many of the weakest state enterprises had been closed in the late 1990s and early 2000s, making China's state capitalism relatively efficient. Chinese firms alone, nearly all of them state owned, occupied eighty-nine of the five hundred slots in *Fortune*'s 2015 annual ranking of the largest companies in the world by revenue.[10] This figure was up from seventy-three Chinese companies on the list in 2012, and sixty-one in 2011.[11] China's score has also steadily risen on the Global Competitiveness Index, the World Economic Forum's ranking of nations' international economic competitiveness.[12] This score has risen in part because China has liberalized some areas of the economy, allowing private companies to flourish and weeding out the state companies with the worst returns on capital, but also because the remaining state companies have become more efficient.

Most important, although free-market advocates argue that the invisible hand will always be more efficient than state capitalism, China's leaders, like their models in Singapore, have now established a long record of relatively forward-thinking, tough economic decision-making; as Beijing responds to its 2015 economic slowdown and stock-market crisis, it will need to display that forward thinking for the state to retain its legitimacy. Even in the wake of the 2015 stock-market drop and economic slowdown, China's economy retained significant strengths. Economists Donna Kwak and Tao Wang of the international bank UBS examined China's manufacturing shipments, electricity use, and other indicators of growth. They found that, despite China's bubbles in infrastructure spending and housing construction, and despite the stock-market slowdown, China's manufacturing and electricity use remained strong. They also found sales of retail goods in China actually climbed during the stock-market meltdown in the summer of 2015, and that China's job market remained tight throughout 2015.[13] Chinese stocks only accounted for about 12 percent of Chinese households' wealth, far less than in most wealthy nations. Nicholas Lardy, an economist at the Peterson Institute for International Economics, noted during China's summer 2015 stock-market slowdown that wages and disposable income were all still rising in China, suggesting that the country was far from economic collapse.[14] Lardy's research revealed that in the first half of 2015, the Chinese economy added over seven million jobs, extremely strong job creation. In fact, he noted, "The pace of creation of non-agricultural jobs is stronger than in any recent year."[15] (Other China specialists, like George Magnus of Oxford University's China center, argued that China's unemployment statistics are underreported, and that true unemployment rates in China are rising and job creation is stagnating, especially for young university graduates.[16]) "Rather than a financial and economic meltdown, China is experiencing an overdue correction in its equity market," Lardy wrote.[17] The Chinese equity markets had, over the past year, experienced a massive increase, and some fall was normal, but the stock-market gyrations—the Shanghai index in particular had long witnessed wild fluctuations—said little about China's economic fundamentals.[18]

What's more, if China had been quicker to open its economy during its three decades of reform, it would have exposed itself to risks that other nations who did open their economies rapidly faced. For example, although China does eventually need a truly convertible currency for its companies to prosper worldwide on the level of Western or Japanese multinationals, the fact that China's currency is still relatively controlled and that the state has moved slowly in opening up currency markets and stock exchanges means that bad economic news cannot create the kind of runs on Chinese yuan and Chinese exchanges that destroyed countries like Thailand in the Asian financial crisis. Short-sellers of the kind who played a role in bringing down the Thai economy in 1997 by betting against the Thai baht cannot do the same to the Chinese economy today, even when China's stock markets are plummeting. The Chinese government also has worked to cull state companies and make the remaining state firms more competitive, though there is still work to be done in this process. In some economic sectors where private companies compete against state firms, private Chinese firms have demonstrated greater profitability than state companies, especially considering that many private companies do not benefit from low-interest loans provided by state banks to state companies. In other sectors, state enterprises have demonstrated competitive profitability.[19]

This is not to deny that China's economy could be more efficient by reforming its state sector, slashing subsidies (including easy credit), and empowering private-sector and foreign companies to compete in many more industries where state companies are now protected; or that I personally think China's state capitalism is the most efficient economic strategy. It also does not mean that China is best governed by an authoritarian government, even if that government is somewhat responsive to public sentiment, or that state capitalism is the best way to promote development in China. We will see the damage that China's type of state capitalism has done to some Chinese entrepreneurs, the limits state capitalism places on China's economy, and the risks China's state capitalism poses as a model for other countries. I am simply suggesting that China's state capitalism has been successful enough—indeed, quite successful, by the standards of developing countries at any time in history and certainly in the period of the past thirty years—to allow for growth, that it can be maintained for a long time, even decades, and that it has created a degree of legitimacy and stability for the government. That record of growth was one reason why, despite significant anger among Chinese investors about the 2015 stock-market slump, most of the Chinese blogosphere was filled with calls for the state to come up with strategies to right Chinese equities rather than calls for economic liberalization.

In the June 2013 crisis, the decision-making qualities that have helped make China's economy relatively efficient were apparent once again, though if the crisis showed Beijing was capable of making tough decisions about some aspects of the economy, the period after the crisis demonstrated that it was still incredibly difficult for Chinese leaders to make tough decisions about state companies and about reducing the role of the state in general. This difficulty in stepping back was evident, once again, in the summer of 2015, as China's government apparently vacillated between extensive measures designed to prop up China's equity markets and allowing the markets to operate freely, even if that meant the Shanghai and Shenzhen exchanges would fall significantly from their debt-fueled highs.

In 2013, Beijing responded to growing worry among Chinese and foreign investors about the health of China's economy and financial sector—ATMs in several Chinese cities reported huge runs on cash—with clear direction and a willingness to stomach some economic pain. Premier Li Keqiang, a former economist, and President Xi Jinping vowed to cut the economy's dependence on debt, and promised to enact policies to boost consumer spending and services and reduce dependence on exports.[20] Along with this push to rebalance China's economy away from its dependence on credit and exports, Li ordered the National Audit Office to analyze and audit all government debt in preparation for measures to cut bad loans.[21]

Indeed, Beijing showed that just because the Chinese state is playing a big role in the economy does not mean that the state will save everyone, or that the state is not interested in competition and profits; some Chinese leaders seem to understand that if their economic strategy is not efficient, the government's legitimacy will be undermined, and so maintaining efficiency is critical to the top leadership. Even as the interbank lending rate skyrocketed in mid-June 2013, and many Chinese corporate leaders and traders publicly complained about the People's Bank's hawkishness, the Chinese central bank did not inject more cash into the system.[22]

THE EVIDENCE FOR CHINA'S CONTINUED STATE CAPITALISM

China's recovery from the 2013 credit crunch, and from its 2015 stock-market plunge, suggest that its economic model remains resilient enough to survive. Indeed, China's model may well survive for decades without making a transition to completely free-market economics. Even some researchers who argue that China's private companies are becoming more important to growth and that China is becoming more of a market economy tacitly admit that state companies remain enormously powerful; the stock-market crisis of 2015 showed again how extensively Beijing can control the economy during times of economic stress. Nicholas Lardy argues that private companies are receiving a growing proportion of all bank loans from Chinese banks, and that in some parts of the Chinese economy, the private sector has largely displaced state companies.[23] Yet even as Lardy, who made his calculations before China's 2015 stock-market crisis, argues that the private sector is becoming more important to China's growth, he admits that, by his figures, state companies still take in about half of all bank lending in China. This is a figure higher than the state companies' percentage of China's total economic output. In addition, he admits that the government in Beijing, working through the party's Organization Department, "controls the top 50 firms in terms of the appointment of the three main (executives.) Provincial (officials) control a much, much larger number of appointments."[24]

A close review of the evidence confirms that China's economy has in some respects become more state controlled since the 1990s and early 2000s, when reformist premier Zhu Rongji shuttered many bankrupt state enterprises, laying off at least forty million workers, and when China joined the World Trade Organization (WTO) and vowed to reduce government control of the economy. In the mid-1990s, China's SOEs contributed only about 10 percent of the country's annual GDP, but by the early and mid-2010s, even though the number of state enterprises had decreased as unprofitable SOEs were shuttered, the remaining SOEs had grown so much that they now contributed nearly 25 percent of the country's annual GDP.[25] As we saw earlier, SOEs received by far the largest share of China's massive 2008–2009 stimulus package, while also receiving tax breaks and getting favorable treatment on loans from China's four largest state-owned banks. (Many SOEs also pay no rent on the land where their factories, headquarters, and offices sit, an enormous de facto subsidy from the state.[26]) Almost as soon as the Chinese government announced its stimulus package responding to the 2008–2009 global financial crisis, China's big four state-owned banks boosted their lending to state enterprises, according to a study by the Washington-based China consulting group Capital Trade Incorporated. As one study for the congressionally mandated United States–China Economic and Security Review Commission found, between December 2009 and December 2010, the average monthly lending prime rate in China was 5.36 percent, yet SOEs received loans from Chinese banks during that period at effective interest rates ranging from 1.13 percent to 2.7 percent, well below the prime lending rate private entrepreneurs would receive.[27] While critics like Lardy argue that the 2008–2009 stimulus package did not benefit only state companies, even they admit that state firms got a far larger share of the credit handed out in the stimulus package than state companies' total share of the Chinese economy, while private companies received less than their share of the Chinese economy.

The Chinese government also has publicly stated that, even given Xi and Li's stated desire to make it easier for private companies to compete, SOEs will be the main drivers of outward Chinese investment around the world, the strategy known by the government as "going out." The annual survey of leading Chinese multinationals by Columbia University and Fudan University in Shanghai has found that fourteen of the sixteen largest Chinese companies operating outside China are SOEs. SOEs operating overseas usually are the largest recipients of loans from state-owned China Development Bank.[28] These national champion companies, in surveys, generally enjoy significant public support in China for their international expansion; even some private Chinese businesspeople express pride in the large state enterprises' abilities to compete all over the world.

Beijing also has launched a raft of new industrial policies designed to place more restrictions on foreign investment in certain sectors, in order to protect and incubate large state companies. These new restrictions have occurred at the same time as the government has allowed the private sector to flourish in industries that it does not deem strategic. The restrictions were codified in the Party's eleventh five-year plan, released in 2006, and have been put into place in the decade since that plan.[29] As a congressionally mandated United States–China Economic and Security Review Commission study showed, in the past decade the Chinese government has increasingly capped the percentage that foreign investors can purchase in Chinese companies in many different sectors, such as telecommunications, petroleum production, and many others.[30] In these sectors, the government has decreed that the state "must maintain at least a 50 percent ownership stake in each firm."

Although former premier Zhu Rongji, who was in office between 1998 and 2003, was probably the most free-market-oriented leader to emerge in modern Chinese history, even he did not fundamentally reform China's state capitalism. "China has never embraced privatization of state-owned enterprises as a central policy goal," notes a study of Chinese SOEs by the Bank of Finland.[31] A branch of the central government known as the State-owned Assets Supervision and Administration Commission, known in China as SASAC, continues to directly oversee the largest SOEs. And as the government privatized some nationally owned SOEs in the late 1990s and early 2000s while simultaneously giving more decision-making power to provincial and subprovincial officials, provinces and subprovincial areas often responded by creating their own government-controlled entities rather than encouraging local private firms. Indeed, China now has more than 100,000 provincial- or subprovincial-controlled companies, many of which Beijing actually encouraged to grow in 2013 and 2014, contrary to the stated economic reform goals. The central government also has encouraged the big four state-controlled banks to lend more to these companies, and it utilized state banks to plow money into Chinese equity markets and Chinese brokerages as China's stock exchanges tumbled during the summer of 2015. This continued government control of important components of the economy is why critics of China's state capitalism like Lardy urge reform of the state sector's power even as they argue that the state sector is not that important to China's economy any more.

Even when the Chinese government has listed SOEs on stock markets, it has taken care to maintain government control of either a majority of the total shares or a majority of the voting class shares that really determine corporate direction. These listings, copied in some ways from Singapore's efficient state capitalist model, allow Chinese firms to raise new sources of funds and interact with foreign investors and advisers—and to potentially bring in new business ideas and models while still allowing the state to maintain the final say on company decisions. In a way, this strategy resembles the most successful American companies that have created two classes of shares—one for investors, who can buy stock in the company after it goes public but whose shares give them little actual control over the corporation, and one for members of the family that started the firm or the corporate founders themselves. The family or founders' class of shares are structured in such a way that, even after going public, these shares—and thus the family or the founders—control the company. The *New York Times* is one prominent example of such an American company which has dual classes of shares, although the newspaper, which has battled the Chinese government's restrictions on its reporting in China for years, surely would not welcome being compared to Chinese state companies. Yet the newspaper has used dual classes to maintain the Sulzberger family's control of the enterprise, while using the second class of shares to raise capital and, to some extent, force the company to interact with outside investors and obtain their advice.[32] Facebook and Google also have used dual classes of shares to allow their founders to maintain control of the company after going public. This is not to say that dual class shares are ideal for corporate governance or long-term efficiency—some corporate analysts argue that it is an effective strategy because it maintains continuity, while others argue that using dual classes allows the family owners or company founders, like the Chinese government, to sell shares while retaining too much power.

Dual class listings in the West and Chinese state firms' dual class listings are not exactly analogous, of course. The *New York Times* and Facebook issue more extensive, transparent, and regular reports on their operations than most Chinese state companies that have dual share classes, and the *New York Times'* dual listing does not raise security concerns for other countries. The comparison merely illustrates that this kind of listing strategy is not totally alien in Western business, and that many Western companies have used dual share classes and maintained high profitability.

Dual listings by Chinese firms on domestic and foreign exchanges have become common. A study by the Bank of Finland of China's state enterprises showed that, as early as the late 1990s, some nine thousand former state companies had gone through a process of corporatization that made them into companies with stockholders—usually employees and management—but much of their stock remained in the hands of the state. Several hundred of these firms listed on the Shanghai and Shenzhen stock exchanges, but nearly all of them retained mechanisms to ensure state control of the company. In fact, SOEs now constitute around 80 percent of all non-financial companies listed on Chinese stock markets in Shenzhen and Shanghai, a larger proportion of the two Chinese exchanges than they were in the late 1990s.[33] Some state enterprises have used a dual share class in which voting shares are controlled by the state and nonvoting shares are sold to domestic and foreign investors. Other state companies spin off subsidiaries that have 100 percent of their shares listed and sold to domestic and foreign investors, but the parent company, which does not list on any stock markets, remains controlled by the government.[34] "The goal of maintaining state control of these companies] while raising funds was effectively achieved," the Bank of Finland study found. Massive Chinese oil firm China National Offshore Oil Corporation (CNOOC), for example, created a subsidiary called CNOOC Limited, for the purpose of listing in US financial markets; it now trades on the New York Stock Exchange as an American depository receipt, a stock trading in New York that represents shares in a foreign company. CNOOC also has another subsidiary listed on the Hong Kong exchange. As a study by research organization Capital Trade showed, parent company CNOOC still retains over 64 percent of the shares of CNOOC Limited.[35]

CAN A COUNTRY BE SUCCESSFUL AT
ECONOMIC PLANNING?

A key difference between efficient and inefficient state capitalists is that the more efficient countries usually are capable of long-term economic planning, because their governments are able to maximize input from outside experts, establish regular mechanisms for using this input, and make decisions about economic planning with a view beyond self-enrichment. These states usually allow large segments of the economy to be determined by the market, so that the government is not micromanaging every industry. Instead, the government focuses on areas where state support could be potentially positive—industries where economies of scale are important, where private sector capital is hard to come by, where barriers to entry are extremely high. These states fund research and development and push laws that foster investment into practice quickly, without the delays that often come with the democratic process. These states also have created at least some systems of incentives for economic officials who foster growth and some kinds of punishments for officials who steal from the state, take action on economic issues without consulting widely in advance, or simply make foolish decisions. Most of the efficient state capitalists also are not highly dependent on natural resources extraction, a scenario that makes a country more dependent on global economic swings and creates less of an incentive to foster domestic innovation.

It is certainly true that in China, and to some extent in other state capitalists that are in the middle of our autocratic/democratic scale, leaders can set long-term economic policy priorities, through five- and ten-year plans, and can have the ability to implement them. Setting priorities can be critical in infrastructure creation, basic science research, and other areas where either the state or a private company must sink considerable capital before recouping costs—or might never recoup costs directly, since the benefits of this investment accrue to society as a whole. Because of these sunk costs, the state often takes a significant role in funding these areas, even in developed nations. Yet areas like basic science research or infrastructure building often wind up unfunded, or underfunded, in developed democracies' state budgets, because their benefits accrue in the long term and rarely benefit one political party or another. Budgets in countries like the United States, however, are fought over every year, with parties in Congress trying to use the budget process to gain any political advantage they can.

Of course, in countries like China, the government's ability to set economic policy priorities and follow through, even if the benefits of these policies take years to accrue, is due in large part to their not having to hold elections, or holding elections in which the political system has been so configured in advance that it is nearly impossible for the opposition to win. Elections eat up time with campaigns, often focus politicians on short-term policy priorities, and can result in dramatic shifts in policy direction when different parties win office. Indeed, Musacchio and Lazzarini found in their study of Brazilian state capitalism that Brazilian state companies seemed to be less influenced by popular pressures under periods of authoritarian rule than during Brazil's democratic period. Although this popular pressure serves as the best check on government's potential excesses, it can be hard to square with long-term policy planning. With regular transition at the top but no elections, a regime can implement the kind of long-term planning critical for the early stages of economic development and often politically unpopular. In addition, efficient state capitalists like Singapore have been able to overcome the lack of policy shifts and experimentation that naturally come with contested elections through measures like performance targeting for state officials. In fact, argues political scientist Sebastien Heilmann in his comparison of modern China with democratic states, Chinese leaders today have had an "unusual combination of extensive policy experimentation with long-term policy prioritization."[36]

China's planning also has helped some state-linked firms become successful enough to be internationally competitive with leading private multinationals. China has accomplished a rise in indigenous innovation by mandating that products manufactured in a range of cutting-edge industries contain a certain percentage of domestically made content, which has pushed Chinese manufacturers to upgrade their technology.[37] In addition, Beijing often uses the lure of its vast consumer market to convince foreign firms to come to China and participate in joint ventures that eventually help the Chinese partners become technologically advanced—a strategy condemned by many foreign governments and companies but often acceded to by foreign firms.

For example, economists Usha and George Haley document how, in the growing plug-in hybrid automobile industry, Beijing refused to provide General Motors—the biggest foreign carmaker in China in terms of sales—the same subsidies it gives to other hybrid makers, unless GM taught a Chinese car firm how to reverse engineer and then produce some of the key technologies that power the hybrid plug-in Chevy Volt.[38] China's government also has served as a force prodding Chinese auto firms to take over small foreign car companies to gain access to knowledge, and eventually build exportable cars. Over the past decade, China has gone from being a minor player in the international automobile and auto parts industry to growing domination of the international car parts market. In 2012, China exported $13 billion in automotive parts to the United States, up from almost nothing ten years ago.[39] China is now the largest exporter of auto parts to the United States, far surpassing former auto parts giants like Japan. Increasingly, Chinese auto parts makers like Wanxiang Group, from Hangzhou, China, have been buying up bankrupt American auto parts makers.[40]

The massive growth in China's export capacity cannot be explained simply by the country's utilization of cheap labor or by arguing that market forces have become more prominent in China, since the biggest Chinese industries remain dominated by state companies. Utilizing a range of government supports and protections but also fostering domestic innovation through market forces, China has moved into ever-higher-value areas of auto parts, steel, and many other industries. Its exports in these industries, economist Dani Rodrik has shown, have gone far beyond areas where China would have a comparative advantage only because of low labor costs.[41] In other words, China is not gaining ground on the world simply by plowing people and cheap state money into companies. China's exports, Rodrik shows, are rapidly becoming more sophisticated and capital intensive, and many of the state companies now are competitive with private companies from leading industrialized nations in many high-tech areas in which the key to competitiveness is skilled labor, innovation, efficiency, and precision manufacturing.

Whether or not these strategies employed by Beijing are ethical or legal under WTO rules, they seem to have worked. China's indigenous innovation is booming, and not only in carmaking. Indeed, over the past two decades, the number of applications for patents in China grew by more than 1,000 percent, while China has taken the world lead in critical areas like supercomputing and the building of the world's fastest computer, which can be used for everything from predicting earthquakes to modeling the production of an airplane in three dimensions.[42] (The US government's plans to build a faster supercomputer were thwarted by inertia and in-fighting in

Congress, which held up funding for the Department of Energy.[43]) China's score has also steadily risen on the *Global Competitiveness Report,* the World Economic Forum's ranking of nations' international economic competitiveness.[44]

Not Really Reform

Although Xi Jinping announced a broad set of economic reforms shortly after taking over as president in 2013, these proposed reforms did not, as we will see, actually reduce the power of state-owned companies in strategic sectors of the economy.[45] Some of the broader proposed reforms touted by Xi and Li essentially did not happen at all. In the year following the announcement of reforms in 2013, Chinese banks continued to approve loans to highly indebted state firms, particularly those with political connections to top leaders.[46] And despite Beijing's vows of belt-tightening under Xi, the central government in 2013 and 2014 actually *encouraged* local and provincial governments to lay out larger amounts of stimulus spending, and signaled state-controlled banks to support provincial governments in these efforts. The central government also continued to ramp up stimulus spending on large projects (e.g., high-speed rail), which are the lifeblood of state construction and energy companies but which also have contributed to wasteful lending by state banks and the Chinese credit bubble.[47] Private companies trying to bid on energy and construction projects complained that the bidding process remained monopolized by state-owned companies, with private firms having little real chance of winning the largest contracts.

China's own data on subsidies showed that in 2012 China's companies received greater subsidies from the state than in 2011, 2010, or 2009. This growth in state subsidies continued its upward trend in 2013.[48] In addition, the number of industries in which state companies exert influence is mushrooming, even under Xi and Li. As writer John Lee notes, the number of industries that China's government now considers critical or cutting edge, and thus state companies targets for advantages over foreign competitors, is growing. "Since the Chinese Communist Party takes a heavily conflated view of political and economic power, strategically critical economic sectors tend to encompass every sector important for the development of a modern Chinese economy," he writes.[49] A comprehensive study by the Bank of Finland found that the number of protected sectors in China's economy has been increasing in the past five years. The breadth of these protected sectors, the Bank of Finland found, stretches well beyond those normally considered "strategic" by developed economies, such as defense and infrastructure; many of the Chinese state companies in these strategic sectors also have been chosen by Beijing as national champions designated to expand internationally, particularly into the developing world.[50] Meanwhile, China's major overseas state development bank, China Development Bank, appears to have dramatically increased its lending in the mid-2010s to Chinese state enterprises expanding overseas operations.[51] Even critics who argue that China is destined to be an increasingly private-sector driven economy admit that state companies have dominated Chinese firms' overseas expansion, and that China Development Bank and other Chinese banks have given an overwhelming proportion of their loans for overseas expansion to state companies rather than private Chinese firms. Many of these lines of credit are given by China Development Bank to state companies at below-market interest rates or with terms of deferred repayment, making Chinese companies trying to expand overseas more competitive.

Xi Jinping did not try to hide his commitment to maintaining Chinese state capitalism, even as he frequently told Chinese entrepreneurs, foreign investors, and the media that his administration would lead visionary economic reforms. At one session of the National People's Congress—China's rubber-stamp legislature, but a forum used by Chinese leaders to announce policies and, within the Party, win support for their strategies—Xi told attendees, "The strength of the state-owned enterprises cannot be trimmed. Instead, they need to be strengthened."[52]

CHINA'S PROMOTION OF STATE CAPITALISM

China is not the only promoter of a state capitalist model. Despite its small size, Singapore has for years been the de facto leader of the Association of Southeast Asian Nations regional organization, while Indonesia has been distracted by its own domestic democratic transition. Singapore has long been the most important American security partner in Southeast Asia, as well as a force in global economic institutions like the IMF, and a leading investor in other countries in the region. As we have seen, Singapore has for

decades actively promoted its model, with its diplomats and leading intellectuals, like former Singapore ambassador to the United Nations Kishore
Mahbubani, writing lengthy articles arguing that Singapore's statist, "Asian
values" economic and political approach is more suited to East Asian
nations than liberal democracy and free-market capitalism.[53] Singapore
also has played a major role in training Chinese officials as well as economic
and finance officials from every other country in Southeast Asia.[54]

China, however, is by far the biggest and potentially most influential
promoter of a state capitalist economic model. China's shift toward promoting its model has happened quickly. Only ten years ago Chinese officials
stuck to Deng Xiaoping's maxim to keep a low profile in foreign affairs,
and denied they had any model to promote. Deng told one visiting African
leader, back in 1985, "Please don't copy our model. If there is any experience on our part, it is to formulate policies in light of one's own national
conditions."[55]

But today's Chinese leaders are not taking such a low profile in foreign affairs, or in promoting the country's economic model. Along with
more forceful diplomacy, a military build-up, and increasing assertiveness
regionally and internationally in places like the South China Sea and the
India-China border, Beijing has started to proactively promote its model
of development. Since the late 2000s, China has aggressively claimed large
portions of the South and East China Seas, begun patrolling in waters far
across the Pacific, and refused to take disputed claims over territorial waters
to any type of international mediation.[56] China even announced that the
disputed Paracel and Spratly Islands in the South China Sea, as well as another area of the South China Sea, have become a Chinese administrative
area called Sansha City, with its own governing officials and transplanted
Chinese population.

But even as China has become more confident, its leadership still
recognizes that it cannot challenge American military power anywhere
outside its region, at least in the near term. Despite boosting its defense
budget by over 10 percent annually and reforming its military to slim it
down and modernize it, China remains a long way from developing a global
blue-water navy or expeditionary forces capable of fighting far from China's
borders. Recognizing that China remains decades away from challenging
the Pentagon outside of China's neighborhood, Beijing's leaders compete
in other ways: by promoting their development model for other countries

to learn about and adopt, Beijing's leaders can reap diplomatic support. The economic crisis of the late 2000s, Chinese economist Cheng Enfu told reporters, "displays the advantages of the Chinese model."

By the early 2000s, China had already developed training programs for foreign officials, usually from developing nations in Africa, Southeast Asia, and Central Asia. These officials came to China for courses in economic management, policing, and judicial practice, among other areas. At the time, Chinese officials would not necessarily suggest China had an economic model to impart. But by the late 2000s and early 2010s, many of these courses explicitly focused on elements of the China model, from the way Beijing uses its power to allocate loans and grants to certain companies, to China's strategies for co-opting entrepreneurs into the Communist Party, to China's use of special economic zones to attract foreign investment. On one occasion, according to China scholar Randall Peerenboom, China hosted a forum called the "Shanghai Global Learning Process," where some 1,200 participants from 117 nations attended sessions designed partly to explain how they could learn from China's development experience.

One Vietnamese official who has traveled repeatedly to China for such programs noted how the style of the programs has changed over time. Now, he said, Chinese officials, far more confident than even ten years ago, would introduce the example of one or another Chinese city that had successfully attracted sizable investments, talking through how the city government coordinates all permits and other needs and moves favored projects swiftly through any approval process. Central Asian attendees at Chinese training sessions noted how they increasingly learned about the Chinese judicial system, in which the Party has almost complete control, and then returned to their home countries, where their governments used similar types of control measures over their judiciaries.

Other attendees at these sessions described how unlike in the past, their Chinese counterparts explicitly contrasted Beijing's ability to pursue long-term goals with the gridlock of Western governments and emerging democracies. Some Chinese officials would compare Beijing's rapid approval of foreign investment projects with India's sloth, noting how hard it was to get approvals for even the smallest investments in many parts of India. Many of these participants in trainings and other classes in China come home impressed by Chinese decision-making, China's mix of state intervention and incentives to create competition among both SOEs and private companies, and China's ability to create an efficient economy while not allowing political liberalization.

Beijing also has built close political party to political party ties with several other developing nations. Increasingly, it has utilized these ties to promote its model of political and economic development. Chinese officials have worked on development planning with leading politicians in neighboring Mongolia, which democratized after 1989 but where the public has become increasingly disenchanted with corruption and weak growth. Chinese officials also have cooperated with United Russia, the main pro-Kremlin party, whose leaders want to study how China has opened its economy without giving up political control. In 2009, United Russia held a special meeting with top Chinese leaders to learn Beijing's strategy of development and political power. Previously, the Chinese leadership reportedly had sent intelligence agents to Georgia, Ukraine, and Kyrgyzstan to analyze why the mid-2000s color revolutions had occurred in these nations. Beijing later reportedly commissioned several state-linked think tanks to produce analyses on the color revolutions. At a symposium, Chinese think-tank experts and intelligence officials presented recommendations for how China could forestall its own popular revolt, and Chinese intelligence agents reportedly shared some of what they had learned from their analyses of the color revolutions with officials from United Russia, who had themselves commissioned intelligence studies of the color revolutions to determine how Russia could help turn back democratization in its near neighbors. Together, Russia and China used the Shanghai Cooperation Organization, a regional group linking the two powers with several Central Asian nations, to make the argument that color revolutions, and democratic change in general, were violations of national sovereignty. The Chinese Communist Party also held several conferences with United Russia members to discuss government-linked organizations (also known in development parlance as GONGOs), which Beijing had increasingly created to compete with and, in many cases, supplant actual civil society organizations in China. United Russia began, in the late 2000s, to copy some of these types of government-linked faux civil society organizations.

In Vietnam, which has applied many strategies used previously by China, top Communist Party leaders have, since the 1950s, enjoyed close party-to-party ties with Beijing, even as the two countries have had disputes over land borders, the South China Sea, migration, and other challenges. These ties continued as Hanoi explicitly modeled Vietnam's economic reforms, first launched in the late 1980s, on those pioneered by China in the 1970s. Despite historical enmity and modern-day tensions, for nearly three decades the Vietnamese Communist Party has sent hundreds of top officials every year to China to study economic management.[57]

As Vietnam began to open its economy in the late 1980s, allowing individual citizens to launch private companies, welcoming foreign investment, and eventually joining the WTO, the state kept control of the largest companies in strategic industries similar to those that the Chinese government continued to dominate: shipping, energy, banking, and other sectors. Closely following strategies learned at China's major universities and schools linked to the Communist Party, the Vietnamese government often offered cheap or free land, low-interest loans from state banks, and enormous tax breaks to state companies—state shipping giant Vinashin simply was exempted from paying its taxes for several years.[58] Like Beijing, Hanoi also pushed smaller state-owned companies to consolidate, to create firms that potentially would have the economic scale to compete regionally and even internationally, and then pushed these state firms to lead Vietnamese outward investment.

China has built party-to-party ties with and held training sessions for many leaders whose autocratic leanings have become stronger in recent years. In particular, according to a number of Cambodian activists, advisers from China's Communist Party have given suggestions to Prime Minister Hun Sen's party about how to utilize laws for libel and defamation to scare the independent media, how to create a network of senior officials who can rotate in and out of major companies and essentially control them, and how to train special police forces to combat street protests.

These efforts to promote a China model of undemocratic development build on a decade-long effort by Beijing to amass soft power in the developing world. Among other efforts, this strategy has included expanding the international reach of Chinese media, by launching new China-funded supplements in newspapers in many different countries and by vastly expanding the reach and professionalism of the Chinese newswire *Xinhua*. Today, according to its own figures, China's state-backed international television channel reaches over sixty-five million viewers outside the country. This strategy also includes broadening the appeal of Chinese culture by opening Confucius Institutes—programs on Chinese language and culture—at universities from Uzbekistan to Tanzania. The number of Confucius Institutes has expanded from 1 in 2004 to 429 in 2013.[59]

This soft power effort has involved a rapid and substantial expansion of China's foreign aid programs, so that Beijing is now the largest donor to many neighboring nations, including Cambodia, Myanmar, and Laos. An analysis of China's overseas lending, compiled by the *Financial Times* in 2010, found that China lent more money to developing nations in 2009 and 2010 than the World Bank had, a stark display of Beijing's growing foreign assistance. And the soft power initiative has also included outreach to foreign students, in the form of scholarships, work-study programs, and other incentives to young men and women from developing countries. The number of foreign students studying in China grew from roughly 52,000 in 2000 to 240,000 in 2009 to over 400,000 in 2012.

Over the past decade, too, China has set up networks of formal and informal summits with other developing nations. These summits are not theoretically supposed to be training sessions like those hosted by Chinese institutions for visiting foreign officials and academics. And at first, the summits offered China the opportunity simply to host gatherings of opinion leaders and, to some extent, woo investment and trade. But over the past five years, some summits, like those with Southeast Asian and African leaders, have also subtly advertised China's model of development and state companies, according to numerous participants. Several Thai politicians who have attended the Boao Forum for Asia, a kind of China-centered version of the World Economic Forum in Davos, noted that some of the discussions at Boao in recent years has shifted from a kind of general talk of globalization and its impact in Asia to more specific conversations about some of the failings of Western economic models exposed by the global economic crisis, and whether China's type of development might be less prone to such risks.

China's development model and soft power has proven increasingly attractive in Thailand, both to elites and to working-class Thais. A 2014 survey of Thais, conducted by the Center for Strategic and International

Studies, a Washington think tank, found that Thais had the most positive views of China and of China's impact on the region of any people from the nine Asian countries studied, other than China itself.[60]

But China is hardly the only example of state capitalism. In places with stronger democracies than Thailand, leaders are looking not to China but instead to the most successful democratic state capitalists, who manage to blend economic centralization and political openness.

6

The Democratic State Capitalists—A Closer Look

In the spring of 2013, Brazil seemed to have much going for it. After years of hyperinflation and weak growth in the 1980s and early 1990s, the country had righted its economy, stabilized its currency, and gone through over a decade of high-powered development. Foreign investment was flowing into the largest country in Latin America, growing from $22.5 billion in 2001 to $65 billion in 2012.[1] With higher growth and less inflation, Brazilian governments were able to use state spending for pioneering cash transfer programs to the poor, which helped slice poverty in a country that had been infamous globally for its sharp wealth divides and massive underclass. Brazil's growth allowed it to claim a larger role on the world stage. Along with China, Russia, and India, it founded the annual BRICS (later expanded to include South Africa) summit of leading developing nations. In its own region, Brasilia no longer deferred to the United States as the dominant power. In the 2000s, Brazilian companies poured into neighboring states such as Venezuela and Bolivia, among others. Meanwhile, as the United States mostly ignored the region, Brazilian presidents Luiz Ignacio Lula da Silva and Dilma Rousseff became the most important voices in regional diplomacy. In recognition of Brazil's arrival as a major player on the world stage, the country was selected to host the two biggest athletic showcases on earth: the soccer World Cup in 2014 and then the Summer Olympics in 2016.

Yet on the streets of many of Brazil's biggest cities, the mood was not so sunny in the spring and summer of 2013, and it continued to darken over the following two years—with the World Cup not exactly lightening Brazilians' moods. Massive protests numbering in the hundreds of thousands of people rocked cities in 2013 from the country's upper Atlantic coast to the Amazon interior to sites right outside of the landmark parliament building in Brasilia. The protests began organically, with demonstrators sparked by everything from local incidents of police brutality to rises in bus fares in some cities to widely publicized articles about corruption in parliament. Demonstrators in many cities were scuffling nearly every day with police, who fought back with tear gas. The clashes sometimes led to all-out riots in the streets.[2]

Yet amid the specific sparks of the Brazilian street protests, several overriding themes emerged—themes that, to an outsider, might seem contradictory. Many of the protestors called for greater government investment in Brazil's infrastructure, education system, and corporations, essentially asking for the state to take a far larger role in social welfare and job creation. Yet at the same time, many of the protestors bashed President Dilma Rousseff, who had never held elected office before winning the presidency in 2010. She had served as Lula's chief of staff, and then essentially was anointed as the Workers Party's candidate for president by Lula. Demonstrators, echoing the complaints of many Brazilian politicians, criticized Dilma for her autocratic style, her circle of aides alleged to have profited from state funds and state companies, and her political tin ear. Her style had much in common with elected autocratic leaders like Thaksin Shinawatra, though Brazil's democracy was far sturdier than Thailand's, and the protestors in Brazil were not calling for a military coup. Despite several years of street protests, and a cascade of arrests on corruption charges that ultimately ensnared some of the most powerful figures in Dilma's Workers Party, coming close to the president herself, the president seemed stonily in denial of the extent of the graft scandal. In mid-2015, she submitted a budget to Brazil's legislature that expanded state spending but also increased funding for the very state enterprises in which the graft scandals had originated.

The Brazilian protestors were touting a seemingly mixed message—they wanted more state intervention in the economy, yet they were angry about the overweening, sometimes self-dealing, political style of that same state.

This mixed message, however, would have resonated with people in many other emerging democracies like Indonesia, Thailand, and South Africa, among others. In Indonesia—which since the late 2000s has passed several laws restricting foreign investment and promoting state enterprises—protestors have repeatedly called for greater state control of resources, while also criticizing two-term president Susilo Bambang Yudhoyono and his Democrat Party for corruption, self-dealing in government contracts, and a domineering political style. "SBY [a common nickname for the president] was popular in the beginning, just because he was stable [after several failed presidents], but now he's just seen as totally out of touch with people, he's like a king," says one prominent Indonesian politician.[3]

Searching for the anti-Yudhoyono, a politician who would be both more in touch with ordinary Indonesians while also taking firmer control of the economy, many Indonesians started to follow the exploits of a populist governor (mayor, in the American parlance) of a medium-sized city, Solo, on the island of Java. The Solo governor, who would burst into prominence in the early 2010s, was known to all by his nickname, Jokowi. (Jokowi's real name is Joko Widodo, but even in formal settings, almost no one calls him that.) A diminutive, slight man with an easy smile on his gaunt and lined face, Jokowi ascended from modest means in central Indonesia, first making his living manufacturing furniture before eventually turning to politics. In contrast to the aloof manner and elitist hobbies—golf, cooking lavish foreign foods—of many Indonesian politicians, Jokowi played rock guitar and walked the streets of Solo in his trademark checkered collared shirt and ratty running sneakers nearly every day to chat with regular people. He engaged in an immensely popular type of political theater on his walks as well. Often Jokowi popped in, unannounced, to the offices of many local government agencies, usually with reporters in tow, and confronted local bureaucrats, pushing them to work harder and vowing to fire them if they did not.

But Jokowi, though relatively new to politics, was not a political naïf; he intuitively understood his regular-guy appeal and sensed that Indonesians were looking for both a more populist and a more economically interventionist type of leadership. He called for the government to take back control of much of the economy, in what he called a "people-centered economy."[4] In Solo, and as he moved up the political ladder, Jokowi publicly highlighted his rough hands, casual clothes, and unwillingness to accept lavish gifts from supporters. Jokowi's clean politics stood in sharp contrast with many other top Indonesian politicians, who had come of age during the Suharto dictatorship and had developed reputations for corruption. When the bassist of the heavy metal band Metallica, one of Jokowi's favorites, presented him with a bass guitar, he very publicly handed the guitar to the state Corruption Eradication Commission to demonstrate to the public that he was so pure he would not even take presents from rock gods.[5]

Jokowi's message and down-to-earth style proved so popular that he moved to Jakarta, the capital, and won an election in 2012 to become the city's mayor. Soon, many Indonesians were backing him as a possible presidential candidate for the next election, though he had no national or international experience.

No matter. Jokowi's immense popularity propelled him to a presidential candidacy, with other potential candidates, like former president (and Sukarno daughter) Megawati Sukarnoputri giving way for Jokowi, who hailed from the same political party as Megawati. Sensing that she could not stop a political dynamo, Megawati endorsed Jokowi in early 2014, despite her own obvious desire to run for the presidency again herself. As Jokowi's presidential campaign gained speed in 2013 and 2014, his desire for a more interventionist economic strategy proved popular with the public. Indeed, the desire in Indonesia for a more state-centered economic strategy helped fuel the campaigns of *both* of the presidential candidates in Indonesia's summer 2014 elections.

The other candidate, former general Prabowo Subianto, who seemed to take his style cues from past Indonesian strongmen like founding father Sukarno, outlined an ambitious, state-capitalist strategy during the spring 2014 campaign season. If anything, Prabowo's ideas for entrenching state capitalism in Indonesia were even more far-reaching than those of Jokowi. In some ways, Prabowo seemed to want to return the economy to the days of Sukarno, when an overweening state dominated all economic policy-making instead of the state merely playing a big role in a percentage of the corporate sector. Sukarno's brand of state capitalism was also highly inefficient; Indonesia's economy had staggered under his economic centralism, which led to massive outflows of investment and serious famines.[6] If elected, Prabowo vowed his administration would potentially nationalize investments in Indonesian natural resources, invest $75 billion in new, state-funded megaprojects similar to China's giant infrastructure projects, and impose tough new regulations on foreign investors who still wanted to invest in the country.

Prabowo's opponent, Jokowi, did not attempt to match the grandiose, bombastic speaking style of the former general, or his immensely detailed policy proposals. Jokowi stuck to presenting himself as a regular guy, just as he had during his successful campaigns in Solo and Jakarta: the pragmatic problem solver and former furniture salesman who would diagnose the country's ills and fix them. During one-on-one debates with Prabowo, Jowoki highlighted his famed style of traveling all over Jakarta to personally confront bureaucrats in order to make sure projects were being completed and government workers were not skimming funds. If government workers were not performing up to task, Jowoki promised, he would sack them, just as he had sacked inefficient bureaucrats in Jakarta.

Although fighting corruption and improving efficiency were fine goals in a country where graft and bureaucratic sloth have held back the economy's tremendous potential, Jokowi went much further toward economic nationalism in his campaign-trail promises. Although Jokowi frequently stressed that he had himself been a small businessman and understood the needs of businesses, including an environment free of graft and excessive regulation, Jokowi promised that as president he also would impose new restrictions on business. He suggested the government retake control of some natural resources, launch plans to make Indonesia self-sufficient in staple foods, maintain an export ban on mineral ore from Indonesia, pass legislation that would protect Indonesian banks from competition, and help Indonesians escape the "market forces" that had trapped Indonesia into dependence on foreign capital.[7] Liberal economic policies, Jokowi wrote in an op-ed in a prominent Indonesian newspaper, had been disastrous for Indonesia in the past and would need to be rethought.[8] Jokowi conceded that some degree of economic openness and investment was needed in the country, though he also made clear that the Indonesian government should increasingly control Indonesian companies and decide what foreign investment to allow.

Despite a late run by Prabowo closing the gap between the two candidates—a run fueled by Prabowo's allies repeated smearing of Jokowi—Jokowi was elected president in July 2014 by a significant margin. Prabowo and his supporters hotly contested the result and filed a lawsuit against

Jokowi in the Constitutional Court. However, Indonesian democracy pre-
vailed, and the challenge was resolved without violence. Jokowi was sworn
in as president in October 2014.

As president, Jokowi quickly instituted some drastic changes in
Indonesian governance, including posting information about government
workings online—a first for transparency in the country. He also promised
a range of reforms designed to cut red tape and make investment easier,
and he proposed cutting fuel subsidies. These subsidies had for years made
the price of gas in Indonesia among the cheapest in the world, but also had
made the government's deficit balloon out of control. And because they cut
into profit margins, the subsidies had contributed to the breakdown of the
state petroleum company. This turned Indonesia from an oil exporter in the
1980s and 1990s into an oil importer today.

But Jokowi also stuck to many of the nationalist proposals he had outlined during campaign season. He vowed to make upgrading Indonesia's
physical infrastructure a top priority of his new administration, including
overseeing the building of some 1,200 miles of new paved roads in the
country. This was not, in itself, a bad idea; as a former mayor, Jokowi had
experience pushing through infrastructure projects. Infrastructure is
critical to any developing economy, and Indonesia's crumbling physical
infrastructure was a major reason why the country lagged behind other
Southeast Asian nations in attracting foreign investment, despite its size,
resources, and untapped consumer market. Yet Jokowi planned to facilitate infrastructure creation through massive new state investments that
were not just designed to build infrastructure but also to build up certain
state companies. This sent a mixed message about his economic views. He
also met with the biggest resources companies in Indonesia and bluntly
told them that the state would be playing a much bigger role in controlling
the resources industry. He expanded the number of sectors where foreign
companies were banned and warned many foreign companies that they
would not find their contracts renewed unless they handed over much
larger portions of their revenues to the state. The new president raised a
range of non-tariff trade barriers and decided to renegotiate bilateral investment treaties with a number of countries. Jokowi even embraced the
idea of Indonesia developing a state-run automotive company that would
build a "national car" similar to Malaysia's Proton, a state enterprise that
poured billions of dollars into building a national car that few Malaysians
seemed to want to buy.

BUILDING ON A HISTORY OF STATISM

Although each emerging democracy has its own unique political and economic history and culture, there are reasons why state capitalism has become more popular, and more entrenched, in the past decade in many young democracies. For one, as we have seen, the first generation of elected leaders in many emerging democracies has shown little commitment to democratic norms and institutions. Leaders like Thaksin Shinawatra and Bangladesh's Sheik Hasina Wazid, admittedly popular with their publics, have destroyed many of the checks and balances necessary for functioning, long-lasting democracy. Whether they built on a history of state capitalism or developed it themselves, in these new democracies the elected autocrats' political power can potentially (though not always) benefit from state control of major companies. We will shortly examine whether, in the more robustly democratic state capitalists, like India and Brazil and Indonesia, state capitalism inexorably leads to curtailed political freedom as well.

In some cases, leaders in many emerging democracies have built on long histories of state intervention in the economy. Countries like India and Indonesia, which had led the non-aligned, anti-Western camp in their early years, had followed socialist models during the early part of the Cold War. Although these socialist models had produced poor growth, the intellectual legacies of Gandhi, Nehru, and Sukarno remained strong, at least among some Indians and Indonesians. The intellectual legacy of Gandhi and Nehru remained strong enough, in fact, that even into the 2000s, communist parties that based their ideologies in part on socialist economics still ran West Bengal, one of the most populous states in India, as well as the states of Kerala and Tripura.

In addition, the deep legacies of socialism in India left in place statist policies so entrenched that it was politically near impossible for even the most reform-minded and powerful prime ministers to change them. Prime Minister Narendra Modi took office in 2014 with the largest mandate in modern Indian history. Unusual in India, where coalition governments are common, Modi's BJP had won an absolute majority of seats in parliament and was not beholden to smaller parties' demands. In addition, Modi had made the election a kind of presidential referendum between him or Congress leader Rahul Gandhi, even though India remains a parliamentary democracy and voters do not directly elect a prime minister. Modi's strategy worked in the election—as we have seen; post-election questionnaires showed that many Indians had voted for the BJP simply because of their preference for Modi over Gandhi.

As a result, Modi entered the prime minister's office in 2014 riding arguably the most favorable climate for reforming statist policies in Indian history. Shortly after becoming prime minister, Modi announced his economic priorities in a national speech full of vows of economic liberalization— reforms he proposed would boost India's annual growth rate back up to the 8 percent per year mark it had reached in the mid-2000s. Though Modi's speech contained promises to slash state intervention and promote market forces, his government's first budget, released shortly after he became prime minister, told the real story. The budget revealed that he was merely going to tinker around the edges of Indian state capitalism, avoiding any attempt to reform it wholesale. Although some investors and analysts had expected the prime minister's first budget to contain massive overhauls of state economic policies, Modi's first budget actually contained only minor changes from previous governments' policies. Modi kept in place some $43 billion in state subsidies that are enormously popular among poorer Indians. Modi also kept in place India's complex web of capital controls that keep Indians from investing their money outside the country, as well as requirements that Indian banks keep more than one-quarter of their deposits in governments bonds and other government securities. These rules, India's version of financial repression, create a huge pool of capital for the state to draw upon and channel to subsidies, state companies, and other state projects.[9]

Modi also vowed to make massive, Chinese-style state investments in new infrastructure projects like high-speed rail lines and building one hundred new cities across India. Although India desperately needs to upgrade physical infrastructure, these types of projects, in China, have served to further build and entrench state companies. Beijing has, over the past two decades, built hundreds of new Chinese cities and extended road and rail networks across the country, even to many places where there was little need for train lines. These projects have helped keep the economy growing, but they also have increased debt and made China's economy too dependent on state spending. Several Modi advisors indicated that the prime minister not only saw a need to improve India's decaying physical infrastructure but also believed that by getting contracts to build such massive infrastructure, India's biggest companies in sectors like construction, steel, oil, and other areas would gain the experience and the size to compete with Chinese state companies around the globe. Many of these Indian companies that would benefit from the new infrastructure building were state enterprises. "Mr. Modi has made clear he wants to emulate China's building of infrastructure," noted *Financial Times* columnist Victor Mallet after hearing the formal roll-out, in India's parliament, of Modi's economic priorities.

Modi's budget suggested either that he was hardly an orthodox free marketer or that he was a believer in the market but was convinced that the power and popularity of statist economics among many Indians was hard to transcend.[10] Indeed, several Modi advisors admitted that Modi was not pursuing the free-market policies many had expected of him. "It is too hard to just get rid of state capitalism in India," said one of Modi's economic policy advisors. "We can make small changes, but not more than that, it is impossible to just erase state subsidies, this is a democracy, this isn't China ... If you cut the state subsidies for the poor that would be it [a loss] in the next election—that is just the reality in India."[11]

South Africa also has a long history of statism. During apartheid, the African National Congress (ANC) had close links to communist parties around the world, as well as to the South African communists; many leading ANC members publicly promoted socialist economic ideas. But after the end of apartheid, South Africa's ANC leaders, who had no serious political challengers and who also could ride President Nelson Mandela's enormous popularity, pursued privatization and free-market economics rather than the socialism that the ANC had long advocated. In post-apartheid South Africa, where white-dominated parties no longer had legitimacy and no black-dominated party could rival the ANC, ANC leaders controlled an overwhelming majority of parliament and no one could stop them from adhering to a more free-market path.

South Africa posted some of the highest growth rates in Africa during Mandela's terms as president and the first term of his successor Thabo Mbeki, who even in exile had been more of an advocate of free-market capitalism than other ANC leaders. Between Mandela's first inauguration in 1994 and 2002, South Africa grew by between 3 and 4 percent most years— impressive growth for a country facing a challenging political transition and the flight abroad of some of the wealthiest (white-owned) companies. Under Mandela and Mbeki, South Africa's finance minister, Trevor Manuel, won wide acclaim from international investors and global financial experts for his consistent and sound macroeconomic policies, which helped the country run a budget surplus in the late 2000s. But expectations among South Africans that the end of apartheid would drastically alter social and economic inequality were not met. During the period 1994–2014, in fact, economic inequality in South Africa's black population actually widened even though the country posted solid annual growth rates.[12] Of course, some of this inequality was simply a byproduct of growth—when nearly all black South Africans had been desperately poor, there was less inequality in the black population—but the inequality still stung South Africans who had believed that ANC rule would usher in drastic change for poor blacks. By the early 2010s, some sixteen million South Africans, out of a population of fifty million, still lived in poverty. By 2014, unemployment in South Africa was over 25 percent, and the rate was far higher for black men under age thirty.[13]

As in Brazil, critics of economic policies adopted by Mandela and Mbeki saw state intervention as a solution to endemic poverty. This devotion to state planning, of course, had a long history in the ANC and had hardly been erased by the Mandela and Mbeki presidencies. South Africa also was developing much closer ties to China, which became the largest foreign investor in the country by 2013, and many top ANC leaders, such as economic development minister Ebrahim Patel, traveled frequently to China and marveled at Beijing's rapid growth and seemingly streamlined decision-making.[14] The South African government, in the early 2010s, began encouraging growing numbers of provincial and local-level politicians to attend training courses in Chinese universities on economic development and management. By the time Jacob Zuma was elected president in 2009, the most pro-interventionist ANC members were calling for the dismissal of ANC leaders who had supported the economic reforms of the 1990s and 2000s. Critics further called for a massive shift in economic planning designed to redistribute wealth, empower a broader swath of South Africans, and roll back some market reforms. The ANC expelled the most vocal critic of its economic policies, youth leader Julius Malema. Malema strutted around in Che Guevara apparel and a Hugo Chavez beret calling for outright nationalization of nearly every leading South African energy, telecommunications, infrastructure, and mining company. (Malema did so while also amassing collections of luxury watches and meeting journalists for lavish meals at boutique hotels in the Johannesburg outskirts.[15]) Malema would leave the ANC to form his own, Hugo Chavez-esque political party—or personality cult—but the ANC would move to co-opt similar populists.

Under Zuma, the government took more significant interventionist steps in 2012, 2013, 2014, and 2015. Those steps co-opted some of the populist sentiment and helped the ANC retain its dominance of parliament in the 2014 national elections, even though its mandate had been significantly reduced. Zuma's government developed a new economic policy platform, released in time for Zuma's 2012 State of the Nation speech. The new policy platform declared that the state needed to play a more activist role in the economy, proposing that the prime minister's office take personal control of several of the largest South African companies. In addition, Zuma's government vowed that the state would take a larger stake in resource companies and would impose steep new taxes—as much as 50 percent of profits—on resource firms operating in South Africa that would not allow the government to take a stake in them. South Africa's public enterprises minister Malusi Gigaba told the *Mail and Guardian*, the country's leading highbrow newspaper, that South Africa had to move closer to the Chinese and Singaporean models of state-capitalist development. "If you look at the developmental state that we have in Southeast Asia . . . they reached the level of development because the state played an active part in the economy. It didn't sit back and say to the private sector that all we do is establish regulation," Gigaba said.[16]

Pretoria took other steps as well. The government created a national oil company modeled on those in Brazil and China, while increasing the state's stake of the national telecommunications firm Telkom. But even this approach was not enough for many younger ANC members. At ANC meetings, they have proposed spending more state resources on control of state-owned mining firms and increasing state control over other sectors like power generation, banking, and telecommunications—even though South Africa's state-owned power company is struggling to maintain its infrastructure, resulting in regular blackouts that hurt South African manufacturing.[17] These firebrands draw on the strong current of public anger at the failure of the ANC to address inequality. As one former labor and ANC leader, Jay Naidoo, wrote:

> The people in our townships, rural areas and squatter camps are bitter that democracy has not delivered the fruits that they see a tiny elite enjoying. Many of the [ANC] leaders they revered have abandoned the townships for the Armani lifestyle previously exclusive to leafy white suburbs. They have long lost touch with the disgruntlement brewing in society.[18]

MISTAKEN LINKS BETWEEN DEMOCRACY
AND GROWTH

In addition to the history of state intervention in many developing nations, other factors have fostered a climate ripe for statist economics in emerging democracies. Many of the leaders who came into office in the post–Cold War democratization in Eastern Europe, Africa, and other regions promised that democracy also would lead to higher growth and greater socioeconomic equality. These promises were based on little actual evidence showing any link between democratization—at least in its early stages—and economic growth. Indeed, while democracy tends, over the long term, to produce longer life expectancies, greater public spending on health and education, and reductions in child mortality, preventable disease, and famine, no one has ever definitively shown that democratization leads to economic growth in the short term—within five to ten years. Yet that is the lifespan of the first generation of elected leaders in most countries. Indeed, Princeton economist Dani Rodrik has examined a wide range of case studies and concluded that democracies historically neither outperform nor underperform dictatorships in promoting economic growth.[19]

Still, after the end of the Cold War, leaders in many emerging democracies, as well as leaders in the United States and other Western nations, frequently linked democratization and short-term growth, suggesting that there was a correlation between the two. Sometimes, they further suggested that democratization would not only promote growth but also help cut economic inequality. Even when top leaders did not make such promises, populations came to assume these links, as prominent intellectuals both in developing countries and in the West repeatedly linked political change with economic growth and economic equality. As a result, even when leaders like Nelson Mandela specifically warned people in their countries that political freedom did not necessarily mean the economy would change overnight, it was hard for them to alter the public mood.

Western leaders seemed particularly eager to promote the linkage between democratization and economic growth. During his first term, which began with the United States as the sole remaining superpower, US president Bill Clinton frequently spoke of how economic prosperity and democracy would come together to developing nations.

During the same early post-Cold War years many emerging democracies also launched periods of privatization, often to shrink state sectors left over from communist eras, or to cut down government budgets that had been bloated with state projects ordered by dictators like Pakistan's Zia ul-Haq or Indonesia's Suharto. Almost inevitably, these initial rounds of privatization involved some layoffs and public pain; leaders, now democratically accountable politicians rather than the previously unaccountable dictators, saw that the privatizations often were extremely unpopular. It was a lesson that would be imbued in the minds of these countries' politicians, particularly after many of the first wave of leaders elected during these privatization periods were roundly tossed out of office in their nations' second presidential or parliamentary elections.

Indeed, when developing nations did not grow quickly in the early years of democracy, the public often expressed enormous discontent, which could now be channeled into evicting politicians at the ballot box. And after a very early period of economic reforms in the 1990s in Eastern Europe, parts of Africa, and even in India, the same realities that limit decisive economic action in the United States—the need to build political consensus behind a bill, the influence of many different interest groups, and the power of populist politics—began to weigh on the first generation of elected leaders in these countries. Of course, these same "limitations" on decisive action also ensured that the public had a voice in policymaking, that no dictator again emerged, and that if a leader could create public consensus behind a policy, it would enjoy long-term support. But economic change moved slowly, far more slowly than many people in developing nations had expected with the onset of democracy.

Even in emerging democracies that experienced growth in the early post-Cold War period, this growth often was not enough to soothe public anger. Though many emerging democracies in Africa, Latin America, and Asia grew relatively strongly in the early 2000s, this growth also came with rising inequality in nearly every developing nation. Overall, the United Nations Human Development Program reports, in the 2000s, income inequality rose in virtually every state in the world.[20] So, despite growth and reductions in poverty, like the sharp cuts in extreme poverty in Brazil in the 2000s, average people in emerging democracies from Nigeria to Thailand to Brazil also witnessed widening inequality. This created the perception that their standards of living were declining even when they were not, a critical perception, and one that drove the protests in places like Brazil and Indonesia.

In Brazil, for instance, the reforms of the 1990s and early 2000s had sparked sharp growth and massive rises in foreign investment. But as state companies shed jobs and the labor market became freer, unemployment rose to nearly 13 percent in the early 2000s in the wake of the Asian financial crisis. The Asian financial crisis reverberated around the globe and affected Brazil in particular, as a major exporter of commodities to fast-growing Asian nations. Brazil's economic bumps would then facilitate the election of left-leaning Workers Party candidate Luiz Ignacio Lula da Silva in 2002, who had lost three previous tries for the presidency.

In some places, this widening inequality and unhappiness with the level of growth led publics to turn against democracy itself, blaming the political system for the economic problems and experiencing authoritarian nostalgia. But even when publics in developing nations were angered by democratic governments' failure to produce higher growth or to fulfill promises of equity, they did not always turn to autocrats for salvation. In some developing countries, like Brazil and Indonesia, democracy had set down firm roots in the 1990s and 2000s, publics had come to value their social and political freedoms, the military was clearly back in its barracks, and the countries had created solid democratic institutions. So, there was no turning back to dictatorship. Instead, without yearning for a strongman, publics called for greater state intervention in the economy, to control a larger swathe of companies and make corporations play dual roles: making profits and also serving a greater social good. This state capitalism, publics in countries like Brazil and Indonesia believed—and demonstrated in polling time and again—would cut inequality and cushion the effects of the privatization era.

THE DEMOCRATIC STATE CAPITALISTS LOOK TO EACH OTHER

State intervention by leading emerging democracies impacted the efforts of other countries, just as China, the largest authoritarian state capitalist, has served as a model for many authoritarian capitalists. Despite China's successes in promoting growth, cutting poverty, and sparking development, many emerging democracies are wary of studying its model too closely.

Indonesia, for example, is perhaps the greatest democratic success story in the developing world over the past two decades. Since the collapse of the Suharto regime in the late 1990s, the country has gone from a political tinderbox poised to disintegrate into civil wars and endemic violence to a (relatively) stable and consolidated democracy, with vibrant public participation and strong civil society.[21]

Though many Indonesian academics study China's model, Indonesia's leaders, like Jokowi, are not going to openly model the country on an authoritarian system—especially not at a time when China's assertions that it controls nearly the entire South China Sea increasingly conflict with Indonesia's own claims and are provoking conflict between Jakarta and Beijing. Instead, since the early period of democratization in the late 1990s, Indonesian leaders have been careful not to pursue too close a relationship with China, partly for fear of damaging their credibility as democrats. Jokowi's opponent in the presidential election, Prabowo, openly demonized China; Jokowi was more reticent but still would never openly model his economic plans on China's state capitalism.

Still, Indonesia's leaders and public have come to view the Indonesian economy, particularly in resource extraction, as too dominated by foreign firms and not serving to reduce poverty, though the country has posted annual growth rates of almost 6 percent for about a decade. In the past five years, many top Indonesian politicians have traveled to Brazil to study Brazilian state capitalism, looking for ways to promote growth while also cutting inequality. Ultimately, top Indonesian politicians hope to help Indonesia reclaim its rightful role (in Indonesian minds, at least) as Southeast Asia's natural leader. They have studied how, since Lula first won election in 2002, Brazilian governments have taken greater state control of natural resources companies and other companies, created a government coordinating council to provide guidance to even Brazilian private-sector companies in key industries, and drastically increased the lending portfolio of the state-controlled development bank to state companies, all the while (thus far) maintaining a vibrant political democracy. The Indonesian officials are not alone: leaders and officials from Argentina, Ecuador, Bolivia, and many other Latin American states have traveled to Brazil to study Lula's economic models. Meanwhile, under Lula and Dilma, Brazil has sent teams of economic advisors to several of its closest partners in Latin America, including Bolivia, Ecuador, and Peru; this outreach has not been dimmed by Brazil's corruption scandals or Dilma's declining popularity within Brazil. Many different Indonesian officials were interested in Brazil's economic strategies; both Prabowo and Jokowi's presidential campaigns had economic advisors who had studied Brazil's and China's models. Several of Jokowi's top advisors, drawn from think tanks in Jakarta, visited China and Brazil to study their economic models in the year before Jokowi's election as president, as the Jakarta mayor was learning about national policy and being groomed for the presidential campaign; the corruption scandals in Brazil did not seem to faze Jokowi's advisors, perhaps because they thought graft was a normal part of doing business. Several Indonesian leaders and policy analysts were particularly impressed with the Brazilian government's use of Brazil's state-controlled development bank to support Brazilian companies that found it hard to attract private capital, despite the fact that several of these companies wound up embroiled in graft scandals. They also were impressed by how Brasilia managed to exert influence over firms that, though partially privatized, still came under de facto control of the government, which controlled boards of advisors and helped shape these firms' major decisions.

To many visiting Indonesians, Brazil under Lula seemed to be an ideal form of government—open and democratic, managing a culturally and ethnically diverse society and a geographically far-flung nation, and yet still keeping strong control over many companies. Jokowi and Prabowo realized that the Indonesian public's mood supported increasing state capitalism, which was why both candidates—shrewd politicians—emphasized their own versions of state capitalism in several head-to-head debates on economic policy. Even before Jokowi was elected in July 2014, his predecessor, Susilo Bambang Yudhoyono, who had come into office in 2004 with free-market leanings and several reformist top advisors, already had given into the public mood. In the early 2010s, the Yudhoyono government passed a series of new regulations forcing foreign investors to sell stakes in their Indonesian resource extraction operations and reinstituting state control over some Indonesian resources and manufacturing companies.[22] This state intervention, both under Yudhoyono and then under Jokowi, has not pleased many foreign firms. In the most recent country-by-country and sector-by-sector rankings of economic openness by Canada's Fraser Institute, which studies economic freedom around the world, Indonesia was ranked as the least attractive country in the world to be involved in resource extraction.[23] Several of the largest foreign resources companies have furiously protested the growing statism and tried to enlist senior Japanese or American or European leaders to intervene with Indonesia's president on their behalf.

Still, the country has continued to attract foreign investment because of its enormous reserves of gold and other minerals, though Jokowi's protectionism probably kept Indonesia from becoming an even larger recipient of foreign investment. The biggest US resource companies operating in Indonesia, Newmont Mining and Freeport McMoRan Copper and Gold, initially protested government plans to rip up deals that were supposed to last into the 2020s and impose new taxes and other regulations. But the US companies mostly eventually agreed to new deals with the Indonesian government in which they paid higher taxes to Jakarta and agreed to build new mineral processing plants in Indonesia. The plants in Indonesia would create jobs and train Indonesians, even though these plants made no sense for the firms' bottom lines. And, seeing that the biggest foreign companies have given in, Indonesian leaders are likely to continue with greater state control of companies in many sectors, including resource extraction.

Under Lula, the Brazilian government had launched policies that put state agencies, including Lula's own ministry and new coordinating agencies created by Lula, at the center of economic development. The Lula government had more than doubled infrastructure spending as compared to its predecessor, with infrastructure spending boosting the expansion of Brazilian state construction and manufacturing companies. Lula also either took back state control of many Brazilian state companies that had been partially privatized or boosted the government's stake in companies until, even if Brasilia was not the majority shareholder, the government had enough of a stake to assume de facto control of the firm.

Brazil's state development bank, the National Bank for Social and Economic Development (BNDES), had taken a stake in over two hundred of Brazil's biggest companies by the end of Lula's two terms, up from less than one hundred before he took office, giving the government control of many more firms.[24] With the state bank's backing, Brazilian state companies also began looking overseas for acquisitions—their balance sheets flush with loans from BNDES provided to the companies at below-market rates. Increased government ownership of companies also came along with increases in spending in many other areas. Instead of cuts in social welfare programs, as had occurred in previous Brazilian administrations, Lula's administration created a successful new conditional cash transfer program to help the poor; the program slashed extreme poverty from 21 percent of the population in the early 2000s to around 11 percent by 2009.[25]

The Brazilian government also promoted state oil company Petrobras' development of cutting-edge deep-sea technology, which would have found few private investors at first. When Brazil discovered massive off-shore petroleum reserves deep in the Atlantic—reserves that could make the country one of the ten biggest oil exporters in the world—Lula passed legislation allowing Brasilia to create a new state-owned company designed to coordinate new oil exploration.[26] In May 2013, Petrobras sold some $11 billion in bonds, the largest corporate debt sale from a company in any emerging market in history. The bond issue was wildly oversubscribed: in retrospect, it became clear that Petrobras could have sold as much as $50 billion in bonds.[27] Among state-owned and private companies from all nations in the world, only titan Apple had a larger bond sale in 2013, selling $17 billion in bonds.

In 2014 and 2015, however, Petrobras ran into serious troubles, re-vealing some of the potential intrinsic flaws in state capitalism, and add-ing to the problems faced by the government of Brazilian president Dilma Rousseff. The government already confronted street protests angry about Dilma's autocratic style, the massive state spending on prestige projects like the World Cup, and other challenges. The company amassed tens of billions in debts, partly to fulfill state-directed mandates about using Brazilian sup-pliers. Its debt rose more than 200 percent between the beginning of 2012 and early 2014. Petrobras also became embroiled in a web of corruption al-legations, sparking an investigation into the company's practices by Brazil's Federal Police, the country's version of the American Federal Bureau of Investigation. Additionally, one of the company's former directors was arrested by the Brazilian police on charges of money laundering, and soon a raft of top company executives and Brazilian political figures were ensnared in the investigation and charged with corruption; the head of Petrobras quit in 2015.[28] The company's problems seemed, to many Brazilians, as indica-tive of a broader kind of cronyism that supposedly plagued Dilma's govern-ment and contributed to Dilma's sinking popularity. Still, Dilma's brand of statism proved popular enough for her to win re-election in 2014, despite low personal approval ratings, anger over her management style, and a strong campaign run by her main challenger for the presidency.

Under Lula and Dilma, Brasilia also increased the state's stake in sev-eral of the largest chemical and agribusiness companies, such as chemical

giant Braskem.[29] Lula further declared that Brazil's state electricity company, Eletrobras, needed, through infusions of state funds, to become a
global electricity giant.[30] "Policies based on selection of priority areas for
[state] investment, subsidized credit . . . and stimulus for the creation of
large, globally competitive national conglomerates . . . [These policies were]
deemed undesirable and market-distorting during the 1990s" in Brazil,
writes Glauco Arbix of the University of Sao Paulo and Scott Martin of the
New School in New York City in a study of Brazil's statist policies.[31] "Yet
they have made a comeback [under Lula]," even though Brazil's political
system and economic environment are more open than they were during
the autarkic military dictatorships in the 1970s.[32]

Dilma increased state spending, as compared to the Lula administration. In fact, her government allocated so much government stimulus
funding that during several years of her first term, Brasilia could not even
spend all the money she had directed for infrastructure.[33] Before the wave
of national protests in 2013 and 2014, Dilma also boosted the number of
seats that the government controlled on boards of leading companies like
Petrobras. She further reduced the independence of the Central Bank of
Brazil, which under Fernando Henrique Cardoso and under Lula (in his
first term) had been given the freedom to set fiscal targets without state
interference. The bank's independence had been critical to the efficiency of
Brazil's growing state capitalism, since it had fostered macroeconomic stability and reassured investors, who still remembered Brazil's years of hyperinflation during the 1980s and early 1990s. Yet Dilma publicly bludgeoned
the Central Bank into cutting interest rates exactly as the government
wanted, raising fears that the bank no longer enjoyed independence, and
potentially threatening the economy's long-term efficiency. Some Brazilian
economists speculated that to address the spiraling economic downturn,
Dilma would call for the government to print more money, a major concern
given Brazil's history of hyperinflation.

Pushed by the street protests, Dilma increased public spending on social
welfare programs and sought to cut unemployment not only through stimulus measures but by prodding state companies to expand and hire more
Brazilians, regardless of their need for more workers or the overall state of
the Brazilian economy. The interventions may have helped Dilma retain her
job as president even though she waged a weak campaign in the 2014 election. She expanded Brazilian state capitalism, prodding the finance ministry to boost outlays to BNDES and other state banks, which then would give

even cheaper loans to state companies.[34] BNDES grew larger and larger; by 2015, its annual disbursements reportedly were larger than that of the World Bank.[35] Some critics of the government charged that Dilma's administration was using the state bank to hide budget deficits, essentially having by having the bank "pay dividends to the government from treasury bonds that [the bank] keeps on its books" in order to bolster the state budget, according to a report in the *Financial Times*.[36] Dilma also announced new state spending on make-work construction projects, linked to helping state companies, and stopped Petrobras from raising the price of fuel it sold to Brazilian drivers. According to several reports, her administration pushed the state bank to even more aggressively fund large, "national champion" Brazilian companies.

These interventions were not effective at goosing the economy. In fact, in 2015 and 2016, Brazil's economy posted its worst performance in nearly two decades. Many of the large construction projects remained incomplete or, in the case of new municipal buildings, unoccupied. By 2015, after winning re-election, the Dilma government was debating plans to cut the size of Brazil's civil service and to junk some new municipal buildings in order to save money.

By 2015, Petrobras alone had amassed more debt than any other oil and gas company in the world, and its web of contractors, fueled by state money, had grown enormous—and also allegedly become a sinkhole for corruption. Petrobras's stock price fluctuated wildly, and it became one of the most volatile stocks in the world, according to an analysis by *Bloomberg*.[37]

DEMOCRACY REINFORCING STATE CAPITALISM

Brazil's experience under Lula and Dilma demonstrate one of the important paradoxes of modern state capitalism. Once state capitalists become completely democratic and their governments highly responsive to the public will, it is hard to maintain efficient state capitalism. A country can, it seems, have relatively efficient state-capitalist economics and some degree of political freedom, or it can have real political freedom and only some degree of economic efficiency. But it cannot have both. At the same time, the most autocratic state capitalists are the most inefficient and potentially the most dangerous—economically and strategically—to the world economy.

Both the Lula and Dilma administrations, despite their state capital-ism, and despite Dilma's tin political ear, ranked as the most democratic in the country's history. Under Lula and Dilma, Brazil received its highest scores in Freedom House's annual surveys of political freedom around the world. Notably, the Lula and Dilma administrations did not try to stop graft investigations into state companies and senior figures in the Workers Party. Other studies of the state of political freedom in Brazil, both by interna-tional organizations and Brazilian rights organizations, also suggested that the Lula and Dilma administrations were, measured by a range of indica-tors to judge political and civil liberties, the most open and democratic in the country's history. In fact, Lula and Dilma responded to public opinion which clearly had turned against the privatizations of Lula's predecessors, and which called for greater state intervention in the economy.

Yet both the Lula and Dilma governments found themselves almost trapped by public opinion; once they launched their new state interven-tions, the Brazilian public mood favored even more state intervention in order to address more and more economic challenges, whether or not the state could effectively tackle other problems. The Brazilian governments responded by increasing state spending and continuing to pour money into infrastructure, state companies, and other state programs. This increased spending came despite the fact that the initial success of Lula's state capi-talism lay in its combination of a somewhat greater degree of state interven-tion with orthodox fiscal policy and a willingness to set limits on how much the state was willingto intervene in various sectors. In other words, Lula's initial state capitalism had resembled the efficient state capitalism previ-ously practiced in places like Singapore, where the state played a major role in leading companies but did not totally dominate the private sector.

Whether or not they wanted to, neither Lula nor Dilma seemed capable of applying the brakes to state interventions when it was necessary. Had they been willing to defy the popular mood—to be modestly undemocratic, in a way—rather than continuing to, as one news article put it, "power up the bulldozers" for state projects, creating make-work jobs and helping state companies, and piling up debt, Brazilian governments might have main-tained the successes of Lula's initial, somewhat more limited, state capital-ism. Of course, even in a more free market-oriented democracy, politicians can be pulled by the popular will, or by what they think will make them popular, to push all sorts of economically inefficient, or just outright foolish ideas—trying to spend $400 million on a bridge to an Alaskan town with fifty residents, or shutting down the whole US government. (This was an idea that turned out not to be so popular with the American public but was popular with the political base of many Republican congresspeople.)

But in countries where the state does not own companies outright, or has relatively little influence over the corporate sector, democratically elected politicians normally have far less influence how the economy performs than does a state-capitalist system like Brazil, India, or Indonesia. And as we will see, when even democratically elected politicians who had supported elections and other democratic institutions are handed the enormous economic powers that state companies offer, they can be tempted to use those powers to entrench their own political positions, keep their party in office indefinitely, or lavish funds on their friends and allies.

7

The Lesser Threats

State Capitalism and Its Threat to Democracy

State capitalism poses five types of threats to democracy, global security, and the global economy. Having taken a closer look at the major state capitalists, we will examine each of these threats in order from the least worrisome to the most threatening.

STATE CAPITALISM AND EROSION OF DEMOCRACY IN ESTABLISHED DEMOCRATIC NATIONS

One of the fears about state capitalism is that the state's control of the economy in democratic nations will inexorably lead to state control of politics and a reduction in democratic freedoms. These fears are not totally misplaced. But when Western writers, politicians, and other opinion leaders examine state capitalism, they tend to take an undifferentiated approach, treating all state capitalists alike, rather than examining each country in detail. In Ian Bremmer's work on state capitalism, such as his book *The End of the Free Market* and his subsequent articles, he tends to fall into this undifferentiated approach. He and others often suggest that state capitalism will inevitably erode a country's democratic freedoms or prevent a country from becoming democratic in the first place.

It is true that in state capitalist nations leaders often have greater access to state funds, more potential largesse to hand out to supporters, and wider leverage over some of the most important companies in their countries. In part, maintaining democracy as state capitalism becomes entrenched depends on the commitment of individual political leaders to democratic norms even as they gain control of more economic tools—potentially too thin a reed upon which to base democracy.

Of course, presidents, prime ministers, and other politicians in new democracies always have a potentially larger role to play in democracy's survival than in more established democracies. More established democracies do not have to contend with the public's memory of—and possible nostalgia for—an authoritarian period. Additionally, they have the benefit of institutions like the judiciary, the civil service, the press, and others to mediate political tensions and prevent political rollback. For example, Corazon Aquino's and Fidel Ramos's personal commitment to democratic norms in the face of multiple coup plots and other threats helped entrench democracy in the Philippines. Whether or not nations are state capitalist or free market, leaders in young democracies often display some of the same traits as autocrats who came before them; the democratic leaders may come from longtime opposition parties and have all the paranoia and almost-autocratic instincts, born of trying to keep their parties alive in the past. And emerging democracies' weak institutions naturally may offer more possible opportunities than developed democracies for elected leaders to use aspects of the state's economy to entrench their political power.

Still, in democratic state capitalists, the state's control of so many companies vastly increases the potential for politicians' abuse of economic tools. Though some leaders, such as Lula, could boost state economic intervention while holding back their own instincts to use state companies to amass personal power, others could not resist the temptation to seize more political control as they gained power over the economy.

Thailand is a prime example of the potentially corrosive impact of state capitalism on democracy. In Thailand in the early 2000s, former prime minister Thaksin Shinawatra coupled interventionist economics with an increasingly autocratic political style. Like many other state capitalists, Thaksin seemed to believe that as long as he delivered strong growth, he and his party would remain popular, and he should be able to use economic institutions to bolster his party and his own personal power.[1]

Indeed, as the Thai government under Thaksin took back more and more control over the economy, Thaksin had increasing leverage over the largest banking, agricultural, cement, and construction companies. He pushed those companies over to use their advertising budgets—which were critical to Thailand's print media—only on those newspapers, magazines, and websites that backed him and his party. Songpol Kaoputumtip, a former top editor at the *Bangkok Post*, one of the two leading English-language newspapers in Thailand, said that the few reporters at the *Post* who were writing articles investigating Thaksin's family business or his dictatorial control of his party soon were told by top editors to move on to other subjects, lest the *Post* lose critical advertisers.[2] It was a more delicate means of controlling the paper's coverage than the tactics once adopted by Thai military juntas, which would simply close newspapers down or force the media—at gunpoint—to run flattering articles. Nevertheless, the leverage of advertising dollars was powerful, and for much of Thaksin's time as prime minister, the *Bangkok Post's* normally vocal political reporters and columnists remained docile. Most other Thai-language and English-language media outlets became even tamer on Thaksin's watch, with only a small number of elite outlets, with low readerships, continuing to seriously investigate his administration.

Similarly, Thaksin used his government's control of the economy to reward allies in the judiciary and the civil service. Traditionally, the Thai judiciary and civil service had maintained a degree of independence from political leaders, even during periods of military rule. But when Thaksin was charged early in his tenure with concealing his assets, he was acquitted by Thailand's top court in a very close decision. Following the verdict, several of the justices alleged that they had faced intense pressure from Thaksin's allies and were promised rewards, such as jobs at state companies, if they acquitted him. Later, as Thaksin became more entrenched, he began purging formerly independent government agencies. The government, which had increased state spending and taken control of many of the largest companies, would dangle the possibility of cushy, retirement-age jobs at state-owned or state-linked companies for civil servants, as long as they supported whatever policies Thaksin promoted.[3]

As Thaksin used his economic power to consolidate his political power, the impact on political freedoms in Thailand was severe. A country rated "free" by Freedom House in the late 1990s, one of the only in Asia to receive that designation, was downgraded in the 2000s to only "partly free."[4] In rankings of freedom of speech, press, Internet, and assembly by groups like Freedom House, Reporters without Borders, and the US State Department, Thailand plummeted even further.

Thaksin's sister Yingluck, who won an election as prime minister in 2011 but was generally considered a stand-in for her brother, combined interventionist economics and an autocratic political style. Her interventionist economics further undermined democracy and sadly set the stage for a military coup that erased democracy in Thailand entirely. Under Yingluck, the government took control of the rice sector, one of the most important in the country, which for years had been the largest rice exporter in the world. Buying up Thai producers' rice crops and promising a guaranteed rice price ran up huge budget deficits and led to Thailand being warned by credit rating agencies that they would downgrade the country's sovereign rating.[5] But the rice buy allowed the government to use outlays for rice crops as a tool to promote Yingluck's party—the rice policy understandably remained very popular with farmers, since the state was lavishing money on them. Although it was a government program and theoretically nonpartisan, somehow the Shinawatra party's logo and Yingluck advertisements would be handed out at events related to the rice scheme.

Meanwhile, the government continued to use state firms' advertising budgets and other powers to pressure the media, while looking the other way as state companies essentially paid favorable media outlets for coverage. Thailand fell from being a nation with one of freest media climates in Asia in the 1990s down to number 135 of 179 nations ranked in Reporters without Borders' 2013 rankings of global press freedom.[6] In the 2013 and 2014 Freedom House global surveys of Internet freedom, Thailand ranked among the ten least free nations in the world, alongside highly repressive states like Saudi Arabia and Syria.[7] No one, of course, doubted that Yingluck had been fairly elected; like her brother, she had won a massive victory and enjoyed a large base of support in parliament. In one high-profile speech, Yingluck vehemently defended electoral democracy, arguing that Thailand had descended into political crisis because the army and other elites had not respected voters' wishes by deposing her brother.[8] Yet at the same time she continued to curtail the media through draconian laws limiting freedom of speech and press, and she sued a prominent political cartoonist for defamation, chilling the climate of speech even further.[9]

The growing restrictions on civil liberties, the government's use of state enterprises as piggy banks for supporters of the prime minister's party, and the amassing of massive debt to fund state companies all contributed to making it easier for Bangkok middle classes, elites, and the Thai military to overthrow Thailand's elected government in May 2014. Of course, not all of the demonstrators who helped foster the environment that sparked the coup had noble reasons for gathering in the sweltering Bangkok streets. Many of the middle-class and elite men and women who held large, often violent street demonstrations in the six months before the coup did so not because they were angry about the state's control of the economy, wasted spending, and the elected government's disregard for the opposition and the rule of law but simply because they detested Thaksin Shinawatra and his family, and they could not tolerate the increasing political power of the poor majority in Thailand, a development they had never anticipated. Some wanted to undermine the elected government: Many demonstrators called for democracy to be abolished and replaced by long-term military rule or an absolute monarchy.

But the use of state enterprises and state spending to favor cronies and dominate opponents of Thaksin and Yingluck did indeed drive some of the demonstrators' anger. These real grievances about how Thai governments were using state money and allegedly fostering corruption also provided some degree of legitimacy in the eyes of the outside world to the demonstrations that led up to the coup, even if a significant percentage of the demonstrators were motivated primarily by disdain for the rural masses.

In fact, after the military launched its coup in May 2014, a coup that clearly had been planned well in advance (it was not, as the military claimed, a spur-of-the-moment operation conceived after Thai politics reached an impasse), the putsch received significant support, at least at first, from a relatively wide spectrum of Thais, though not from hardcore Thaksin supporters. Many Thais, including even some liberal and reform-minded men and women, were willing to tolerate the coup at first because they thought the military would actually use its immense powers to crack down on corruption, including corruption at state enterprises, which had been used as political tools by politicians.

These reformists wound up bitterly disappointed. The junta quickly realized that though some of the Thaksin-era use of state enterprises for political gain had been unpopular with Bangkok elites, statist economics overall remained extremely popular with most Thais. Although the junta was not elected, it also wanted to minimize any potential opposition to its rule. So, while army leaders claimed that their coup would allow for serious political and economic reforms, the coup leaders simply evicted Shinawatra allies from leading Thai state companies and replaced them with military cronies or military men themselves. Generally, they left Thai-style state capitalism in place.[10] The military regime even launched a Thaksinesque proposal to spend $75 billion on new infrastructure projects, funded largely by the state and designed to boost the fortunes of many leading state companies as much as to actually improve Thailand's infrastructure.[11] The junta government's projects were expressly designed, as Thaksin's had been, to inject revenues into a handful of state companies favored by the government. In this case, the favored state companies, which would benefit from no-bid contracts, were ones where the junta had installed current or former military men on the boards, and which also had the closest links to the royal family, whose holdings extended across Thai companies. (According to Forbes, Thailand's King Bhumibol Ayuldayej is the richest royal in the world, with his Crown Property Bureau holdings, which include stakes in many state companies, worth more than $30 billion.[12])

Argentina provides a similar example of the dangers of state capitalism in a place where political institutions are highly centralized—with one city dominant—and democracy has relatively weak roots among political leaders. Argentina's democracy, battered by periods of military rule, a history of authoritarian populism, and frequent economic crises, never developed strong institutions independent from the executive, and always tended to concentrate power in Buenos Aires. Yet in the 1990s, a period of economic liberalization, the Argentine government's economic powers were reduced substantially. This economic reform helped democracy flourish as well, since the ruling party could hand out less political patronage, and had little ability to use state companies to punish critics of the government.

But after Argentina endured an economic meltdown in the early 2000s, the government of Nestor Kirchner and his wife Cristina Fernandez de Kirchner—although only Nestor was actually on the 2003 presidential ballot, the couple campaigned and acted like a team—won office in 2003 vowing to end the chaos. At the time, the Kirchners' relative obscurity—they had led the far-away, barely populated Patagonia province—helped them win the election. They could portray themselves as a breath of fresh air compared to the rest of the candidates, nearly all of whom were well-known names in Buenos Aires.

In office, the Kirchners promised to use the power of the state to promote Argentina's economy and Argentina's state companies, even if that
meant defaulting on the country's international debts. The ruling couple
harkened back to the populist tradition of Juan Peron while also promising
that greater state control of the economy would position Argentine firms
to compete in the global commodities market—particularly in selling to
China—and to obtain better deals from foreign investors for Argentine resources like gas and wheat. The Kirchners made good on their promises,
defaulting on Argentina's debts and infuriating creditors while also taking
greater state control of Argentine oil and gas companies, agricultural companies, and other firms. As this book was published, many foreign creditors were still trying to get some of their money back from Argentina. But
even if they obtain judgments against Argentina in their own court systems,
it was proving very hard to find Argentine government assets to seize in
payment.[13]

At first, the Kirchners' embrace of state capitalism angered only foreign creditors and some Argentine businesspeople, while proving popular
with the Argentine public. But it soon became clear that state capitalism
was allowing the Kirchners to strangle democracy as well. As the Kirchners
gained more and more control of the economy, by closely controlling banks'
deposits, nationalizing more private funds, and nationalizing everything
from airlines to trains to shipping firms, the formerly obscure first couple
found they could use their economic power against opposition parties,
prominent newspaper outlets, critical economists, and many other critics.
The press, which had battered the Kirchner's predecessors, became tamer
and tamer. As in Thailand, the first couple pressured Argentina's media
outlets to quash negative stories or face a drop in advertising from state
companies, which were major sources of revenue for print and broadcast
outlets.[14] The Kirchners banned the publishing of independent Argentine
assessments of the country's economy or any independent economic data
at all. The Kirchners took over state companies producing the actual paper
needed by major media groups. This gave the government more power over
critical media outlets, such as Clarin, a media group that had long been
critical of the Kirchner's patronage politics and alleged corruption. As the
Kirchners nationalized companies, many business leaders who previously
had served as major voices of criticism of Argentine government's economic policies stopped offering commentary for fear that the government
could turn on them next.

The Kirchner machine ultimately slowed down, as Nestor died suddenly in 2007. Fernandez, though she won an election as president after Kirchner's death, left office in December 2015, replaced by a former Buenos Aires mayor who pledged to reverse some of the Kirchners' statist policies. Yet the Kirchners' state capitalism had a lasting effect on Argentine politics. Without the Kirchners' use of government companies to intimidate the media, other types of civil society, private businesses, and opposition politicians, the couple never would have been able to amass such political power and undermine democratic institutions, according to numerous Argentine politicians and officials, including several from the Kirchners' own political party. The Kirchners had no other ways to intimidate opposition and take control of politics; unlike the Democrat Party in Thailand, the Kirchners had no particular links to the Argentine military or security forces, who had largely bowed out of politics since the period of the "Dirty War." The Kirchners had no rabid national political base before Nestor Kirchner's first election as president, and they did not have a particularly charismatic style of politics. So, unlike a leader like Hugo Chavez, who could use his charisma and fervent political base as well as growing government control of state companies to crush the opposition, the Kirchners could never have relied on their political appeal. And, unlike in some other countries like Malaysia, Saudi Arabia, or Thailand, the Kirchners could not play on ethnic and religious divisions to demonize opponents and gain support for restricting democratic freedoms for certain segments of society. Their only strategy for amassing political power was to slowly dominate more and more of the Argentine economy and then use that domination to intimidate critics from every sector of society.

STATE CAPITALISM IN SOUTH AFRICA AND MALAYSIA

Even in South Africa and Malaysia, where the public retains a strong commitment to democracy, state capitalism has had a corrosive impact on political freedoms. Average South Africans clearly support democracy. A 2013 study by Freedom House, which polled a broad socioeconomic range of South Africans over several months, found that "South Africans take their human rights for granted and retain faith in the democratic system, with strong support for voting."[15] Yet at the same time as the South African public continues to support democracy as the best means of governing, the growing state capitalism in South Africa has been a major factor in the country's democratic regression. Indeed, South Africa's score in Freedom House's annual ratings of political and civil liberties has continually dropped since the end of Nelson Mandela's presidency in 1999. Growing state capitalism has played a role in facilitating South Africa's regression of political freedom. The South African media is rife with allegations of senior ANC members, including the inner circles surrounding President Zuma, siphoning funds from state enterprises and using state companies at polling time to hand out cash, promises of jobs, and other benefits to people who pledge to vote for the ANC. Areas where the vote goes against the ANC are allegedly denied critical services, provided by state enterprises like electricity and water. In addition, ANC leaders allegedly have used promises of jobsat growing state enterprises, as Thaksin did in Thailand, to silence critical bureaucrats and civil servants—a powerful means of silencing dissent.

This use of state companies as vote banks is a tradition in several other hybrid autocratic/democratic state capitalists, including Malaysia, where the same coalition has ruled since independence five decades ago, and has made great use (in terms of staying in power) of state companies for the ruling coalition's own ends. According to numerous Malaysian politicians, both from the opposition and from the ruling coalition, in the run-up to parliamentary elections, Malaysia's ruling Barisan Nasional (BN) coalition makes sure that state company executives remind workers that their jobs rest on BN victories, and after elections state firms usually expand projects—and create jobs—in areas that gave the BN the most support. Areas that vote for the Malaysian opposition often find state companies pulling out investments, closing plants, and simply shutting off basic services. The fact that state companies are used as vote banks becomes obvious when one maps where many state firms make investments in Malaysia. State firms' investments closely track the areas that voted most heavily for the BN, even though many of those regions, particularly in the Malaysian states on the island of Borneo, are poor choices for most types of investment, given their remote locations, poor quality of workforce, and lack of infrastructure. (In the 2013 national elections, the BN won nearly every parliamentary seat in East Malaysia.) By contrast, many Malaysian state companies have made relatively few investments in the past six years in the states of Penang and Selangor, which happen to be two of the wealthiest and most educated states in Malaysia, and seemingly natural places for all types of investment. After all, foreign investors have flocked to these states because of their educated workforces, high-quality infrastructure, and wealthy consumers. There is little doubt that state companies would have higher profit margins investing in these states. Yet the federal government has not encouraged government companies to expand in these two states. Why? Because people in these states mostly support the opposition coalition in national and state elections, and these two states are governed, at the state level, by the opposition.

Malaysian politicians from both the opposition and the ruling party admit this is the case. "This has become an accepted part of Malaysian politics and the economy by now," says opposition member of parliament Nural Izzah Anwar. "The BN [ruling coalition] barely even has to suggest before the elections that areas that vote for it will win from the state companies, since it is so established that this is what always happens . . . Then the state companies invest there, hand out money in those areas, no matter whether it's profitable or not, or they ignore a place like Selangor."[16] Although he was unwilling to put his name on the record, a prominent politician from the ruling coalitionechoed Izzah's sentiments. "Sure, the GLCs [government-linked companies], there's no pressure from the federal government for them to do more in Selangor, since that's an opposition state."[17]

HOW DEMOCRACY AND STATE CAPITALISM COULD COEXIST

Although the examples of Thailand, South Africa, and Argentina seem to suggest that state capitalism inevitably erodes democratic freedom, in some countries economic statism coexists with political openness, indicating that state capitalism is not such a threat to democratic freedoms in countries that already have strong democratic institutions and cultures. State capitalism is one factor that may foster democratic regression, but in itself it does not automatically cause political regression; it is not even necessarily correlated with political regression.

Although individual leaders play a role in maintaining democratic politics in a state-driven economy, they are not the only guardians of democracy in countries like Indonesia, Norway, or Brazil; if they were, state capitalism would inevitably undermine every democracy, since the quality of leadership in any country ranges widely. But, if state capitalist countries are also able to create independent institutions insulated from the power of the executive—and thus insulated from the executive's control of state companies—these institutions can help preserve democracy even as statist economics expand. For example, Indonesia has created a truly independent agency to investigate graft cases; the Corruption Eradication Commission has wide-ranging police powers that, in some ways, exceed those of the regular Indonesian police. The commission, established only a decade ago, has quickly become a powerful check on the use of state economic tools for patronage and self-dealing. Though Indonesia still suffers from serious graft problems, a legacy of the Suharto regime, the Corruption Eradication Commission has pursued some of the most powerful politicians and has notched a 100 percent conviction rate in its cases. Unlike the Directorate of Special Operations, the elite police unit created in post-apartheid South Africa to combat graft and organized crime, Indonesia's anti-corruption commission is not directly controlled by elected leaders and so cannot be easily manipulated; in recent years the commission has launched high-profile investigations into some of the closest allies of Susilo Bambang Yudhoyono, during Yudhoyono's time as president. (The Directorate of Special Operations, known in South Africa by its nickname, the "Scorpions," were defanged and then essentially disbanded at the end of the Mbeki era, just as it was investigating allegations of bribery by political allies of South Africa's next president, Jacob Zuma.) To Yudhoyono's credit, he did not block the commission's investigation into his political allies, and in late 2014 the commission announced it was investigating Yudhoyono's son on allegations of accepting bribes.

Singapore, though not as democratic as Indonesia, long ago created checks on state power that are relatively insulated from the reach of individual politicians. These checks have remained strong as the city-state has become more open politically, with a real opposition party and a much freer atmosphere for speech and expression than even a decade ago. The Political and Economic Risk Consultancy, a leading Asia-Pacific business analysis firm, has consistently ranked Singapore's judiciary as the fairest in Asia.[18]

Norway, perhaps the most successful example of combining state capitalism with vibrant democracy, uses similar strategies as Singapore. Even as Norway's economy has become more state dominated over the past two decades, with the exploitation of oil riches and the expansion of Norway's SWF, the country has maintained its ranking in Freedom House's annual survey of global democracy, holding among the five or ten freest nations in the world. Norway's state companies have policies written into their charters that are designed to limit government's ability to use the state firms for political purposes. Norway also has put into place some of the most robust open-government laws in the world, which allow Norwegian citizens and foreigners to gain extensive insight into the workings of Norwegian state companies, Norway's SWF, and the Norwegian government. (Norway's freedom-of-information and open-government laws are far broader than those in the United States, for instance.) Indeed, Norway's open-government laws are so thorough and transparent that the *New York Times* was able to use the process to obtain an enormous trove of Norwegian government officials' internal emails, explicit agreements between the Norwegian government and American think tanks, and internal reports produced by Norway's foreign ministry laying out strategies for lobbying in Washington for policies that would benefit Statoil, Norway's giant state oil company.[19]

Norway's Statoil has set high governance standards that even many publicly traded multinationals could not meet. Like the Norwegian government, Statoil is subject to Norway's extensive transparency and open-government laws. Statoil also publishes all of its financial statements and major decisions online, has several directors on its board elected by employees, holds frequent press conferences and other consultations with the public, sets aside a percentage of revenues for corporate social responsibility programs, and opens its shareholder meetings (the state is the largest shareholder, but Statoil also trades on the Oslo stock exchange) to the public.[20]

The Norwegian example has caught on, as rich Norway has sent teams of advisors to several nascent democracies to help them balance political openness and significant state intervention in the economy. One of the most notable examples of Norway's influence has come in tiny Timor-Leste, the former Indonesian province of East Timor, which has only about 1.2 million people in one half of an island. Timor-Leste came into existence in 2002 after decades as part of Indonesia. It remains the poorest nation in Asia, but one with a significant share of the profits from oil exploration in the seas between Timor and northern Australia. Since its founding, Timor-Leste, whose leaders previously were guerillas fighting the Indonesian army and who have a great deal of legitimacy due to their role in fighting for independence, has relied on significant state intervention in the economy, as well as heaps of donor aid, to survive.[21] But in order to prevent future governments from taking advantage of the state's role in the economy and plundering the money from its petroleum riches, Timor-Leste's government has created a state fund with Norway's assistance. All of the proceeds that go into the fund must be invested abroad in financial assets and cannot be transferred back into Timor without parliamentary approval. Even then, Timor's law says that any money from the fund transferred back into Timor-Leste must go into the central government budget and must be reported to the public, creating a high degree of transparency in how the fund is used.[22]

In addition to taking tough measures to ensure transparency even when the state owns large portions of the economy, some democratic state capitalists, like Indonesia, have effectively combined state control of a percentage of companies with political decentralization, thereby preventing too much power from being concentrated in the capital and in the executive. In Indonesia, democratic governments have indeed amassed greater control of Indonesian companies in the past ten years, but at the same time Jakarta has allowed provinces and smaller regions to take in larger shares of tax revenues and to create their own local legislatures, governors, and other elected local offices. This process has allowed Indonesians to make decisions locally about a broad range of issues once determined by Jakarta—permits for resource excavation, infrastructure creation, tax policies, local corporate and civil law, and many other issues. To facilitate this process, Indonesia has in the past two decades of decentralization created sixteen thousand public service buildings and facilities for provincial, sub-provincial, and city-level governments, and hired at least thirty thousand new provincial and city-level government officials to staff these facilities. This process of decentralization thus has also brought government services closer to people across the country.

This political decentralization has been wildly popular in a diverse and geographically large country that, under Sukarno and Suharto, had become accustomed to total political dominance by Jakarta. Political decentralization also has been the major check on the power of the presidency, no matter how many state companies Indonesia creates. Even with greater central government control of many companies than existed in the early 1990s, the Indonesian presidency is still far less powerful than it was in Suharto's time, or even in the early post-Suharto period.

Decentralization also has naturally improved budget transparency, since it is harder for a larger number of officials to keep data secret from the media and from the public. In addition, as we have seen, the independent Corruption Eradication Commission, probably the most popular institution in the country, has played a major role in ensuring that even in a country with serious remaining problems with corruption and patronage, independent institutions can serve as a check on power and can limit the threat statist economics pose to democracy.

Indeed, though Indonesia's economy has become more closed in the late 2000s and early 2010s, its democracy has become stronger during the same time period, by nearly all estimations. The country has held three straight free and fair direct presidential elections, and is now routinely touted by political scientists as one of the most successful examples of democratization in the developing world. The country has surpassed every other nation in Southeast Asia in Freedom House ratings of the state of democracy.

Indonesia is not unique. Comparing annual ratings of countries' political freedom in Freedom House's *Freedom in the World* index and annual ratings of countries' economic freedom in the Heritage Foundation's *Index of Economic Freedom* suggests that there is no clear correlation between economic statism and political authoritarianism. Although the *Index of Economic Freedom* measures many types of restrictions on economies, some of which do not necessarily imply state capitalism, in general it is a broad barometer of whether a country is becoming more economically statist or more free market oriented. Looking at a country's score on the index over time gives a general sense of whether it is becoming more or less state capitalist, although this is not a perfect measure.

Over time, what the Heritage Foundation index and the Freedom House scores reveal is a fairly complex picture. Some developing nations have regressed on the *Index of Economic Freedom* over the past decade, and their Freedom House scores for political freedom and civil liberties have dropped as well. These countries include some of the notable examples we examined above, like Thailand, where statist economics has gone hand in hand with growing authoritarianism. But comparing these two indexes also reveals that some state capitalists have been able to maintain strong democratic institutions and culture over time even as their scores on the *Index of Economic Freedom* have dropped because of their growing economic statism. Several countries whose political freedoms, as judged by Freedom House, have increased since 2000 also have dropped on the *Index of Economic Freedom*. Indonesia is the most obvious example of this trend, but Brazil and other countries also fall into this group.

Although the number of countries whose economic freedom and political freedom have fallen simultaneously is larger than the number whose political freedom has risen or remained the same as their economic freedom has declined, the difference in size between this first and second group is not large—not enough of a difference to see a clear correlation between rising state capitalism and declining political freedoms in developing nations.[23] There is, as we have seen, anecdotal evidence that state capitalism can make it easier for leaders to amass political power and possibly undermine democratic institutions, but this evidence remains only anecdotal, and not comprehensively supported by these indexes.

STATE CAPITALISM IN DEMOCRACIES AND THE THREAT TO SECURITY

State capitalism, then, is possibly but not necessarily a threat to democratic freedoms. State capitalism is not inherently anti-democratic per se—witness Brazil can foster democratic regression because of the ways in which it concentrates too many types of power in the hands of political elites. But state capitalism is at most one factor in the global democratic decline that has taken place over the past decade.[24] Since it remains unclear whether state capitalism is even necessarily a cause of democratic regression, a link between economic statism and democratic regression should be a concern for policymakers around the world, but a lesser concern than some of the other threats of state capitalism. In the final chapter, we will examine how to address state capitalism's potential impact on democracy in developing nations.

Some politicians and analysts also worry that state capitalism will allow countries to use state companies as weapons, as de facto means of warfare. But there is little evidence that this fear is justified in the case of the democratic state capitalists. The democratic state capitalists, even those where state capitalism has contributed to a degree of political regression, are not serious threats to regional and international security just because of their statist economics. (Later chapters show how government control of the economy can make the undemocratic state capitalists serious threats to regional and international security, however.) The democratic state capitalists are no more likely than free-market democracies to use their companies as weapons, to engage in trade disputes, or to pose threats to regional and international security. The United States and other Western nations should learn to distinguish among state capitalists, examining them based upon their political regimes and not their economic strategies.

In fact, the most democratic state capitalists, like Indonesia and Singapore, have proven themselves as highly effective partners for the United States and for other democracies, and as generally responsible members of the international community. Both Singapore and Indonesia have at times taken on leading roles in the Association of Southeast Asian Nations, the main regional organization, with Indonesian leaders in recent years quietly urging other Southeast Asian nations to embrace more open and responsive government. Meanwhile, neither Singapore nor Indonesia have any history of using their state companies, like Singapore's banks or Indonesia's state gas company, as weapons in strategic disputes, such as Indonesia's dispute with China over claims to areas of the South China Sea. In contrast, as we will see in the following chapters, the most autocratic state capitalist nations surrounding Singapore and Indonesia, such as Vietnam and China, do have a recent history of using their state companies as weapons in strategic disputes over the South China Sea.

Take Brazil as another example of a country where growing economic intervention has proven little obstacle to either democracy or warming ties to the United States. Although Brazil's economy was sputtering by the end of 2014, the government was no threat to its own people or to other nations. Brazil's recent governments have invested considerable state funds and rhetorical support for Brazilian state companies, but there is no evidence that Brasilia had attempted to use state companies as weapons to punish neighboring nations with whom it had political or strategic disputes.

Meanwhile, over time, Brazil's maturing democracy has made it far more vocal on some international democracy and human rights issues (e.g., women's rights and abuses) by other South American governments; this responsible rights advocacy has come even as Brazil has become more statist economically. And despite some cracks in the United States–Brazil relationship over revelations of Americans spying on Brazil, the maturation of Brazil's democracy has generally fostered better relations with the United States during the course of Lula's and Dilma's terms. The political nature of the Brazilian government, not its state capitalism, has largely determined its role in hemispheric stability and its relationship with the United States.

Irrespective of the composition and management of its economy, Brazil has become one of the largest aid donors in Central and South America, focusing its regional assistance on key development goals such as disease eradication. Between 2005 and 2010 alone, Brazil's international aid outlays grew from around $150 million to over $4 billion.[25] In some respects, Brazil in South America has come to resemble France, another regional power with some global power ambitions that has a large state sector but still manages to create some world-beating companies. In fact, although all European economies were hit hard by the economic slowdown that began in 2009, France, as economist Paul Krugman noted, recovered decently well: between 2009 and 2014 France's economy far outperformed the euro-area average, including many European economies with much smaller state sectors and tighter fiscal policies, like the Netherlands.[26]

Singapore, Indonesia, and Brazil fit a pattern. The past sixty years of history show that democracies, whether state capitalist or free market, almost never go to war against each other, because such wars require the support of the population, which is hard to obtain. And democracies tend to work better, over the long term, with other democracies in international economic and security institutions. Over the past six decades, governments with strong public legitimacy have formed lasting partnerships with the United States, whether or not these countries have state capitalist economies. The North Atlantic Treaty Organization (NATO) works well together in large part because most of its member governments historically have been democracies with similar political cultures. At institutions like the United Nations, where there is a wide diversity of opinion among leading actors, the United States has tended to vote, on most issues, in similar ways as other democracies, whether or not those democracies practice a form of state capitalism. Indeed, at the United Nations Security Council, democracies, including many of the most prominent democratic state capitalists, have over the past ten years voted with the United States three times more often than authoritarian nations, a rate similar to the confluence of democracies' votes at the UN Human Rights Council.[27]

Authoritarian rule can, at times, provide a kind of stability in bilateral relations, especially in places like Saudi Arabia or Jordan where it is unclear whether, given the level of anti-Americanism in the population, an elected government might actually be far more anti-American. In nations like Jordan it could be convincingly argued that autocratic rulers generally have been better for American strategic interests than elected politicians would be.

But because governments with weak public legitimacy, like authoritarian regimes, are inherently unstable, they make poor long-term partners for the United States or any other major democracy, even when the two countries' opinion leaders have many common interests, as is true with Amman and Washington. The United States' partnership with these countries usually rests on ties to a small handful of leaders, who could be removed in rapid and violent turns of events that throw the bilateral relationship into disorder.

In addition, in most of the developing nations where state capitalism is entrenched, there is little evidence that the elites—and in autocratic nations, authoritarian rulers—are more pro-American than the average population and thus are holding back a tide of anti-American sentiment. In particular, young people in many developing nations, especially in Asia, tend to have relatively positive views of the United States and of potential economic and strategic ties with the United States.[28] This desire for close strategic ties to, and even a formal alliance with, the United States is particularly strong among young people in Vietnam, for instance. In fact, Vietnam's top leaders, who are usually older and have some memory of the war with the United States, tend to be more hesitant about building ties with the United States than young Vietnamese.

It is thus unlikely that, as might happen in a place like Saudi Arabia, free elections in Malaysia, Thailand, Vietnam, or many other state capitalists would bring to power politicians who would be more anti-American than the authoritarian leaders currently in place. For instance, Anwar Ibrahim, the longtime opposition leader who probably would have been prime minister in Malaysia if elections in 2013 were not stolen, spent extensive periods of his life in the United States, had strong democratic credentials, and publicly desired close economic, political, and strategic ties between Malaysia and the United States.

EROSION OF POLITICAL FREEDOM BREEDS INSTABILITY

To be sure, in some democratic state capitalists where political freedom has eroded—erosion facilitated by state capitalism—the breakdown in freedom can contribute to political instability and thus make these countries worse strategic partners. This is the second potential threat of state capitalism, although it is not the greatest threat. Thailand, for example, is a US ally and a country that long was one of the most reliable American partners in Asia. The Obama administration has struggled to work with Bangkok on many important strategic and economic issues, largely because Thai leaders are so preoccupied with domestic crises that have come along with Thailand's breakdown in political freedoms, a breakdown partly caused by the expansion of Thai state capitalism under Thaksin. The Thai government has been unable to participate in the United States' regional trade agenda because Bangkok is consumed, even after the coup, with domestic politics. Similarly, in Malaysia, the ruling coalition has been so distracted since the 2010s by domestic political turmoil, itself a result largely of political regression and scandals surrounding alleged misuse of funds from a Malaysian SWF, that Kuala Lumpur has in recent years proven an often useless partner for the United States on trade talks, regional economic cooperation, and security issues.

Still, although the breakdown of political stability in countries like Thailand and Malaysia, a breakdown often facilitated by state capitalism, is a serious problem for the United States and other democracies, it is one of the lesser threats of state capitalism for several reasons. Most importantly, as we have seen, the strongest democracies, like Brazil and Indonesia, probably will not have their political freedom undermined by state intervention in the economy. Several of these strong democracies—such as Brazil, Indonesia, and India—also are at the head of the emerging giants of the developing world, and their political stability matters far more than that of Thailand and Malaysia. Indeed, although there are states beyond Thailand and Malaysia where political stability and the ability to partner with the United States are endangered in part because of state capitalism, this list is relatively small: Argentina, several Central Asian nations, and perhaps Myanmar, whose growing economy is in danger of being dominated by a small group of government-controlled companies.

Most of these state capitalists also have managed to muddle along economically, even through their political crises, and nearly all observers believe they will continue to do so. They have more efficient economies, more attractions for investors, and greater macroeconomic stability than the more economically troubled state capitalists, like Russia, Venezuela, or Egypt. What is more, no country in this group is actively trying to undermine regional and international stability, use state companies as weapons, dominate neighbors, or drastically change international institutions, as some autocratic state capitalists are doing.

Indeed, as we will see, there are several countries whose political and economic stability is precarious, in part because of their seriously flawed versions of state capitalism. These countries are far greater dangers to their regions and to the world.

8

State Capitalism's Long-Term Economic Future

A Threat to Countries' Own Long-Term Development and to the World Economy?

Although the democratic state capitalists pose little strategic threat to the international community, and indeed often can prove effective partners for the United States, their brands of state capitalism could potentially pose a threat to their own economic well-being. The third potential threat of state capitalism is that as an economic model, it is not as effective in the long term as free-market capitalism, and that it will become so popular among developing nations that it will distract them from pursuing more effective growth strategies. In the worst-case scenarios, state capitalism fails in the long run so badly that it proves not only a distraction from a potentially superior economic model but also a cause of major economic collapses in developing nations, impacting the entire world.

The developing nations embracing state capitalism, remember, are critical to the world economy; Standard Chartered bank estimates that, statistically, about 70 percent of global growth until 2030 will come from emerging markets.[1] Most of the state capitalists we have examined so far fall into this group of emerging markets that are likely to be the highest-growing economies between now and 2030.

Malaysia illustrates this third worry. Malaysia's brand of state capitalism has been moderately efficient but seems to be reaching the end of its utility. This is hardly uncommon, and we will explore in depth in the next chapter the challenges faced by state capitalism over time. Indeed, it can be difficult for even the most efficient state capitalists to maintain high growth rates for two or three decades or more.

Malaysia grew from one of the poorest nations in Asia at the time it gained independence from Britain in 1957 to a middle-income economy with a GDP per capita of over $10,000 today. Among former British colonies that gained independence in the post–World War II era, Malaysia today boasts a higher GDP per capita than all but Singapore and several of the oil-rich tiny former British colonies in the Persian Gulf and Southeast Asia. While using sound macroeconomic policies, Malaysia's post-independence governments created government-controlled companies that allowed Malaysia to develop its natural resources, including gas and palm oil, into higher-value-added products, which probably would have been impossible if the country simply sold oil and gas leases to foreign companies. In neighboring Brunei and Indonesia, the examples closest to Malaysia's, foreign resources companies mined and drilled for oil, gas, copper, and gold; under Bruneian and Indonesian law, these foreign companies were allowed to export raw natural resources. For decades, neither Brunei nor Indonesia developed domestic industries based on their natural resources, such as refining, plastics and petrochemicals, or any other industries. As a result, neither country captured as much of the value of their resources as they might have otherwise.

Malaysia's government also protected many local banks and pushed them to merge into larger, regionally competitive entities. In addition, the Malaysian government used state policies to force foreign investors to work with local companies in joint ventures, helping support Malaysian manufacturing of everything from computer chips to phones. The foreign investors received enough incentives to agree to this deal, and eventually Malaysian manufacturing companies were able to produce more and more technologically advanced items, making them into real global competitors in a range of manufactured goods.

This is an economic success story, but Malaysia's economy has stagnated in the past decade. Some of Malaysia's earlier state-capitalist strategies allowed it to develop a strong manufacturing sector; create sizable, competitive companies in many industries; and use its natural resources effectively. But over time, the negative aspects of Malaysian state capitalism became greater burdens, while these earlier benefits of the statist approach provided less return. The Malaysian government has maintained laws that require any large Malaysian companies to ensure that at least 30 percent of their firms are owned by ethnic Malays, a policy that has created a rentier class of Malays who are given equity stakes and board seats while often doing virtually little work for their pay.[2] (Malaysia, a country of almost twenty-eight million people, is comprised of roughly 60 percent ethnic Malays, 23 percent ethnic Chinese, 7 percent ethnic Indians, and smaller percentages of other groups.[3]) Prime Minister Najib has pushed national oil company Petronas to spend money to support small Malay-controlled companies who could be vendors or suppliers for giant Petronas, the only Malaysian company big enough to make *Fortune*'s Global 500 list of the largest firms.[4] But this ethnic favoritism and lack of meritocratic business practices have badly undermined many Malaysian state companies and the economy as a whole, while foreign investors have become more wary of helping Malaysian partners, and Malaysia has nearly reached the limits of how much value it can get out of its natural resources. Meanwhile, the benefits accrued over decades from using cheap state capital to build up industries like gas processing, electronics manufacturing, and other sectors have started to wane. Malaysia now faces more global and regional competition in these industries.

Malaysia's brand of state capitalism also has failed to modernize, a contrast to that of its neighbor in Singapore. In an earlier era, the Malaysian government effectively pressured and wooed foreign companies to help a select number of Malaysian manufacturing firms develop, and used state policies to modernize Malaysia's natural resources industry. But the government did not help Malaysian individuals to prepare for the modern economy. Malaysia's weak education system does little to foster innovation, and the government has failed to use the cheap credit it has on hand to help build twenty-first-century industries similar to those in Singapore, like pharmaceuticals or nanotechnology. In addition, the Malaysian government has done little to cull uncompetitive state enterprises and force state companies to compete with each other, a strategy employed at times by China and Singapore, among other successful state capitalists.

Many Malaysian state enterprises now are suffering, and the economy as a whole has slowed dramatically since the early 1990s. Petronas has continued to be profitable, as have some other Malaysian natural resources companies, but other Malaysian state-controlled companies are floundering badly. The country's state-controlled flagship airline, Malaysian Airlines, lost money in 2011, 2012, 2013, and 2014, and like many Malaysian state firms has long been plagued by reports of corruption, insider trading, and nepotism in hiring and promotion.[5]

Few people outside Malaysia noticed the endemic problems in this particular Malaysian state enterprise, until a Malaysia Airlines plane, Flight MH370, left from Kuala Lumpur on the night of March 8, 2014, and within an hour had lost contact with air traffic control. The ghost flight then vanished, triggering a fruitless multi-country search for the plane's wreckage. Combined with the apparent shooting down of a Malaysia Airlines plane over Ukrainian airspace three months later, a tragedy that further focused international attention on the state-owned parent company, the twin disasters revealed the economic rot at the heart of Malaysia Airlines. The company had to admit that it had been losing even more money that it had publicly admitted in the past and was forced to ask for massive state assistance to survive after the two disasters.

Malaysia's economic problems do impact the regional and global economy—it is one country in the group of emerging markets projected to, statistically, make up much of the growth in the global economy in the next twenty years. So, if state capitalism undermines Malaysia's economic potential, it also undermines Malaysia's contribution to global growth and regional economic leadership, threatening the world economy. Malaysia, with the twenty-ninth-largest economy in the world, is followed closely by investors. Malaysia also historically has been a leader in Asia in promoting free trade. Rising economic nationalism in the country thus imperils its ability to be a leader on regional trade integration.

A far greater worry would be if one of the bigger state capitalists—Brazil, India, or Indonesia—saw their growth stagnate so badly that their economies collapsed, taking down the rest of their regions and seriously undermining the world economy. Statist economics seems, at least in Brazil, to be running out of steam, with Brasilia allocating far too much cheap capital to infrastructure projects of minimal utility designed to create jobs and boost state companies. State projects have helped keep Brazilian unemployment down but are becoming an enormous drag on the economy. Indeed, both the Indian and Brazilian economies have slowed down from their periods of high growth in the 2000s. Yet India actually is poised for faster growth in 2015 and 2016 than it had been in the early part of the 2010s.

The possibility of the large, democratic state capitalists suffering severe long-term economic slowdowns, and thus seriously damaging the world economy, is not great, and it does not appear to be any greater than the potential of economic collapse in more free market-oriented developing nations. State capitalism's advantages, such as the ability to focus state funds on certain industries, provide capital to areas where the market will not go, and build up companies with economies of scale often seem to peter out within a decade or two. Still, the democratic state capitalists have generally produced at least moderate long-term growth going back to the end of the Cold War and the spread of democracy throughout much of the developing world. State capitalism seems to have a limited life span as an economic tool for many countries. Few of even the efficient state capitalists have not been able to maintain annual growth rates above 4 percent for more than twenty-five years. That number is chosen as a benchmark because many of these larger developing nations need to maintain 4 percent annual growth to continue to create jobs for people entering the workforce; however, 4 percent is not an absolute figure but one chosen as a tool to show generally how substantially these countries are growing. But the relatively democratic state capitalists—Indonesia, Singapore, Malaysia, Norway, Thailand— have averaged more than 3 percent annual growth for the past twenty-five years. This evidence suggests that the democratic state capitalists have been able to sustain growth for extended periods—growth that, if not at China levels, is high enough to promote development and largely avoid economic meltdowns.

As we have seen, the more politically open state capitalists tend to produce relatively strong economic efficiency, in part because if their statist policies are so bad for domestic businesses, leaders in more open state capitalists either have to change their policies or face removal from office. It is also much harder, in the more open state capitalists, for the government to hide massively ineffective or graft-ridden policies from the public, even between elections. This openness helps prevent total economic meltdowns.

In Brazil, for instance, corruption in state-owned companies like Petrobras may have contributed to these firms' recent poor performance and affected the whole economy, but that corruption has been exposed, aired, and investigated at great lengths, demonstrating the strength of Brazilian democracy. In democratic Indonesia, corruption remains endemic, and state enterprises are rife with graft. But the public finds out about the wrongdoing, corrupt officials are often brought to justice (though surely not often enough), and the public is able—through national, provincial, and local elections—to regularly render its own verdict on corruption and economic management. In contrast, in Russia, Venezuela, Vietnam, and other highly autocratic state capitalists, graft becomes interwoven with state capitalism, endemic corruption is never punished, and officials continue to loot the state with little fear of being ousted from office. These are the types of state capitalists, we will see, that really threaten the world economy with their potential collapses.

THE RUSSIA MODEL

Here we can see the chart first examined in Chapter 2. We can see that the most efficient state capitalists also tend to be the more open and responsive state capitalists, although not the most democratic of the group. The least efficient state capitalists in this chart also tend to be the most politically repressive. In this second group of nations—Russia, Vietnam, the United Arab Emirates, Saudi Arabia—corruption and rot inside state enterprises goes unexposed. In these countries, leaders can oversee massive misallocations of capital without the public knowing it and trying to correct it, and economies thus can become massively distorted, as has happened in Vietnam, without any real public understanding of who is making economic decisions at all. It is in these countries that severe and rapid economic contraction is most likely.

Indeed, several studies comparing the growth trajectories of authoritarian and democratic nations have shown that autocratic states tend to be more prone to drastic swings in their economic fortunes. Meanwhile, democracies tend to have smoother growth trajectories, in part because the transparency that comes with democratic government makes it harder for leaders to conceal, and thus avoid addressing, massive economic problems.

In perhaps the most thorough analysis of democracy's benefits and demerits and growth trajectories, political scientists Morton Halperin, Joseph Siegle, and Michael Weinstein found that even in the poorest countries in the world, sustained democracy over decades is linked to "less volatility in growth rates than autocracies . . . The strength of democracies' economic performance is as much their ability to maintain steady growth [i.e., avoid disastrous outcomes] over time as it is to achieve relatively rapid progress."[6] They found that going back to the 1960s, only five of the twenty worst-performing economies in the world, in terms of per-capita growth rates, were democracies. The rest were all authoritarian regimes. And even when democracies did face serious economic challenges, they respond more rapidly and effectively than most authoritarian nations. Following the Asian financial crisis of the late 1990s, democracies in East Asia generally recovered from the crisis more rapidly than autocracies and hybrid regimes. In part, studies suggest that democracies recover more quickly because they use elections to restore confidence in their governments. That confidence spreads through the population and ultimately leads to confidence in government reforms, which helps rebalance economies and put them on a path back to growth.[7]

The value of political openness in times of crisis was first examined more than thirty years ago by Indian economist Amartya Sen in his famous essay on famine and political systems. He showed that even when they face serious crises like famine, democratic governments are better equipped to handle them, ensuring that their citizens do not starve. Democracies have more incentive to learn from their mistakes and adapt, he showed, and are designed to take in information and respond to it, making it highly unlikely that a democratic government can simply ignore a famine or other catastrophe.[8] Halperin, Siegle, and Weinstein call this ability to take in information and respond horizontal and vertical accountability—democratic governments, unlike autocratic ones, are moderated by checks on the regime's power and by their need to obtain the support of much of the population to continue governing.

This smoother growth trajectory tends to be true whether the democracies have free-market or highly statist economies. It is the political nature of the government that is related to how the country handles economic crises, not whether that government intervenes or not in the economy.

Indeed, the international community should be worried about the most authoritarian state capitalists rather than the democratic state capitalists. Authoritarian state capitalists' possible economic collapse is not the greatest of all potential threats from state capitalism—we will examine the greatest threat in the next chapter—but it is a real and serious worry about all authoritarian state capitalists, even those still growing strongly.

Russia is the most obvious example of how the most authoritarian state capitalists threaten to sabotage their own economies and drag the world economy down as well. Russia's failures are the reasons why, while leaders of many nations may come to China or Singapore to study these countries' state-capitalist models, no one talks of a "Moscow model," unless they are discussing how to avoid going down the same path.

As in many other developing nations that began to democratize in the early 1990s, Russian leaders at the time frequently suggested that the end of the Soviet Union would not only usher in vast changes in personal, social, and political freedoms, but that the opening would also spark economic revival. Russians did enjoy enormous gains in political, social, and economic freedoms in the 1990s, under the presidency of former Moscow mayor Boris Yeltsin. The country held its freest elections ever—far freer than the elections today—and average Russians could travel where they wanted, read what they wanted, say what they wanted, and meet whomever they wanted. A vibrant print and radio media culture emerged, so vibrant that even more than a decade of Putinism has not fully extinguished it. Yet radical economic restructuring in the 1990s, without first building a strong rule of law and private property protections, created a brutal kind of wildcat capitalism. Cities like Moscow and St. Petersburg boomed, but many of the state's biggest companies in oil, gas, manufacturing, and other heavy industries were privatized and grabbed in deals with minimal transparency by former government insiders who became known as "oligarchs." Many average Russians saw their real incomes decline in the mid-1990s, while at the same time they watched the small handful of oligarchs who had emerged live some of the most ostentatious public lives in the world. Inequality in Russia increased far more quickly in the 1990s than in any other former Eastern Bloc nation.[9]

A series of brutal wars in Chechnya, the frequent absence of Yeltsin from public appearances, and the appearance that graft was becoming more common only further soured the public's mood. Corruption might not actually have been increasing, despite the insider dealing of the oligarchs. But because Russia's media had become considerably more open than in Soviet times, there was now more reporting of alleged corruption. This sunlight actually created the impression that graft was spreading far more than in Soviet times. This is not an unusual phenomenon. In many developing countries the initial transitions to democracy and/or market economics often leads to a kind of liberalization of graft. The opening of the press leads to greater public knowledge of corruption, the first step toward actually combating it. But before the country has created the institutions necessary to fight graft—like an independent and empowered anti-corruption commission—constant media reports of corruption that seems to never be resolved creates a public perception, as in 1990s Russia, that graft is out of control.

The economic chaos and inequality of the Yeltsin era and the perceptions of widespread graft all contributed to the Russian public souring on both democracy and, to a significant extent, on free-market economics. Many polls taken in the late 1990s and early 2000s revealed Russians' growing distrust for democratic politics and their association of free-market economics with corruption and inequality.

By New Year's Eve in 1999, when Yeltsin appeared on Russian television to hand power to his (then) little-known deputy Vladimir Putin, the climate in Russia was perfect for the emergence of a statist strongman. In a country where the population already had a strong inclination toward an authoritarian ruler, the chaos and inequality of the 1990s had fueled a desire for greater state intervention again. Putin took advantage of the hangover from the 1990s. He gradually took back state control of both the political and the economic sphere. Putin and his aides framed the state's resurgence in nationalistic terms, even though most of the companies and assets they seized actually were owned by fellow Russians who had launched firms in the 1990s. Russia's natural resources "belong to the state—they are not private property," declared defense minister Sergei Ivanov, one of Putin's loudest acolytes.[10] The Kremlin took back control of Russian energy companies that had been at least partially privatized during the 1990s, and forced prominent foreign investors, like Shell, to hand over blocks of oil and gas they had previously bid for to Russian state companies.[11] The most politically active and sophisticated private company, Yukos, saw its managers hauled into jail and its assets confiscated by the Kremlin. The giants that survived Putinism, like Sberbank and Gazprom, usually were handed to managers drawn from Putin's circle of former officials from the KGB (now known as the FSB), where Putin had served during the Soviet era.[12] Business leaders who resisted Putin's state capitalism were punished severely.

But rather than using state intervention to promote effective development, Putin relied on natural resources. And for a time, this strategy worked. The price of oil, which went from below $10 per barrel in the late 1990s to over $120 in the early 2010, drove the economic resurgence of Russia, one of the largest producers of natural gas and crude oil in the world.[13] Putin basked in the black, oily glory, as the Russian economy grew by around 6 percent annually from 2000 to 2008, during Putin's initial two terms as president. Russia built up hundreds of billions of dollars of foreign currency reserves, some of which were plowed into a new SWF called the Russian National Wealth Fund. This growth created large, new classes of consumers in Russian cities, brought a degree of stability to the country, and also seemed to lull most Russians into an apolitical trance. Despite the early 2010s riots protesting Putin's return to presidency and the increasingly autocratic ways of the Kremlin, these protests never really caught on outside Moscow, where they were limited to a small group of liberal activists. Although Putin used all the tools of the state to ensure his win in the 2012 presidential election—the election was rated as unfree by observers from the Organization for Security and Cooperation in Europe—he took a commanding 64 percent of the vote.[14] Even without any ballot-stuffing or fawning media coverage, Putin probably would have won a majority of Russian votes, as he remained popular with Russians outside of the largest cities. Indeed, well into the 2010s, Putin still enjoyed favorable approval ratings from the majority of Russians.[15]

Russia grew strongly in the 2000s, but it did almost nothing to create long-term, sustainable development. The oil revenues accruing from the spike in the price of a barrel could have helped put Russia on a path to sustainable long-term growth. But Putin's Kremlin capitalism employed few of the strategies of successful state capitalists like Singapore, Abu Dhabi, or China. The Russian government did create an SWF, but it did not upgrade the country's physical infrastructure, particularly in the Russian East, which became depopulated, dominated by criminal gangs, and increasingly dependent on Chinese capital and migrant workers.[16] Unlike in Singapore, Russia did not use its SWF to provide seed capital to entrepreneurs in twenty-first-century industries, or to encourage entrepreneurship at all. Today, small and medium-sized enterprises only employ about 25 percent of Russians, a miniscule figure that shows how hard it is to launch and maintain a small business in Russia; in most developed countries, small and medium-sized enterprises employ half of the workforce or more.[17]

Even the Russian oil and gas giants, with their enormous reserves, have begun to fall behind competitors from other countries. Illustrating another potential problem with state capitalism—state firms, with their monopolies on domestic markets, may find it politically unfeasible to invest in the most capital-intensive, cutting-edge technology.

This is what has happened in Russia. As other countries have developed new technologies like fracking for shale gas and expanding exploration into the most challenging terrain, Russia's gas and oil giants have fallen behind. Their production has stagnated, their pipelines and rigs have creaked and rotted, and they have lost many chances to compete in emerging new markets thirsty for oil and gas. The Russian firms still dominate the Russian oil and gas market, but this market is shrinking, as Russia's population shrinks.[18]

Russia's dependence on oil and gas sales, which account for more than half of the government's budget, was most clearly illustrated in 2008 and 2009. As global oil prices fell sharply due to decreased consumption in the West, Russia's GDP plummeted by nearly 8 percent in 2009.[19] Only after global oil prices rallied in 2009 and 2010 did the Russian economy recover, growing by 4.3 percent in 2011 and 3.4 percent in 2012.[20] In addition, new discoveries of shale gas in the United States and other locations have cut into Gazprom's dominance of global gas markets, and the falling price of oil in 2014 and 2015 has hurt the Russian economy badly once again. The Center for Global Energy Policy, a New York think tank, estimated in 2014 that if the United States started exporting its liquefied natural gas, these exports would trim about 18 percent off of Gazprom's annual revenues.[21] American gas producers are expected to start exporting liquefied natural gas by 2016.

In the long term, as the world transitions away from fossil fuels for power and transport and new technologies allow countries to explore for gas in shale and other locations, Russia's statist and undiversified economy will become even more vulnerable to a severe slowdown or a total collapse. The fact that Russia has the largest amount of illicit capital flight in the world suggests that Russians with money know that the economy could face collapse in the near future and do not trust Russian banks and other financial institutions to hold their money in case the collapse occurs.[22] Western sanctions on Russia, due to Russia's takeover of Crimea and de facto invasion of eastern Ukraine, will hit the Russian economy hard as well, and already have begun to bite by the middle of 2015. The falling price of oil led to repeated runs on the ruble in 2015, although not an outright economic collapse. Indeed, the Kremlin staved off total collapse, at least for a time, only by sharply raising central bank interest rates while also using the state's currency reserves, to support several large state companies.

But Moscow may not hold off economic collapse much longer, and even interest rates of 17 percent could not convince many Russians to keep their deposits in the country. "The catastrophically declining effectiveness of the economy is likely to be a key factor in this process [of Russia's decline]," writes prominent Russian businessman and former Duma deputy Konstantin Borovoy.[23] Indeed, Russia's current account surplus, almost totally dependent on oil and gas, has been declining from its mid-2000s highs. The state still has significant capital reserves, but these may not be enough in the long run to defend the ruble against speculation, help state companies pay off their debts, and also increase government spending on social welfare, job creation, and other means of keeping the population happy as the economy shrinks.

What's more, since heads of companies like Gazprom, Rosneft, or Transneft were chosen not for their corporate skills and managerial expertise but because of their absolute loyalty to Putin, few heads of state firms have been sacked, even as their companies have become less competitive. With the same leadership, Gazprom had to shelve its potentially giant Shtokman gas field in the icy northern Barents Sea because it lacked the infrastructure to exploit it in a cost-effective manner. Indeed the company's total annual production of gas has not grown since 2001.[24]

In the wake of American and European sanctions enacted on Russia in 2014, Putin cracked down even harder on large private-sector companies, even those whose heads had been slavishly supportive of the Kremlin. Putin thus further ensured that Russian state companies would never pick executives based on skill rather than loyalty to the Kremlin. In September 2014, Russian police arrested Vladimir Yevtushenkov, head of privately owned oil and telecommunications conglomerate AFK

Sistema, for money laundering. Russian analysts said the arrest was simply a tactic by the Kremlin to get Yevtushenkov to sell his company's oil and gas assets to struggling state petroleum giant Rosneft, whose oil and gas production is stagnating and, in some fields, decreasing. (In the summer of 2014, Rosneft had been forced to ask the Kremlin for an injection of over $40 billion in capital from Russia's SWF to stay alive.) Yevtushenkov's company, by contrast, had modernized its oil and gas infrastructure and was getting much more efficient production out of its fields than Rosneft.[25] Yevtushenkov had little choice but to sell the oil and gas company he had built up. "With Russia under threat from sanctions, no one dares argue against the case that strategic assets like this one [Yevtushenkov's oil and gas assets] must be in state hands," one Russian tycoon told the *Financial Times*.[26]

The Russian state giants' low market valuation reflected how investors, both foreign and domestic, recognized their shortcomings and problems with long-term competitiveness. Although in 2010 and 2011 Gazprom had been the most profitable or one of the most profitable companies in the world, depending on how its profit and state subsidies were calculated, the company was still valued on the Moscow stock exchange at only about 2.9 times its earnings—extremely low by the standards of most large petroleum companies. (Gazprom's profitability has dropped in the mid-2010s.) By comparison, multinational petroleum giant ExxonMobil was valued on the New York Stock Exchange in 2015 at about eleven times its annual earnings.[27]

CONTAGION FROM THE AUTOCRATIC STATE CAPITALISTS

If Russia were simply statist, like the old Soviet Union or like North Korea and Cuba, its authoritarian, inefficient state capitalism, which could ultimately lead to a collapse of the Russian economy, would matter primarily to suffering Russian people. Cuba's economy has been in slow meltdown since the end of the Cold War and the removal of Soviet subsidies, and it has been sustained only by cheap energy from friendly Venezuela, remittances, and tourism and foreign trade, often conducted outside legal channels. But since Cuba is not highly integrated with the world economy, and only the sixty-eighth-largest economy in the world (slightly bigger than the economy of miniscule Luxembourg), its suffering mostly remains its own.

But the state capitalists today are not just statists—as we have seen, they are capitalists too, and even the more inefficient ones are open to world trade and integrated with the global economy. Russia is still the eighth-largest economy in the world by total GDP and is highly integrated with the economies of Europe.[28] European Union countries export more than $195 billion worth of goods and services to Russia each year, and while sanctions will reduce that trade, if Russia's economy were to collapse altogether, it would be an enormous blow to Europe's economy. Russia normally is one of the five biggest destinations for Polish exports, while the economies of Ukraine, the Baltics, Scandinavia, Hungary, the Czech Republic, and many of the nations in Central Asia are highly dependent on selling to Russian markets. European nations are also highly dependent on Russia for energy; Gazprom gets about 40 percent of its annual revenues from sales to countries in the European Union.[29] If a Russian economic collapse led Gazprom's production to decline sharply due to severe shortages of capital and an inability to maintain its infrastructure, it would have enormous repercussions for European energy markets.[30] This dependence on Gazprom's energy, surely, is a major reason why Europe has exempted the Russian gas giant from the sanctions imposed on Moscow in 2014. (We will examine later the potential impact of Gazprom being used as a weapon and reducing gas exports to Europe on purpose, rather than Gazprom's production declining because of failing infrastructure.)

Russian investors also are key players in global capital markets and Russian companies are central to many investment funds' strategies. So, a Russian economic collapse would impact capital markets as well. Russia's rich have plunked an estimated $75 billion of capital into real estate, stocks, and other assets in Britain alone, a major reason why the British economy was not hurt more by the downturn that began in Europe in 2008 and 2009.[31] (This figure takes into account only the money sent out of Russia to the United Kingdom legally; Russia's illicit capital outflows likely exceed its licit capital outflows significantly.[32])

Shares in Russian companies also are central to broad emerging market funds sold in the United States, Europe, and other rich nations. These funds spread their investments among the largest emerging markets in the world; investors outside Russia have plunked nearly $200 billion into broad emerging market index funds that include Russia among the places they invest.[33] And Western banks and other financial institutions have played a central role in financing Russian companies' listings on stock exchanges, while Western hedge funds and other active investors have also poured money into Russian firms.

A Russian collapse would dramatically impact global capital markets and probably scare investors away from funds involved in other emerging markets, such as India, China, Brazil, and Southeast Asian nations. In 2014, a year when Russia's economy wobbled because of the conflict in Ukraine but did not actually collapse, some analysts estimated that investors pulled around $100 billion of capital out of Russia, a sum far less than what would be withdrawn if Russia's economy collapsed.[34] Although these other emerging market economies are not necessarily directly linked to Russia's economy, the recent history of emerging market financial crises suggests that shocks to one emerging market economy almost always lead investors to pull money out of other emerging markets as well. In the late 1990s' Asian financial crisis, for example, a severe contraction in the Thai economy, which suffered from an unregulated banking sector awash in bad loans and unproductive companies bloated with credit, led foreign investors to pull money out of nearly every economy in the region, whether or not other Asian economies suffered from the same problems as Thailand.

History provides a guide to what might happen in the event of a Russian economic collapse. Russia's economy already melted down once in 1998, a time when its economy was far smaller than it is today, and Russia was not as economically integrated with Europe as it is today. Yet Moscow's near-bankruptcy and subsequent default on its debt in 1998 badly roiled world markets and neighboring economies. Ultimately, it took the IMF and the World Bank to save the Russian economy and to prevent the 1998 Russian collapse from triggering more serious economic downturns in Europe and possibly around the world.

Russia is hardly unique as an authoritarian state capitalist linked to the world—links that all but ensure that autocratic state capitalists can do serious damage to other economies. Venezuela is another of the more authoritarian, nontransparent, and less efficient state capitalists, yet it is also the thirtieth-largest economy in the world and the fifth largest in Latin America. Venezuela is a country whose bonds are owned by investors around the world, and whose wells make it a major international provider of oil and gas. Although a Venezuelan meltdown would not have the global impact of a Russian collapse, on a regional level its effect would be significant. A Venezuelan collapse likely would damage investor confidence in South American markets more broadly, and possibly push much of the South American continent into recession. There are precedents for this contagion effect in Latin America. When Argentina's economy, the third largest in Latin America, suffered a severe crisis in 2001 and 2002, investors fled stock markets in many neighboring nations, including Brazil, leading to a period of severe financial and economic volatility in Brazil and other Latin American nations.[35]

Such a collapse is not hard to imagine. Indeed, in early 2015, Venezuela's government could barely meet its international bond payments after years of rolling up huge budget surpluses to channel cheap capital into state projects, with little accountability or transparency about how the money was spent. Caracas was struggling to have enough cash on hand from week to week to pay the interest on its debts. Many investors already were speculating that Venezuela would have to default on its debt, a catastrophe for any country that needs to borrow on international capital markets.[36] Argentina defaulted on its debt in 2001, and the country still cannot borrow on international capital markets, a crippling blow to the Argentine economy.[37]

It is not hard to imagine the same type of regional economic downturn in other parts of the world, with the meltdowns caused by opaque, authoritarian state-capitalist economies imploding. In Southeast Asia, the trigger likely would be an economic implosion in Vietnam. Although Vietnam copied many of its initial economic strategies from China's state capitalism, as Hanoi began to open up the Vietnamese economy in the 1980s and 1990s, Vietnam's state companies have remained, almost universally, uncompetitive, bloated, and poorly managed. On the scale of openness among the state capitalists, Vietnam, though not as autocratic as Egypt, Qatar, or Russia, is far more opaque and unresponsive to its public even than China.

Vietnam's lack of responsiveness and its authoritarian political and economic culture is hurting it, and a Vietnamese collapse is far more likely, in the near term, than any serious meltdown in China. Unlike China or Singapore, Vietnam has not culled the least efficient state companies. Hanoi has refused to let unprofitable state firms die, to encourage competition among state enterprises, or to instill modern management techniques—and modern managers—at the top of many state companies. Compared to the chief executives of Chinese state enterprises like oil giants PetroChina and CNPC, the leaders of most Vietnamese state enterprises have minimal global experience or understanding of modern corporate management and accounting methods. In the most notable example of little transparency or modern management, state-owned shipbuilding giant Vinashin ran up debts of over $4 billion with the help of totally opaque state banks before its international creditors, who held a fraction of Vinashin's debts, even realized how troubled the company was.[38]

Vinashin is only one of many such indebted stumbling state firms. Corruption continues to eat away at the top levels of state firms. The Vietnamese stock market plumbed new lows in the early 2010s, and the country's currency weakened rapidly against the dollar and other leading currencies.[39] With Vietnamese savers having few places to put their money other than real estate, thanks to a collapsing market and untrustworthy state banks, a network of underground lenders sprung up, many of whom simply stole investors' money or just collapsed. By late 2012, both Vietnamese and foreign economists focusing on Vietnam were predicting that the Vietnamese economy could suffer a serious downturn, perhaps even a major recession.

Although the stock market and the Vietnamese currency have stabilized somewhat in the mid-2010s, a more serious economic collapse is hardly out of the question. The Vietnamese economy has only avoided a more serious downturn because of easing monetary policy, a global economic recovery, and the country's diligent and resourceful workforce, which makes Vietnam highly attractive to foreign investors even when Vietnam's macroeconomics remain shaky. (In 2014, global mobile telecommunications giant Samsung announced plans to drastically scale up mobile phone production in Vietnam, even as it was cutting production in neighboring China.[40]) Still, slowing growth has left Vietnam, which has one of the youngest populations in Asia, unable to create enough jobs to absorb the number of young men and women entering the workforce.[41]

A government plan announced in 2013 to reform state enterprises had little obvious impact in the two years since the plan was proposed.

Like a Venezuelan meltdown, a Vietnamese collapse would have a significant impact on its region, if not on the world. Vietnam, a country of ninety million people, has become a major trading partner of all the other large economies in Southeast Asia and is one of the biggest potential engines of global growth. Vietnam also has become a favored destination of individual large investors in emerging markets, as well as funds that invest in emerging markets. As with a downturn in Venezuela, a Vietnamese economic collapse, like the one foretold in 2012 and barely avoided at that time, would seriously shake investors' confidence in other economies around Vietnam, whether or not such a reaction would be rational.

One could list five or six other autocratic state capitalists that are regionally important economies—and that could face severe economic slowdowns within the next decade. All of these countries, including Saudi Arabia, Egypt, and Kazakhstan, fall on the autocratic end of our chart, and though each economy is different in some ways, they all share some of the problems of Russia and Venezuela—undiversified and inefficient economies, dependence on natural resources, and a complete lack of transparency in policymaking. These factors make it harder for investors to gauge government decisions, and possibly lead investors to panic more than necessary when these economies begin to fall. All of these economies, too, are regionally (and in some cases, globally) important. Their meltdowns would have major repercussions for their regions and for political stability in some of the most strategically important parts of the world.

China, however, does not make the list of countries whose economies may collapse; China's economy appears to be slowing, but it is unlikely to go into recession. In the next chapter we will see why China's brand of state capitalism, which has more in common with that of Singapore than it does with Vietnam, will remain relatively successful in the long term—and could pose a serious challenge to the free-market model.

9

A Greater Threat

State Capitalism's Long-Term
Effectiveness and State Capitalism
as a Model

The fourth possible threat of state capitalism is not that it will fail as a model, causing economic chaos in countries like Russia—and impacting the whole world economy—but just the opposite, that it will succeed as a model. The possibility that state capitalism will succeed as a model is a concern particularly in China, a state that is authoritarian, extremely powerful, possibly interested in promoting its economic model as a means of enhancing its overall power, and in some ways antagonistic to the United States and other leading democracies. Indeed, state capitalism's combination of economic strength and adaptability in China make the Chinese model a genuine challenge to free-market capitalism. And if state capitalism succeeds in the long term, particularly in China, it could help Beijing—and to a lesser extent other authoritarian but efficient state capitalists—remake the international economic system, amass strategic power, and potentially use state companies as weapons.

Can state capitalism work economically for developing countries for extended periods? Can it work effectively enough to not just maintain decent growth and prevent an economic collapse, and not just spark a short-term boom fueled by cheap credit and construction and other state-capitalist tools? And if state capitalism can work for an extended period of time, with growth rates well over 4 percent annually, are the most efficient state capitalists actually challenging fundamental assumptions about the superiority of free markets and the structure of the international economy?

Most leading Western economists, until the past decade, argued that state capitalism could not succeed in the long term. Further, they argued, since state capitalism could not work in the long term, its resurgence did not challenge assumptions about the superiority of the market.

Overall, the evidence on state capitalists' economic record since the end of the Cold War suggests a mixed conclusion about state capitalism's long-term viability. First, just the fact that few of the state capitalists, most of them developing nations, have kept their growth rates above 4 percent annually for decades does not mean state capitalism cannot work in the long term. Few countries maintain such sustained growth, no matter how their economies are structured.

The evidence instead suggests that state capitalism *can* work as a long-term economic strategy, past a decade or two, given the right conditions—success that suggests that the state-capitalist model could be a viable challenger to purer free-market economics well into the twenty-first century. These conditions are not easy to create, so advocates of state capitalism who argue that it is the best strategy for developing countries—advocates like prominent economist Paul Krugman and many Asian leaders—are as glib in assuming that state capitalism will work for developing nations as advocates of the Washington Consensus were in the 1990s in assuming that the Washington Consensus formula could work everywhere. State capitalism *is* hard to make work over the long term, but it can work.

In fact, many leading Western institutions that have voiced doubts that state capitalism can succeed in the long run have, at the same time, actually given more credit to state capitalists than one might think. Though the World Bank's leadership and missions in most developing nations consistently argue that both economic and political freedom are critical to growth, the Bank's own annual *Ease of Doing Business* reports, which analyze countries on such issues as property rights, ease of incorporating a company, protections for investments, and so on, regularly reveal that one-quarter to one-third of the countries ranked in its top thirty—the easiest places to do business—are actually state capitalists. According to the Bank's analysis, countries that rank near the top of the *Ease of Doing Business* reports are countries that have put in place economic policies that will allow for high growth. Singapore has topped the *Ease of Doing Business* survey year after year. Other state capitalists like Malaysia, Thailand, and Qatar routinely rank highly.[1] Even the Heritage Foundation, which is more politically and economically conservative than the supposedly politically neutral World Bank, allows that Singapore, Malaysia, the United Arab Emirates, Qatar, and Norway all fall among the forty most economically free nations in the world, as defined by a wide range of measures including regulation, openness to trade, and environments conducive to launching a business.

In addition, studies by economists Aldo Musacchio and Sergio Lazzarini have shown that state capitalism can have as many advantages as disadvantages in promoting growth, particularly when states, like Singapore, take minority shares in leading companies rather than owning all of them. Having "government as a minority owner can have positive effects," their macroscopic study of fifteen countries showed; government as a minority owner reduces the likelihood that state firms will just feed a government or business kleptocratic elite, as in Russia.[2] Their study concluded that companies where the state has taken a stake in the corporation do not have any worse long-term performance than wholly private firms in the same countries. In several cases, companies that had formerly been private or partially private firms actually were taken over by the state and nursed into profitability. Similarly, a meta-study comparing privately owned and state companies in the former Eastern Bloc found that there was little difference in performance—in terms of profitability, efficiency, productivity, and employment—between state companies and companies that had been privatized.[3]

Other recent studies have shown that state capitalism, in the form of a clear industrial policy that protects infant industries while slowly embracing free trade, may be the most viable strategy for developing nations. As globalization makes supply chains in many industries longer and necessarily faster, and creates the need for economies of scale, "for [developing nations'] firms attempting to enter export markets, it cannot be assumed that simply achieving low cost is sufficient to realize foreign sales [anymore]," notes one study of developing nations and industrial policy by the World Bank's own internal think tank.[4] In addition, although free-trade agreements theoretically lower barriers for all signers, thus boosting growth, many developing nations rightly complain that, when many of today's richest economies began to develop, they were not subject to such free-trade agreements. The Bank's internal think tank admitted, "Developing countries have to contend with several multilateral agreements that were not in existence when the rich countries of today were developing." Such agreements include those that prohibit tariffs and other protections for nascent industries—strategies that many rich countries, like the United States, France, and Japan once used to protect their own infant manufacturing sectors.[5] "The international policy environment today imposes constraints on the use of national [economic and industrial] policies that were absent even fifteen years ago," the Bank admits.[6] Of course, by pursuing state-capitalist policies, developing nations also potentially are able to push state companies and state funds to direct some of their profits toward social welfare programs, a control the government would not have with private companies. But with state corporations, governments are able to both collect taxes and compel the companies to make donations to social welfare programs or other government initiatives, like Brazil's program of cash transfers to the poor.

These studies suggest that the conventional wisdom on which policies are critical to long-term growth—privatization of state companies, reducing tariffs and other protections for domestic industries, keeping the tax burden low—should not be taken for granted. *Some* of the successful state capitalists have adopted *some* of these policies, but others have not, and few of the successful state capitalists have embraced one of the conventional wisdom's biggest keys to long-term development: reducing all state supports for domestic industries.

CHINA'S SUCCESS, AND WHAT IT MEANS

These research studies are corroborated by industrial statistics from China, the biggest state capitalist. According to economist Jonathan Anderson:

> Even when we adjust for sectoral differences there is almost no visible difference between state-owned and private profit performance . . . And sectoral data suggest that overall productivity and margin growth have been a good bit faster in heavy-industrial state sectors than, say, in foreign-funded light manufacturing export firms [in China.][7]

This China model—in many respects a similar model to that used in Singapore—has promoted growth for an extended period of time, but it will be hard for other nations to replicate. As I noted, I am simply suggesting that China's state capitalism has been successful enough—indeed, quite successful by the standards of developing countries at any time in history. China's state capitalism has allowed for sustained growth, created a degree of legitimacy and stability for the government, and given China a potential model to advertise to other countries.

Although the economies of Brazil and Indonesia, two of the four other large (population-wise) state capitalists, have not matched China's historic gains, they still each have more than doubled in size in the past twenty years, making enormous inroads into poverty—inroads that have not been rolled back even as Brazil and Indonesia have witnessed economic slowdowns. The percentage of Indonesians living in poverty has shrunk since the late 1990s, from around 23 percent of the population to around 14 percent today.[8] In Brazil, meanwhile, the combination of fifteen years of growth and intervention to reduce inequality has resulted in the poverty rate dropping from 23 percent in the early 2000s to 7 percent by the end of that decade.

China is not going to collapse any time soon. If it so desires, China could use its economic strength, and strategic and diplomatic influence, to challenge the Bretton Woods institutions that have undergirded the international economy since the end of the Second World War. Singapore and some other state capitalists may continue to succeed, but they are neither large enough nor interested enough in promoting their model as an alternative to the Washington Consensus to foster real changes in the international economy and international institutions.

Why won't the China model collapse anytime soon? For one, although graft remains a huge problem in China, it will not necessarily be fatal to China's economy. Certainly, corruption is a major problem. Claremont McKenna professor Minxin Pei estimates that corruption in China costs the state over $86 billion in lost revenues every year.[9] Yet the current Chinese leadership has, for the first time in two decades, cracked down on high-ranking officials allegedly engaged in graft, making a real statement about fighting corruption. Under Xi Jinping, Beijing has arrested former security chief Zhou Yongkang, the first member of the Politburo Standing Committee, to be jailed for graft.[10] In 2014, China's police also filed charges of graft against Ling Jihua, who had served as a top aide to former Chinese president Hu Jintao. Ling's arrest also marked a first—the first time such a senior aide to a former president had been charged with corruption so soon after a Chinese transition to power.

This crackdown on corruption is designed in part to consolidate power around President Xi Jinping, and in part to actually root out corruption, but it is still having the effect of exposing graft among top leaders. Even before the crackdown and the shocking arrests of Zhou and Ling, the level of corruption in China had remained low enough that the economy still functioned effectively; China does not rank near the bottom of countries in the world in Transparency International's rankings of the most corrupt nations. In fact, in the most recent Transparency International Corruption Perceptions Index of nations around the world, China ranked 80th, roughly in the middle. The lowest-ranking nations—Somalia, North Korea, and Afghanistan—came in tied for 175th. China came in just below South Africa; not far behind Italy; and ahead of India, the Philippines, Thailand, and Colombia.[11]

Ranking ahead of India or Colombia or Thailand in levels of graft or just behind Italy, no bellwether of clean government, is not a great victory, to be sure. But China's ranking, alongside other countries that have posted sustained high growth rates despite some degree of corruption, suggests that graft is not as crippling in China as some scholars might believe, and that China's economy, like that of Thailand, can continue to grow for years despite a sizable degree of corruption.

In addition, in the long run, state capitalism does not ensure corruption, so China does not necessarily need to privatize much of its economy to reduce graft. Indeed, in the most recent Transparency International ranking of the most and least corrupt nations in the world, the countries listed among the cleanest states included state capitalists Singapore, Qatar, the United Arab Emirates, and free-market countries like Denmark, Hong Kong, and Australia; the defining feature that all the least corrupt countries shared was that they had very rich economies, not how they got rich. At the bottom of the list, the most corrupt countries in the world included some where the state plays a major role in the economy, like Nicaragua, some where the state does not, like Nigeria; and some where the state barely exists, like Somalia and Afghanistan. The one variable linking all the most corrupt countries was that they were poor; how and why their economies became impoverished did not determine whether they were more or less corrupt.

Critics charge that along with corruption, state capitalism will lead to extreme income inequality in China, a situation in which the small number of businesspeople with close ties to the government will become incredibly wealthy, while the majority of the population does not make such economic gains. This inequality, critics argue, ultimately will upend China's model. It is true that income inequality in China has widened vastly since the mid-1970s. But China may not remain so unequal forever. No evidence suggests that in the long run state capitalists are necessarily any more unequal than free-market capitalists, particularly those free-market countries, like the United States or Britain, that have limited social safety nets and relatively regressive taxation policies.

Worldwide, rankings of nations with the greatest levels of income in-equality include, at the top, many free-market economies, including Hong Kong (whose economy is not controlled by Beijing), which has the largest income inequality of any wealthy nation or territory. Some state capitalists rank among the more unequal nations, but the twenty more economically unequal nations in the world are a mix of free market-oriented countries and statist countries. Several prominent state capitalists, such as Indonesia and Vietnam, have relatively low levels of inequality.

Since the late 1970s, when China's period of reform began, consistent high growth rates have helped cut extreme poverty—defined by the United Nations as making less than US $1 per day—from over 80 percent of the population to less than 12 percent of the population.[12] This is the largest cut in poverty, and one of the greatest creations of wealth, in all of human history. Income inequality has, since the beginning of the reform era in China, widened so much partly because the whole country was so poor in the 1970s. Starting from such a poor base and going through such dramatic growth, no country would have been able to avoid a large bump in income inequality. Even today, more than a century after indus-trializing, the United States still suffers from a level of income inequality roughly equivalent to that of China, and in China income inequality has decreased slightly over the past five years, though it is still far wider than it was in the 1970s. Certainly, developed nations like the United States, Britain, and France, during their periods of industrialization in the nine-teenth and early twentieth centuries, went through similar periods of skyrocketing inequality. They later addressed inequality through reforms designed to create social safety nets, transfer some degree of wealth to the poor through taxation, and minimize the harshest edges of modern-day industrial capitalism. As pressure mounts on the government in Beijing to address inequality, China may very well go through a period of progressive reforms in which the government creates a larger social safety net while maintaining the essence of its state-capitalist system.

Many critics of state capitalism also believe that support for state companies will eventually lead all state capitalists, including China, to amass unsustainable mountains of government debt. Yet some state capitalists' high levels of debt are not so different from debt problems facing developed nations such as Japan and the United States, which have used massive stimulus spending to bolster their economies. Japan, in fact, has a debt-to-GDP ratio of nearly 200 percent, meaning that its public debt is twice as large as the annual production of its economy, greater than the debt-to-GDP ratio of any state-capitalist nation.[13]

In addition, it is clear that countries can run large national debt burdens for considerable periods of time while still growing strongly and without hurting their international credit rating and ability to borrow on international markets.[14] Conversely, several of the world's most prominent state capitalists have relatively low levels of public debt.[15] Several of the countries with the highest debt-to-GDP ratios in the world, including the United States, Singapore, Japan, France, and Belgium, are highly functioning economies that have continued to grow despite amassing public debt for years or even decades.[16] Nearly all of these nations also have AAA or AA ratings from credit rating agencies like Moody's and Standard and Poor's, allowing them to borrow on international markets at very low interest rates.

China's model thus could survive for an extended period of time, even riding out periods of lower growth and equity slumps. Whether China will step up its promotion depends as much on dynamics within the Beijing regime as on the long-term success of the Chinese model.

BEIJING UNSURE OF PROMOTING THE CHINA MODEL

Effective promotion of China's model could, in some developing nations, undermine successful democratization by providing a way for leaders to foster economic growth without political openness, gaining legitimacy through high growth instead of elections. In addition, trainings of officials in China seem to emphasize not only the authoritarian nature of the China model but also provide specific lessons in how to control the judiciary, use the police to stop dissent, and co-opt opinion leaders into a ruling party—the kinds of methods used by the Beijing leadership and potentially by other autocrats. Indeed, several Cambodian officials said that as China has become the predominant influence in Cambodia, and Western donors have lost their leverage over the government of Hun Sen, the Cambodian prime minister increasingly has based his political and economic strategies on China, from his use of his political party to control big business to his use of the court system to dominate the opposition.

Although in theory other democratic state capitalists also could promote their model, in some ways as a counterpoint to China's, this is an unlikely possibility. Although some state capitalists have managed to combine free politics with statist economics, few other than Brazil have touted their models the way that China does, and few have been held up by other world leaders as success stories to emulate, the way that China often is. With Brazil's slowing growth and wave of street protests, it is unlikely to be seen as a model to many, although the state's success in promoting growth and cutting inequality in the 2000s and early 2010s still rank as impressive.

For now, the Chinese government remains unsure of how far to go in promoting a China model, or in trying to offer alternatives to current international institutions. Unless Beijing clearly decides to embrace the idea of a China model and of alternatives to the international institutions that exist today, the China model will not threaten democracies.

Beijing's leaders apparently remain split on how much China should promote the idea that it has a model of development to offer other countries, and how much, in general, China should challenge the international order created after the Second World War and still dominated by Europe and the United States. Until the late 2000s and early 2010s, Beijing had seemed willing to accept the international order; work with international institutions like the IMF, WTO, and the United Nations; and remain agnostic on whether a Beijing Consensus could be a real challenger to the Washington Consensus. As we have seen, for years top Chinese leaders refused to even publicly recognize the idea that China had its own model of development that might be transferable to other nations. They kept quiet in part because making such a suggestion would go against China's own publicly stated policy of "noninterference" in other countries' affairs—a principle that Beijing of course has violated many times but which nonetheless remains at the core of China's official foreign policy.

After all, as numerous Chinese and foreign scholars have noted, China has benefited enormously, since the beginning of its reform period, from that international order. China's early reform period benefited significantly from technical advice and aid from foreign governments and international financial institutions, and foreign investment has been central to China's sustained high growth rates. China's admission into the WTO in 2001 helped speed up foreign investment in China and gave Beijing the legitimacy to negotiate multiple regional and bilateral free-trade deals.

What's more, for decades, China has benefited from the American security presence throughout the Pacific Rim, the Indian Ocean, and other trade routes, since this security presence has largely minimized conflict, prevented piracy, and fostered free and safe trade to East Asia—without China having to contribute much in terms of naval and other military assets.

But since the early 2010s, Beijing has started to challenge both the existing international institutions and, as we have seen, to more actively suggest that China's model could be an alternative to the Washington Consensus. President Xi Jinping is by far the most openly nationalist Chinese leader since Mao's time, and also has consolidated the most power in the presidency of any Chinese leader since Deng Xiaoping. Xi's "Chinese Dream" concept of what he calls a "revival of the great Chinese nation," though potentially benign, is the most openly any Chinese leader since Mao has embraced China's status as a major world power. Xi is the first Chinese leader since Mao to openly challenge, in speeches and written documents, the United States' strategic influence in Asia. In one speech in Shanghai in 2014, Xi declared that the United States should reduce its influence in Asia, presumably allowing China to gain influence—Xi argued that "it is for the people of Asia to run the affairs of Asia."[17] He also has overseen a nationwide effort to reduce Chinese academics' and officials' links with US foundations, think tanks, universities, and other institutions. In addition, Xi has used speeches and other public events to lavish praise on prominent nationalist Chinese writers, such as a blogger who regularly compares the United States to Nazi Germany, and to criticize Chinese artists and writers who do not publicly praise China, China's role in the world, Chinese history, and the Chinese Communist Party.

Under Xi there also are multiple signs that China, if not interested in totally revising the existing international order, will not be content with simply accepting it as it currently stands. In other words, China will no longer be content to remain what some scholars have called a "status quo" power, a country uninterested in changing how the world operates. The nascent BRICS development bank, though small in its initial capitalization compared to the capitalization of the Bretton Woods financial institutions, was strongly backed by Beijing and is a first small step, along with encouraging countries to use currencies other than the dollar as a reserve currency, toward creating alternatives to the World Bank and Asian Development Bank and IMF. In 2013 and 2014, Chinese officials pushed leaders of other Asian nations, from South Korea to Thailand, to join China in creating a new development bank dedicated to financing Asian infrastructure, a bank that would directly compete with the Asian Development Bank, which has traditionally been led by Japanese bankers and dominated by economists and development experts trained in Japan and the United States.[18] The Shanghai Cooperation Organization, a regional grouping linking China, Russia, and Central Asia, has in the past five years become more central to Beijing's foreign policy and likely will soon expand to incorporate new members. According to Chinese academics, top Chinese leaders see the Shanghai Cooperation Organization, which celebrates sovereignty and development over universal ideas of human rights and democracy, as an alternative model to Western-dominated organizations like the United Nations. In addition, Xi has called for a "new type of great power relations" between China and the United States—one in which China gets to determine the shape of international institutions and the world in general as much as the United States did in the post-World War II era. And China's military actions since the early 2010s in the East China Sea and South China Sea—asserting its claims in the Seas, publicly calling on the United States to stop close-in surveillance of China by American planes, buzzing American planes flying over the Seas—also suggest that Beijing is increasingly interested in dominating the region, if not the world.

Given China's increasingly assertive foreign policy in general, the nationalist views of Xi Jinping and his closest associates, the distracted and increasingly isolationist nature of American foreign policy, and, as I predict here, the continued success of China's model, it is increasingly likely that Beijing will promote China's development model in the latter half of the 2010s and the 2020s much more aggressively than it has in the past.

It is important to be clear about what kind of impact China's model could have on other countries, even if Beijing intends to actively promote the China model and if China remains a one-party authoritarian state. More assertive promotion of China's model would pose a potential challenge to democracy in countries like Cambodia and the Central Asian nations, where democratic institutions are not well established, poverty and underdevelopment remain enormous problems, and the appeal of a Chinese model remains powerful not only to leaders but also to citizens looking for any model that promotes high growth. Some of these countries, such as Thailand and several Central Asian nations, are important to the world strategically and/or economically, and so the influence of the China model is a real concern for the United States and other democratic nations; we will later examine which nations are the most vulnerable to the impact of the China model. However, other countries susceptible to the China model are not very strategically or economically important. For example, in Cambodia, China's influence has played a role in helping perpetuate the authoritarian government of Prime Minister Hun Sen. Yet Cambodia's stalled democratic transition is, to be straightforward, of minimal strategic and economic importance to the world, given the country's small size and tiny economy.

More assertive promotion of a Chinese model likely would not pose a real threat to democracy in countries where democratic institutions and culture have been deeply entrenched—Indonesia, Brazil, India, and many others. As we have seen, these countries' opinion leaders may travel to China, be awed at China's growth, and take home some specific lessons about economic strategy from China, but the publics in these nations have become too supportive of democracy for China's authoritarian model to take hold. Indeed, when in the summer of 2014 a group of Indonesian legislators, hoping to restore the power of traditional Indonesian elites, proposed a bill in parliament that would end direct election of many local and provincial leaders, the Indonesian public came out strongly against the bill. A poll by the respected Indonesian Survey Circle of people across the archipelago showed that more than 80 percent of Indonesians supported direct elections and opposed the idea of the bill, and public demonstrations chided the legislators for even introducing it.[19]

Xi Jinping and at least the next generation of Chinese leaders almost surely will have the freedom to promote the Chinese model to the world without the fear that Communist Party rule is threatened at home. Indeed, even growth at a slower pace as China's economy and equity markets correct their bubbles will provide the Communist Party with some degree of public legitimacy, at least with urban Chinese. This legitimacy will allow Beijing to continue its one-party rule, as well as its continuing crackdown on any forms of organized opposition. In this respect, the success of the China model will clearly undermine democracy in one important place—in China itself—even if Xi and future leaders decide not to be as aggressive in promoting China's model internationally as I think they will be.

Not all China specialists believe that growth will continue to provide the Party with legitimacy, though even some of the most ardent advocates of reform in China have begun to recognize that political liberalization is far away, if it happens at all. (This contention, again, does not reflect my own personal beliefs about what kind of government people, including the Chinese, deserve to live under.) Claremont McKenna professor Minxin Pei, one of the most thoughtful and prolific scholars predicting that China is destined for greater political freedom, writes, in an essay that directly echoes Seymour Martin Lipset's original modernization theory:

> The effects of socioeconomic change—rising literacy, income, and urbanization rates, along with the improvement of communications technologies—greatly reduce the costs of collective action, delegitimize autocratic rule, and foster demands for greater democracy. As a result, authoritarian regimes, which have a relatively easy time ruling poor and agrarian societies, find it increasingly difficult and ultimately impossible to maintain their rule once socioeconomic development reaches a certain level. Statistical analysis shows that authoritarian regimes become progressively more unstable (and democratic transitions more likely) once income rises above $1,000 (PPP) per capita . . . If we apply this observation and take into account the probable effect of inflation (although the above PPP figures were calculated in constant terms), we will find that China is well into this "zone of democratic transition" because its per capita income is around $9,100 (PPP) today, comparable to the income level of South Korea and Taiwan in the mid-1980s on the eve of their democratic transitions.[20]

Yet we have seen that evidence calls into question the theory, now often assumed as fact, that economic freedom and affluence will foster political freedom. Indeed, the evidence suggests that the authoritarian Chinese government may be able to survive indefinitely without opening up the political system.

Since the 1980s and early 1990s, China actually has become more closed politically even as its economy has boomed. There was far greater space for public protest and public criticism of the Communist Party in the 1980s than there is today, despite the growth of microblogs, the removal of many restrictions on Chinese people's personal lives, and China's growing interaction with other countries. Just since 2013, when Xi Jinping became president, the Chinese government has launched an intense crackdown not only on artists and writers but also on a wide range of activists, including political activists, religious groups, and ethnic minority activists in regions like Xinjiang.

One of the best-known groups of activists was a small coterie that had formed in 2012 after learning that Xi Jinping, the next president, supposedly planned to make reform part of his agenda. It called itself the New Citizens Movement and tried to launch large street protests calling for greater transparency in Chinese politics. After less than a year on the job as president, Xi Jinping had the leaders of the New Citizens Movement locked up.[21]

Wen Yunchao, a prominent Chinese activist living in exile, compiled a list of high-profile detentions, dating back to 2013.[22] Wen Yunchao's records show that the number of detentions rose in 2013, after Xi became president, demonstrating a growing climate of political repression. Some of the activists rounded up in 2013 and 2014 were forced to "confess" their crimes, such as promoting "foreign" values like democracy, in Cultural Revolution-esque confessions.[23]

Yet there was little sign that many urban Chinese cared about the increased political repression as much as they had in the 1980s, when urban China, not rural China, was at the center of anti-government protests. As Beijing writer Li Datong has noted, the urban population in China today is still relatively happy with the state of the economy—a contrast to the 1980s, when inflation was skyrocketing and the most significant economic growth was taking place in rural areas, which had seen some of the earliest reforms. Indeed, even among China's urban entrepreneurs, who in other countries had been the linchpins of protest for democratic change, there was little support for significant political reform. Even after China's sharp stock market declines in 2015, there was little public call for political change. In studies of Chinese private-sector businesspeople, Johns Hopkins University political scientist Kellee Tsai consistently has found low levels of support for the idea that democracy would be the best political system in China.[24]

In rural areas, which have lagged farthest behind in growth since the late 1980s, tens of thousands of protests occur each year, as even China's own security ministry admits.[25] But protests in rural areas have failed to garner anywhere near the momentum needed to become national movements, in part because the demonstrations have not spread to urban areas.

Urban Chinese businesspeople have become increasingly unwilling to criticize Beijing at all; by producing robust growth concentrated in urban areas, China's state capitalism has helped co-opt these urban middle classes. While in the 1980s, polls had shown significant dissatisfaction with the government among a majority of urban Chinese, by the late 2000s and early 2010s, this dissatisfaction had shifted, in many studies, to satisfaction with the regime. In one study conducted by Chinese political scientist Zhou Xiaohong, nearly half of middle class respondents polled in the late 2000s now said that "participation [in politics] doesn't matter . . . The politics being implemented by the state are increasingly decided upon by intellectuals and specialists. Their thinking and ours are . . . the same. They won't threaten our political position, economic position, or social position. They won't have any [adverse] influence on us."[26]

SINGAPORE—HOW STATE CAPITALISM COULD WORK

In the long term, the threat of the China model to free-market economics and existing international economic and financial institutions will be blunted not only by whether Beijing itself wants to challenge these institutions but also by the difficulty of copying the Chinese model. These Chinese and Singaporean models have well exceeded the period of time in which most of the other state-capitalist economies have slowed down; indeed, China and Singapore have outpaced almost every other economy in the world over the past thirty years. But as we will see, copying all of the elements that have allowed Beijing and Singapore to succeed will be immensely difficult for most nations.

The main "knowledge center" of Hyflux Limited water and environmental company looks like a flash forward to 2030. Located in an area of Singapore of industrial estates, server farms, and mazes of high-speed mass transit projects, the knowledge center, which actually combines ten laboratories, houses over two hundred scientists and other staff. From the windows of the knowledge center, one can look right across the narrow Kaliang River to new high-rise condominiums and state housing blocks, topped with the Singapore's typical orange slate roofs being built by armies of cranes that look, from afar, like the world's biggest Lego project. When I visited the Kaliang area several years earlier, in 2009, most of these new housing blocks—and many corporate buildings—did not even exist.

Founded in 1989 by chemist Olivia Lum, Hyflux began with only four staff and initial capital of around $15,000, which Lum had raised partly by selling her car. (Lum told reporters and associates at the company that after selling her car, she had to cruise around Singapore on a motorbike to tout the new company's products to potential buyers and investors.[27]) The international industry it was entering, water and wastewater treatment systems, did not seem like one that would be easy to crack for a new entrepreneur from a tiny city-state, even one as successful as Singapore. Water treatment for large urban areas around the world was, at that time, dominated by massive private companies with decades of experience and links to political leaders, like French water giant Suez, American monolith Bechtel, and Britain's Thames Water, among others. Bechtel alone had nearly sixty thousand employees around the world, and annual revenues of over $30 billion.[28] Singapore itself had relied on several major multinationals for water treatment.

But unlike in Russia, Hyflux's founders did not have to face off against their own government, or against rapacious state companies in their own backyard. Instead, they benefited from effective, highly supportive assistance from the Singapore government. The government gave the company several small projects to help it build its expertise. As one investment analysis of the company noted, "Hyflux . . . benefited tremendously in its initial stages from Singapore's government projects."[29] Once it got more established, too, Hyflux was given a twenty-five-year agreement with Singapore's state water utility to provide water treatment, a contract designed and approved by the government as part of a broader state plan to incubate Singaporean water and environmental firms that then would become global players.[30] Hyflux also got the chance to build a reverse osmosis plant for the government, desalinating saltwater to make fresh drinking water.

This initial support allowed Hyflux to gradually build its research and development capacities, drawing on Singapore's large pool of skilled engineering graduates and on the city-state's natural need for ever more sophisticated water and wastewater treatment. Singapore has few natural water sources and little room to put large wastewater plants, and although it imports water from neighboring Malaysia, tensions between larger Malaysia and smaller Singapore are often high, and the city-state's leaders never want to be too dependent on Malaysia.

The Singapore government did not protect Hyflux endlessly, as the Kremlin backs Gazprom or Venezuela protects its state champions, often making them uncompetitive, uninnovative, and laden with debts. When Hyflux was founded, Singapore already had allowed many foreign water companies to operate on the island. Despite some initial backing from the state, Hyflux quickly had to prove its competitiveness to gain more contracts in Singapore, and then to expand globally. In addition, Singaporean officials also never tried to exert control over Hyflux's operations.

Building on Singapore's location, close air links to China, and the Singapore government's good relations with China and India—Singapore has trained over ten thousand Chinese officials, many of whom have gone on to be provincial governors or mayors or major cities—Hyflux quickly developed customers in China. It won large water-treatment projects in Harbin in northeastern China and Hejiang County in Sichuan province, among other projects.[31] Winning these projects required the strong backing of top Singapore government leaders, who helped make the sale to Harbin, Sichuan, and other locations by repeatedly traveling to many Chinese cities and advocating for the Chinese to sign deals with specific Singaporean companies. This advocacy, the kind of promotion of specific companies that many Western leaders would avoid for fear of looking like they were beholden to certain firms, has helped not only Hyflux but also many other Singaporean firms win deal after deal to provide infrastructure in China, often beating out larger competitors. Indeed, aggressive advocacy to win contracts in China, as well as the contacts made through so many trainings in Singapore, helped the city-state become one of the few countries in the world to post a regular trade surplus with China.[32]

Meanwhile, using its links to the National University of Singapore's water technology research programs, which had been funded lavishly by the government, Hyflux soon developed cutting-edge filtration products. By the mid-2000s, it had set up research centers not only in the city-state but also in many locations around the world. These labs helped the company expand into desalination, new membrane technologies, and other novel concepts in water treatment.[33] By the 2000s, Hyflux had even more talented water engineers applying for jobs than it had when it started, since the Singaporean government was providing startup capital to small companies in membrane technology and other water industries. Many engineers would train at these small firms and then move on to Hyflux. By the early 2010s, Hyflux held patents in over thirty-seven countries and had expanded its operations to include plants in several Middle Eastern nations, a proposed treatment plant in Nigeria, and a new water desalination plant in Gujarat state in India.[34] It had branched out from water and wastewater treatment into other environmental areas, including biofuels and oil recycling, areas that the government encouraged Singapore companies to enter, offering favorable tax treatment and some seed capital for firms in these sectors.[35]

By 2001, with the government eager to back domestic firms' listing on the Singapore stock exchange (SGX), Hyflux listed publicly. Hyflux eventually listed a subsidiary on the SGX as well. Today, Hyflux has been listed on the SGX for more than a decade, has over one thousand employees, and enjoys a market capitalization of over $820 million.[36]

Just as Russia offers one picture of state capitalism's future—a bleak one—Hyflux's operations in Singapore offer another, more optimistic possibility. Singapore shows that state capitalism can have long-term success and can adapt to the twenty-first century, but Singapore's example, which required many foresighted policies, also demonstrates how hard it will be for other state capitalists to achieve success similar to that enjoyed by Singapore and China.

Like Russia, Singapore's economy has for decades revolved around government-linked companies, government spending, and government decision-making. Like modern state-capitalist failures, including Russia (or Venezuela), Singapore's meshing of economics and politics could have created uncompetitive state firms, opportunities for massive graft and patronage, bundles of red tape, and a climate that inhibited entrepreneurship.

Yet Singapore's state capitalism appears to achieved just the opposite, promoting growth, the rule of law, and an environment conducive to doing business. Because the business environment is clean, easy to enter, and regulated, Singapore has little of the underground gray economy of Russia or even most developed economies. The process of establishing a business in the city-state is transparent and, as long as companies fulfill basic requirements of incorporation, undiscriminating. Much of the paperwork needed to start a company in the city-state can be filled out online in an hour or two; I got halfway to incorporating a company in Singapore in two hours at my laptop in a hotel room off Orchard Road, a large street in the city-state packed with gigantic shopping malls.

An innovative, relatively democratic, highly efficient, trading state capitalist, Singapore has exemplified the brand of state capitalism most likely to produce success, if any state capitalists are going to succeed over decades. Although many visitors to the island nation—including this writer—find Singapore antiseptic, with a government that seems nanny-like and patronizing, the results of Singaporean state capitalism are undeniable. From a GDP per capita of around $500 at independence from Britain in 1965, Singapore has grown to a GDP per capita of over $46,000 in 2013. The country's literacy rates, proficiency in standardized tests, life expectancy, and other measures of development now all rank among the best in the rich world, far above comparable statistics for the United States or most nations in Western Europe.[37] Singapore's government-linked companies, far from turning into creaking patronage machines like Russia's giants, actually have outperformed private companies in the city-state in terms of annual profits, according to comprehensive studies of the Singaporean firms by the IMF and by economists at Nanyang Technological University in Singapore.[38] This despite the fact that, while Singaporean government-linked companies have some advantages over private companies, such as initial inflows of government capital, they also face some disadvantages, such as greater difficulty making international acquisitions because their government links sometimes raise suspicions in other countries in Asia where they want to expand. In contrast, a similar study in a place like Russia or Vietnam, where the playing field is tilted so heavily against private companies, would not be able to effectively ascertain whether state companies were doing well or whether private companies were simply performing miserably because they faced such disadvantages compared to state companies.

"Singapore's government-owned enterprises are comparable to privately run enterprises in efficiency," the Nanyang Technological University economists found. The state companies were comparable in part because the government forced the state enterprises to be competitive with each other and with foreign companies operating in the city-state, and in part because the government firms have long operated under expectations of profitability, with executives punished if profitability is not achieved.[39]

Even between 2004 and 2014, a time of slow global growth, Singapore's economy grew by over 5 percent annually, enormous annual growth for an economy that is already one of the richest, per capita, in the world.[40] Since the early 1970s, Singapore has consistently received among the largest annual inflows of investment of any country in the world, a staggering figure given its miniscule size.

Singapore's state funds and state companies figured heavily in this growth, investing in industries that could diversify Singapore's economy, including pharmaceuticals, nanotechnology, medical tourism, and clean energy. Singapore also has been able to use state incentives to push Singaporean firms to move into industries that, while not necessarily profitable now, will be the emerging technologies of this century, such as clean energy. With state backing, and despite having only about five and a half million people, Singapore is now dominating clean energy research in Southeast Asia.

One example of Singapore's state-driven strategy is the Singapore Biomedical Sciences Initiative, a government project designed to set guidelines for the biomedical sector, cement drug researchers' intellectual property protection, and foster investment through government funding and tax breaks. The initiative led nearly every major pharmaceutical company in the world to set up manufacturing and research centers in Singapore.[41] It also created a climate of support for young Singaporean scientists; between the big companies' investments and new drug developments launched by Singaporeans, the city-state pharmaceutical sector grew from almost nothing in the early 2000s to an industry producing over $16 billion each year by the end of the decade.[42]

Officials from over thirty other developing nations regularly send national-level bureaucrats and ministers to Singapore for training in management, economic planning, and other tools of industrial policy. Singapore has a less corrupt business and political environment than the United States, according to global corruption monitor Transparency International.

But there is reason to believe that, over decades, the strategies employed by Singapore and, to some extent, by China and Norway are extremely hard to copy. As a result, the possibility that state capitalism will prove a viable alternative to the free market for many nations will remain relatively remote. For one, while retaining significant state stakes in many industries and keeping macroeconomic policies stable, Singapore's long-ruling People's Action Party has given executives of these firms great latitude over day-to-day decisions. A relatively hands-off strategy that is difficult for most state capitalists, democratic or undemocratic, to allow to occur.

Allowing for this kind of latitude is very hard for most countries to follow, since in most state capitalists, leaders and government officials, whose legitimacy rests in part on economic success—and thus the success of state companies—are reluctant to hand over total decision-making power of state companies. In Thailand, for example, successive Thai governments, whether military led or democratically elected, have been unable to help themselves from meddling in the leadership of flagship Thai state companies. One Thai leader after the next has shaken up boards of state firms, handpicked leaders of state companies, and interfered in state firms' day-to-day decision-making. "Every Thai prime minister just doesn't feel comfortable having someone they don't know well and feel then they can't trust running state companies, so they just draw upon their friends and family [to run state companies] . . . There just isn't the kind of trust in politics and trust in independent management, so Thai state companies are just packed with cronies," says one prominent Thai private-sector businessman who deals extensively with Thailand's biggest state companies.[43]

And although the Singapore government controls great reserves of capital, entrusted to it from sales of real estate and mandatory contributions to national savings programs, it usually has used its SWFs to invest in Singaporean firms only when private capital markets are shallow or unwilling to do so. In Singapore's early post-independence period, for example, state capital played a major role in launching many domestic industries. Then, the local banking sector was small and many potential foreign investors in Singaporean manufacturing, shipping, or other industries were scared off by the Vietnam war and race riots that had recently occurred in Singapore and neighboring Malaysia. So the Singapore government took stakes in a range of industries that it believed were critical to industrialization and to creating higher-value products in the city-state.

These initial investments, in sectors like shipbuilding, banking, and petrochemicals that the government believed would be critical to industrialization, paid off, creating Singaporean firms like shipping firm Neptune Orient Lines, bank DBS, and air carrier Singapore Airlines. Supported by state funds, able to make long-term decisions, and—sometimes—given domestic monopolies for a period of time, these state champions became regionally and then internationally competitive.[44] Singapore Airlines has grown into one of the dominant long-haul international carriers, frequently ranked by long-haul passengers as their favorite airline in the world, and it has amassed a staggering record, since the early 1970s, of never losing money in any year—a claim that US carriers, constantly in and out of bank-ruptcy, would love to match.[45] DBS, meanwhile, has expanded into the largest bank in all of Southeast Asia, controlling over $275 billion in total assets.[46]

The state's investment vehicles eventually grew far larger and more complex. Singaporean SWF Temasek Holdings, which controls over $170 billion in assets, continued to invest heavily in Singaporean firms, even if the government's interests broadened from areas to now include support-ing sectors like medical tourism, wastewater treatment, and computing servers.[47] But Temasek's commitment to promoting local industries did not stop the SWF from making money: it delivered returns of nearly 12 percent annually between 2005 and 2014.[48]

Again, this strategy is difficult to copy, since SWFs, like state compa-nies, are easily captured by a small group of regime insiders, particularly in more authoritarian state capitalists. They are often then used to fund com-panies with close links to these senior leaders, like Russia's failing petroleum giant Rosneft, rather than companies with the best prospects for long-term success or companies in areas where private capital markets are insuffi-cient and shallow. And once funds and state banks start supporting state companies, it is hard to turn off the tap of capital, the way that Singapore and (sometimes) China have done, since these state companies now have allies in government, workers to support, and substantial political capital. In China, graft-ridden, subsidized state companies certainly do exist, but the government usually is interested enough in promoting growth—not just in enriching officials—to slash subsidies to inefficient state companies. The weakest state firms may be closed altogether. In Singapore, although the government has often given state companies tax holidays for five to ten years after their creation, it has refused to extend these tax exemptions, or even cut them short, if the state-linked companies are not profitable within a certain period of time.[49] This kind of cut-off has proven difficult for gov-ernments to achieve in other state capitalists, like Brazil and Indonesia, once these state companies develop allies in government and labor unions.

The Singapore government also has provided incentives for state firms to lure and retain the most skilled corporate talent from within Singapore and around the world. Singapore's welcoming immigration policies have allowed it to attract the finest talent in the region, and even from compa-nies from the West. Today, nearly one-third of the people in Singapore are first-generation immigrants.[50] To foster export-led industrialization, the government has made it easy for companies to invest in Singapore since independence in 1965, a sharp contrast to larger neighbors like Malaysia and Indonesia, which in the early independence period aggressively nationalized foreign investment. In addition, rather than offering certain groups of Singaporeans entrenched privileges in state companies, the Singaporean government has forced state firms to act like meritocracies. Malaysia, on the other hand, gives ethnic Malays preferential treatment in state firms.

This strategy, too, is difficult to copy. Even today, it is hard for most state capitalists—or any nations, period—to be as welcoming to skilled talent as Singapore, since immigration is rarely popular with the general public. And even without bringing in immigrants, simply copying China's and Singapore's strategies of co-opting leading talents into state companies is not easy for every nation, whether because of vast disparities in pay between state firms and the private sector (Singapore pays extremely well for executives of state companies and government officials), small pools of domestic talent, and public perceptions that working for a state company necessarily involves politics and possibly engaging in graft.

Both the Singaporean and Chinese governments also have used government funds as seed capital to help companies with bright ideas grow and potentially become profitable. In China, for example, the government has provided funding, land, tax incentives, low-interest loans, and other benefits for many companies in specific cutting-edge industries that are not already dominated by firms from developed nations, including lithium-ion battery production and nanotechnology.[51] In these areas, where the global market is not already saturated with powerful firms from Europe, Japan, South Korea, or the United States, Chinese firms and individual entrepreneurs and inventors are receiving much larger amounts of government support than in nearly any other economy in the world, support that helps them scale up into sizable companies. Beijing also has pushed and funded science and engineering universities to boost their research budgets and hire foreign experts in many of these fields. According to an analysis of China's science research by the National Science Foundation, China's share of publications in leading global science and engineering journals has grown significantly in the past ten years.[52] China's total annual spending on research and development, meanwhile, has grown to be the third largest in the world, and is quickly catching up to that of the United States, the largest spender on research and development but a country that is much richer than China and has—for now—far more established elite science and engineering universities.[53]

Singapore's entrepreneurs, though sometimes criticized by some Singaporean businesspeople as too cautious, can be vibrant and innovative: many Singaporean entrepreneurs *have* launched successful start-ups in industries like personal computing, business servers and hardware, pharmaceuticals, and mobile telecommunications, sometimes with the help of backing from government seed funds, state universities, or investments from larger state-linked companies. When these entrepreneurial companies have emerged, no giant, politically backed state firms swallow them up just because they do not pay off the right official, as happens in Russia or even in Malaysia.

THE STATE-CAPITALIST MODEL WILL CONTINUE, EVEN IF IT DOES NOT WIN MORE CONVERTS

Whether or not China tries to convert other nations to its model, it seems clear that the state capitalists that exist today are unlikely to embrace economic liberalization, so many of the world's major emerging markets will remain state capitalists. Indeed, it is wrong to simply suggest that the state capitalists are necessarily headed toward economic systems that will be as free market as those of Hong Kong, Britain, or other free-market-oriented nations. Yes, *some* of the policies that Singapore, China, Brazil, Indonesia, and others have instituted resemble those of more free-market-oriented nations. Most of the state capitalists have created stock markets, signed regional free-trade deals like the China-Southeast Asia agreement or the Mercosur Latin America group, participated in global free-trade negotiations under the aegis of the WTO, allowed for market forces to dictate winners and losers in many segments of their economies, and initiated other policies similar to those in free market-oriented nations. In some sectors of their economies, prominent state capitalists like Singapore or China or the United Arab Emirates have pursued a path of liberalization that will be nearly impossible to reverse. Singapore's banking sector, for example, today little resembles banking on the island in the late 1960s and early 1970s, when the government-linked DBS and other state-linked banks dominated the market and foreign banks were mostly kept out. In the late 1990s and early 2000s, the Singapore government changed many of the laws regarding banking on the island, making it far easier for foreign banks to operate in the city-state. Now, nearly every major international bank, from BNP Paribas to Citigroup to Bank of Tokyo-Mitsubishi, has local operations in Singapore, which has become one of the world's leading private banking locales, jousting with Switzerland for the most private banking assets held.[54] Overall, there are over 120 commercial banks now operating in Singapore, with most of them owned by private foreign multinationals, and the possibility of Singapore reverting to the situation in the 1960s and 1970s, when the banking sector was far more closed, seems unthinkable.[55]

Yet as we have seen, Singapore—even after decades of gradual unwinding of some of the state's assets—is not Hong Kong. (Although Hong Kong is a territory of China, for trade and business purposes it operates like a sovereign nation, and so throughout the book it has been treated as a sovereign state.) The share of Singapore's economy linked to government spending remains far higher than in Hong Kong, and Singapore's government collects vastly more revenues and also forces citizens to contribute to a national savings/pension program; Hong Kong has among the lowest tax rates in the world and no national savings program. Singapore has moved slightly in Hong Kong's low-tax direction, by passing legislation in 2004 that provided significant corporate tax exemptions for the smallest start-ups, a move designed to further encourage Singaporean entrepreneurship, but the city-state has not moved any closer to Hong Kong's laissez-faire style.[56]

In addition, the Singapore government retains far more state companies and funds than Hong Kong—Hong Kong has virtually none—and remains far more involved in the economy and other aspects of the country—including citizens' medical well-being, their access to basic goods and services like Internet connections, and their interactions with Singaporeans of different races—than Hong Kong's small civil service does. After national elections in 2011 dealt a blow to the ruling People's Action Party, the Singaporean government launched what it called a "national conversation" designed to better shape how the multi-ethnic country wanted to shape its social and cultural future.[57] The conversation helped the PAP win elections in 2015. "What are our priorities as a nation? Where do we want to go as a country, as a people?," the ruling party asked thousands of Singaporeans in surveys and face-to-face meetings with top ministers, who spoke of the "national conversation" as if they were elected therapists. "The government wants to make sure they are still able to shape people's attitudes, who they are as Singaporeans," says former Singapore ambassador to Washington Chan Heng Chee.[58]

Just as Singapore is not becoming Hong Kong, China is not Britain, Indonesia is not the United States, and South Africa is not Switzerland. Although countries like Singapore and China, Indonesia and South Africa, have liberalized some sectors of their economies, the state capitalists do not appear to be headed toward fully embracing the market or liberalizing many more sectors of their economies.

By contrast, since 2008, leaders in several Western nations, including some politicians in the United States, have suggested that Western governments should play a more active, Singapore-type role in fostering domestic manufacturing sectors, protecting certain industries, and creating state banks to fund infrastructure and support certain private companies in sectors like clean energy, automobile manufacturing, and other areas.[59] President Obama himself began advocating in 2011 for the creation of a national infrastructure bank similar in some ways to state banks like those in China and Brazil, a bank that would be controlled by the government and would make relatively low-interest loans to companies building infrastructure in the United States—and, possibly down the road, making loans to companies in other industries that it considered critical to American competitiveness. Without control of Congress, and with limited sway over even his own party, Obama was not able to get this idea off the ground, but in 2013 he began aggressively promoting the concept again.[60] Visiting Miami in March 2013, Obama gave a speech touting a national infrastructure bank that would be initially capitalized with $10 billion in government funds, though he hoped that its capitalization would expand exponentially. "What are we waiting for?," Mr. Obama said at the Miami port. "There's work to be done. There are workers who are ready to do it. Let's prove to the world that there's no better place to do business than right here in the United States of America, and let's get started rebuilding America."[61]

Even Hong Kong, the free-market bastion, has in the past five years faced public complaints that the government does too little to manage economic policy, create a social safety net, and regulate housing. With criticism mounting, Hong Kong leaders have considered adopting greater economic intervention, with Singapore as the model.

In democratic state capitalists like Indonesia, Brazil, and South Africa, a move toward further free-market reforms actually seems less likely than in China or even Vietnam, where a slowing economy over the past few years and revelations of corruption scandals at the highest levels of politics have soured some of the public on Vietnam's style of state capitalism. Public opinion matters far more to policymakers facing more or less free elections in democratic state capitalists like Indonesia, Brazil, Singapore, or South Africa. And public opinion in these democracies has over the past decade strongly backed greater state intervention in the economy. In South Africa, for instance, the ANC youth league, which generally reflects sentiment among the South African public more closely than the actual ANC leadership, has endorsed state takeovers of much of the mining, petrochemicals, and steel production in the country. In polls, a majority of South Africans support these interventions; the ANC's lack of movement on having the state play a larger role in the reviving the economy was a major reason why, in 2014's parliamentary elections, the party recorded its lowest share of the vote in any election since the end of apartheid and the advent of democracy in the early 1990s. In late 2013, the swelling public support for greater state control of the mining sector, which comprises the biggest portion of South Africa's economy, led the ANC government to write a new mining law that would force mining firms to sell their raw materials to South African companies at prices set by the state, not by local markets.[62]

Given strong public support for state capitalism in nations like Indonesia, South Africa, and Brazil, it seems probable that these democratic state capitalists will continue with further state intervention, whether in the form of Indonesia's continued nationalization of natural resources firms, Brazil's growing use of state funds to take stakes in powerful private Brazilian companies, or other forms.[63]

Indeed, annual polls of the Indonesian public by the Lowy Institute, a leading Australian think tank, show that a large majority of the Indonesian public consistently supports democracy as the preferable system of government.[64] But numerous polls of the Indonesian public also show that the public supports far greater state intervention in the economy— even greater intervention than already has occurred in the early 2010s, as Indonesia has created new barriers to investment, boosted state control of resources, and facilitated far greater government intervention in some of the country's largest companies.

Even many Indonesian businesspeople, who might actually find their own businesses hurt by these barriers to investment and state control of resources, have advocated for these policies, so strong is this current of support for state economic intervention. In 2013, the main chamber of commerce in Indonesia, which one might expect to be an aggressive advocate of free-market reforms and deregulation, pushed to change the national constitution so that natural resources across Indonesia would become the property of SOEs. Still, even the most nationalistic Indonesian businesspeople do not envision Indonesian state companies as weapons to be used against Jakarta's neighbors, but merely as bulwarks against what they see as predatory foreign competition.

10

The Greatest Threat

Resources, State Firms as Weapons, and the Two Big Authoritarians

The biggest concerns about state capitalism should be that state capitalists will use state companies as de facto weapons of war, as weapons of trade policy, as means of stealing intellectual property and sensitive technology from foreign countries, and potentially as means to undermine international labor, environmental, and corruption norms. These are the most important concerns both because they are the most likely to occur—state companies already are often used as weapons of trade policy and to steal technology— and because, if they were to occur, they would have the biggest consequences for international security, perhaps even fostering a shooting war in East Asia. By contrast, some of the other threats we have examined, like state capitalism causing democratic regression or autocratic state capitalists imploding and damaging the world economy, appear less likely to occur and, if they did occur, would be serious but less catastrophic than a shooting war in East Asia or the former Soviet Union.

These concerns about state firms being used as weapons should focus on authoritarian state capitalists, specifically on Russia and China. Again, it is the nature of the government engaged in state capitalism, not the state capitalism itself, which should worry Western states. The challenge is not simply a challenge because

Russia and China are powerful, although that is part of the reason for the concern about Chinese state companies; this is not simply a story of great power politics. These two nations are international and regional powers, and serious challengers to the United States and its allies. Of all the countries in the world, China and Russia have the clearest interest in challenging existing international institutions and potentially overturning them. This challenge to international institutions and structures can be seen in (relatively) smaller examples like Beijing's desire to create an alternative to the Asian Development Bank and thus reduce American and Japanese influence over Asian aid to bigger and more imminently dangerous examples like Russia's attempts, under Putin, to reclaim its influence or outright control over large parts of the former Soviet Union.

China's and Russia's power, and potential interest in challenging the international system, thus means that their state companies indeed deserve the highest scrutiny. But although power politics is part of the reason for this scrutiny, the two countries' state capitalism potentially makes them far more dangerous to regional and international security than if all of their leading firms were truly privately owned. Even if Moscow and Beijing desired to completely destroy and remake international institutions (which, as we have seen, it is not clear Beijing wants to do), if they were free market-oriented economies, their arsenal would be limited to diplomacy and traditional types of coercion, including military force. Russia under Putin, far more comfortable than China with playing the rogue in the international system, has shown a willingness to use traditional types of coercion. Yet even Russia has relied heavily on Gazprom to bully its neighbors and provide the cash that allows Moscow to modernize its military, launch de facto invasions of other nations, and still prevent the Russian economy from collapsing (for now) and triggering domestic unrest. Less willing to openly utilize its military in the way Russia does, China has relied heavily on state companies in disputed areas like the South China Sea to stake out Beijing's strategic interests and attempt to bully neighboring nations, instead of using only traditional types of coercion to gain what Beijing wants.

Indeed, the wielding of state companies as weapons stems from a dangerous confluence today of this great power politics and state capitalism. To be sure, private companies from these two powers could also be used as weapons, but it would be far harder for Moscow and Beijing to do so, since they are harder to control—which is why Vladimir Putin has systematically tried to eliminate any large, powerful privately owned Russian companies in areas that the Kremlin considers critical to Russian national interests. Since becoming president of Russia in 2000, Putin has assiduously taken state control of all the most powerful Russian companies in oil, gas, and other natural resources precisely because he knows that only state companies can be relied on to make potentially unprofitable and dangerous decisions that could bolster Russia's regional power that make little sense from a corporate viewpoint. Still, even private companies from China and Russia should raise concerns in the United States and other democracies, especially if they make investments in areas critical to national security like physical and telecommunications infrastructure and if they appear to have links to the Chinese and Russian military or government. For example, Chinese private telecommunications firm Huawei has—rightly—come under intense scrutiny in the West for its opaque management structure and possible ties to the People's Liberation Army (PLA). Since Huawei has remained less than transparent about its management structure and its long relationship with the PLA, the scrutiny seems warranted. If the company, however, was completely transparent about its structure, and plausibly had no links to the Chinese government and armed forces, then it could be invited to build infrastructure in any country.

State firms, though, have the greatest potential to be used as weapons, and Western nations should focus scrutiny and possible countermeasures on China and Russia's state companies. The Kremlin already has repeatedly used Gazprom, the biggest gas company in the world and the main gas supplier to former Soviet states and many western European nations, as a weapon to intimidate countries in Russia's neighborhood and to potentially change their political trajectory. When Ukraine was led, in the mid-2000s, by a pro-Western government unfriendly to Vladimir Putin, the Kremlin utilized Gazprom to pressure Kiev, cutting off gas supplies to Ukraine at critical times in a pointed reminder of how dependent Ukraine is on Russian gas. After Ukraine elected a less pro-Western government in 2009, Gazprom's gas deliveries to Ukraine stabilized and there were no further threats of cut-offs. Yet in the fall of 2013, Gazprom suddenly warned it would suspend deliveries to Ukraine again. The company said that this warning came only because Ukraine was behind in payments, but few observers believed the company's statement, since Gazprom had let other countries run credit for a much longer period of time. Instead, most Kremlin observers believed that Gazprom was issuing its warning because Ukraine was moving toward signing a trade deal with the European Union that would draw the country closer to Europe.[1] By signing a deal with the European Union, Ukraine would be rejecting a proposed customs union with Russia and other former Soviet states like Belarus. Even before Gazprom's move, *The Guardian* reported, a prominent Kremlin advisor had issued warnings that "if the [Ukraine–EU] deal is signed 'political and social unrest' will ensue and Russia could cease to recognize Ukraine's status as a sovereign state."[2]

By late 2013 and 2014, Gazprom had become even more intertwined with Russia's growing interference in and outright annexation of parts of Ukraine. As protests in Kiev eventually forced President Viktor Yanukovych, Russia's ally, to abandon his post and flee, and a pro-Western government took power in Ukraine, the Kremlin moved quickly. It apparently inserted special forces into eastern Ukraine and the Black Sea peninsula of Crimea, seized the key port in Crimea that hosted Russia's Black Sea fleet, and used its men on the ground in Crimea to facilitate a referendum in which, prodded by armed men, Crimeans voted overwhelmingly to leave Ukraine and join Russia. Vladimir Putin obliged, signing bills absorbing Crimea into Russia in a lavish Kremlin ceremony shown live on Russian television.[3]

But Putin wasn't done. After annexing Crimea, he continued to apply immense pressure on the weak government in Kiev, with that pressure coming partly from Gazprom. In the spring of 2014, Gazprom announced that Ukraine's bill for gas already delivered to the country was $22 billion, not the $2 billion that Gazprom previously had said Ukraine owed—and that the price for gas deliveries to Ukraine had just gone up.[4] Then in June 2014, Gazprom abruptly cut off gas supplies to the Ukraine, potentially leaving Ukraine desperately short of gas in the coming winter. Meanwhile, Gazprom executives warned that it could do the same to other countries in Europe—a not-too-subtle hint that major NATO states like Germany also were highly dependent on gas from Gazprom.[5] Gazprom again cut off gas supplies to Ukraine in November 2015.

The Kremlin appears to have also utilized Gazprom and other state companies to bully other nations surrounding Russia. For two decades, Georgia and Russia have had extremely tense relations, going to war over the disputed territory of South Ossetia in 2008—a war that, in hindsight, looked like a preview of Russia's tactics in annexing Crimea. Gazprom repeatedly cut off gas supplies to Georgia as the Georgia–Russia relationship hit its nadir, although Gazprom bosses and Russian political leaders sometimes would blame these shut-offs—unconvincingly—on technical problems or on sabotage on Gazprom's supply pipelines.[6] Still, most observers of the Georgia–Russia relationship concluded that the suspicious and repeated nature of the "technical problems" suggested that the cut-offs had been done on purpose.

China, meanwhile, has since the early 2010s become increasingly confident in asserting its dominance over land borders and disputed waters in Asia. As the Chinese government has become more assertive, it has not hesitated to use state companies to bolster its power, even while insisting that these state enterprises operate solely to maximize their profits.

China's disputes with Japan and other nations in Asia over the East and South China Seas reveal how Beijing has utilized its state firms as weapons, and send an ominous signal about the future, if China becomes increasingly powerful and assertive in its own neighborhood. As tensions between China and Japan have risen, primarily over islands and economic zones in the East China Sea claimed by both countries, Chinese companies have on several occasions appeared to withhold shipments of "rare earth" metals—metals critical in the production of modern technologies like cellular telephones, electric cars, computer batteries, and other items—to Japanese buyers. Most noticeably, Chinese firms appeared to withhold deliveries of rare earths in the fall of 2010. (The Chinese government denied that state firms were withholding deliveries to Japan, and at the time it was hard to prove they were withholding.) Again, as the disputes over islands claimed by both China and Japan heated up once more toward the end of 2012, Chinese state firms appeared to have been encouraged to stop buying Japanese products if possible.[7] This time, the evidence that Chinese state firms were purposefully boycotting buying certain Japanese products appeared much clearer than the evidence that China had withheld deliveries of rare earths several years earlier. This Chinese boycott of Japanese products cut as much as 1 percent off of the Japanese economy's total growth in the last quarter of 2012, according to several economic analyses.[8]

In 2013, 2014, and 2015, Chinese state companies played an even more central role as weapons in Beijing's disputes with Southeast Asian nations over claims to the South China Sea. Operating almost assuredly on orders from President Xi Jinping and the State Council, Beijing's highest organ of government, in 2014 Chinese state oil and gas companies sent rigs to portions of the South China Sea claimed by Vietnam as that country's exclusive economic zone. (China claims nearly the entire South China Sea as its own, even areas hundreds of miles from the Chinese mainland and only a few miles off the coasts of Indonesia, the Philippines, and Vietnam.) Chinese naval vessels accompanied the rigs. Many oil-industry analysts speculated that the central government in Beijing would be subsidizing the companies for losses incurred in the rig movement, since it was unclear whether the new rig locations would prove economically viable.

Indeed, it would have been much harder for Beijing—or any government—to get a private company to take as dangerous and potentially costly a decision as moving a major oil rig into waters claimed by another country. Only a state-controlled company, like China National Petroleum Company (CNPC), could make such a choice. Most Western oil and gas executives questioned about the rig move said they would not have made such a decision, since moving such an advanced rig was extremely expensive and potentially complicated, and the potential reserves in the block where the rig was moved were still largely unknown.[9]

The moving of the rigs in the South China Sea led to the most dangerous security situation in the Sea in two decades, including Chinese ramming of hundreds of Vietnamese boats in the Sea and massive anti-China riots in southern Vietnam, in which demonstrators attacked Chinese-owned factories (and, in the chaos, some non-Chinese-owned factories as well). The attacks led China to bolster its naval presence around CNPC's rig and to evacuate thousands of its citizens from Vietnam.

Hanoi sent cutters to challenge China's claims, and Vietnam and the Philippines held a very public meeting of Vietnamese and Philippine soldiers on an island in the middle of the Sea claimed by China—a not very subtle signal that, if pressed, Hanoi and Manila's armed forces might work more closely together.[10] China's government then used Chinese state firms to apply even more leverage on Vietnam to back down to Beijing in the South China Sea. In June 2014, Beijing ordered all SOEs to freeze any possible new investments in Vietnam, according to reports in the *South China Morning Post*.[11] Again, state enterprises were being told to take actions that would probably hurt their profitability, since Vietnam had been an extremely lucrative place to locate factories, given that Vietnam's labor force was both hard-working and generally much cheaper than labor in southern China.

This order could have sizable ramifications for the Vietnamese economy, already struggling due to a population boom, bad debts within Vietnam's own state companies, and a slowdown in investment from other key foreign investors. China is Vietnam's biggest trading partner, and

Chinese companies had invested some $2.3 billion in Vietnam in 2013, up from $371 million in 2012.[12] In all likelihood, Chinese direct investment into Vietnam would have continued to increase in 2014 if not for the freeze.

Other countries took note of China's actions. In the Philippines, several Chinese diplomats quietly warned Philippine officials that, if Manila continued to push back against expansive Chinese claims to the South China Sea, Chinese state enterprises might avoid the Philippines as well. The Philippines began to build even closer military relations with Hanoi, resulting in the announcement of a strategic partnership in 2015 that would solidify military ties. Both Manila and Hanoi also strengthened their strategic ties with the United States, with Vietnam inching closer to abandoning its decades-old policy of hedging ties between Washington and Beijing. As China in 2015 again prepared to explore in disputed areas of the South China Sea, leading Vietnamese foreign policy thinkers openly encouraged the Hanoi government to abandon hedging and embrace its strategic relationship with the United States.

These incidents, involving state companies, could only be the beginning. If China and Russia continue to use state companies in this manner, their actions eventually could lead to real military conflicts. The regions where Russia and China are using state companies to stake out influence are already heavily militarized. In these regions, like East Asia, arms races are already under way, tensions are already high, militaries have gained more power in policymaking, and few countries have designated hotlines to Moscow or Beijing that could be used to cool tempers before they led to war. Arms sales to East Asia are up by more than 100 percent since 2005, according to an annual survey of weapons purchases, country by country, conducted by the Stockholm Peace Research Institute.[13]

Still, even during the South China Sea unrest, the Chinese government claimed that it never uses state firms as weapons against other nations. Yet another fascinating study suggests that, on some occasions, Beijing seems to do exactly that. Researchers at the University of Gottingen in Germany analyzed the relationship between countries accepting a visit by the Dalai Lama, the one figure most demonized by Beijing, and trade between those countries and China. They used media reports of Dalai Lama meetings with countries' heads of state and government, plus twenty years of data on Chinese trade with over one hundred countries around the world. They found that countries that allowed a Dalai Lama visit suffered an 8 percent drop in trade with China for the *next two years*.[14] Though this drop in trade could simply be an accidental correlation with the post-Dalai Lama visit periods, the drop was far greater than the normal fluctuations in trade between China and these countries, suggesting a causal, rather than a correlative, relationship. In addition, much of this drop in trade with China was due to a decline in trade in machinery and transportation equipment, two areas heavily controlled by Chinese state companies. The relationship held true even for major trading partners, with whom an 8 percent drop in trade for two years could be a serious blow to China's economy. "Our empirical results support the idea that countries officially receiving the Dalai Lama at the highest political level are punished through a reduction of their exports to China," the study's authors note.[15]

However, while Russia has used Gazprom and other companies not only to punish other countries but also to back governments it supports, it is much harder to prove that China uses state firms to explicitly support certain regimes around the world than it is to prove that Beijing utilizes state companies to punish nations that have conflicts with it. Why is it hard, for instance, to demonstrate that China's investments are designed to prop up dictatorships? For one, the largest recipients of Chinese overseas investment to date (other than investments in bonds and other securities) are Australia, the United States, Canada, the United Kingdom, and Brazil—all of them democracies. The figures suggest that Chinese firms are making investments to be profitable or to gain access to sources of energy or both, but not primarily to prop up authoritarian regimes.[16]

In addition, although many critics have raised concerns that Chinese investments in places like Sudan, Iran, and Uzbekistan help these dictatorships stay in power, there is little evidence that Western companies would avoid these dictatorial regimes if their governments had not imposed sanctions on investing in places like Iran or Sudan. This is not to say that China's investments in Sudan or Uzbekistan have not played a role in dictators' survival, but that it is doubtful Western companies would act any differently, if given the opportunity. Many major American companies are donors to the National Foreign Trade Council, a Washington-based advocacy organization that has focused on removing US sanctions on trade with authoritarian regimes.[17] Many leading Western multinationals also have for decades operated in some of the most repressive states in the world, particularly in the energy industry. Western companies have dominated investment in Saudi Arabia, Gabon, and Equatorial Guinea—three of the most politically repressive states in the world—according to international monitoring group Freedom House.[18]

UNFAIR ADVANTAGES?

Besides the threat of state companies being used as weapons in conflicts, the biggest and most autocratic state capitalists also may use their power to give their SOEs unfair advantages over multinational competitors. To be sure, many multinationals have failed to distinguish between profitable, well-managed state companies, most of which hail from open, trade-dependent state capitalists like Singapore and Thailand, and state firms that can compete solely because of tariffs and other protections from the state. These weaker, more state-dependent enterprises tend to come from more closed and predatory state capitalists, like Venezuela, where the government has done little to encourage innovation and to make state companies competitive globally, or from state capitalists that, though they may be relatively open and responsive, are so regionally and internationally powerful that they believe they can openly flout trade rules and get away with it—China, for one.

What's more, in a world no longer dominated by the West, state companies from developing nations increasingly interact with each other and learn from each other. If the biggest autocratic state capitalists are allowed to get away with giving their state firms unfair advantages, state companies from other powerful developing nations may be tempted to follow suit.

Myanmar provides an example of how the most powerful state capitalists use unfair advantages to benefit their state companies. Although some Myanmar leaders have actively encouraged Western investment in the country, Western multinationals, many of whom have only focused on Myanmar since the reform process there began in 2011, already believe that they will be unable to compete in many sectors, since they are battling Chinese state enterprises that receive unfair advantages from the Chinese government, which sees Myanmar as strategically important. These advantages include low-interest or no-interest loans from Chinese state banks or outright payments from Beijing and provincial Chinese governments to Chinese state companies to invest in Myanmar.

It is far more common for Chinese state companies to compete unfairly with multinationals than it is for China to try to export its model of development, or for Chinese-style state capitalism to play a role in demo-cratic regression in other nations. In several of the industries deemed stra-tegic by Beijing and thus worthy of state support, for example, a broad range of Chinese state firms expanding internationally have been provided with a wide range of subsidies, soft loans, and other supports that violate trade agreements China has signed. In the solar industry, for instance, a lengthy analysis by the European Union of China–Europe trade found that Chinese firms in the solar industry enjoyed so many state advantages, including financing that was essentially interest free, that it would be impossible for European solar-makers to compete with Chinese firms even if European companies cut costs significantly. Between 2010 and 2013, more than twenty European makers of photovoltaic cells went out of business or had to down-size dramatically because they could not compete.[19] The European Union's policymaking arm slapped initial retaliatory tariffs against Chinese solar companies, although Beijing and Brussels agreed in 2013 to a deal to avoid punitive tariffs and reduce the chance of Chinese state-backed solar com-panies dumping, or selling products below cost, into European markets.[20]

Indeed, even though China has signed WTO agreements and other trade deals that promise not to utilize such extreme subsidies, it has con-tinued to do so in industries it deems strategic. The number of such pur-portedly strategic industries, we have seen, has more than doubled in the past decade. In the same industries where China is using illegal supports to boost its exports to Europe and other developed markets, it is also prohibit-ing foreign firms, including European ones, from effectively competing in these industries within China. One analysis by the European Council on Foreign Relations think tank noted:

> The problem presented by Chinese direct investment in Europe becomes even clearer when one considers Europe's limited access to similar opportunities in China. China's capital market remains largely closed in sectors that the government deems important for its eco-nomic development strategy. . . . In many sectors, ranging from air transport to banks and alternative energy, foreign stakes are limited to 20 percent of capital.[21]

Solar is not unique in terms of its state protections. For instance, the Chinese automobile parts industry, heavily state controlled, has grown by more than 150 percent in the past decade alone and now dominates the world. Ten years ago, China did not produce enough steel to meet domestic demand—China was a net steel importer in 2005—but is now the largest steel exporter in the world, not only meeting domestic demand but also competing successfully with steel multinationals like European giant AccelorMittal.

How much of this competition in auto and steel is due to Chinese firms' natural economies of scale, growing technological sophistication, and proximity to the most important consumer market in the world for steel and automobiles—and how much is due to state supports for auto and steel companies that do not allow multinationals like AccelorMittal or Ford a level playing field? Determining an exact answer to this question would be impossible, but several comprehensive analyses show that in at least fifteen sectors, including machine tools, machinery, clean energy, nanotechnology, mobile telecommunications, auto manufacturing, steel, oil, and others Chinese state firms enjoy far greater supports and protections than most private multinationals—or even most private Chinese companies. Economists George and Usha Haley, who developed perhaps the most exhaustive analysis of data on subsidies to domestic Chinese companies, concluded that over a twenty-year period, Beijing spent around $300 billion in subsidies on state-owned companies in industries Beijing considered essential to China's security and development.[22]

In other industries that Beijing does not consider strategic, however, from household products to personal computers to small appliances, the role that the Chinese government plays in assisting state companies is far less dramatic, and private Chinese companies have far more market share. The state companies that do exist in these non-strategic areas usually receive more minimal assistance from Beijing, and sometimes closely resemble state companies from Singapore or Norway, which enjoy some supports but must be extremely profitable to survive.

In industries considered strategic by Beijing, these subsidies and other state supports for SOEs can make it seem almost impossible for Western multinationals to compete with Chinese state-owned firms in some sectors, particularly when, as in Myanmar, that competition takes place in a developing country, where it is even harder to investigate and enforce agreed-upon trade rules or norms about bribery. Multinational firms have pulled out of many emerging markets where they believe they cannot compete with Chinese state-owned enterprises, avoiding bidding on infrastructure projects entirely where they cannot undercut Chinese state firms' pricing or compete with Chinese firms by lowering environmental and corruption norms.

This lack of competition in infrastructure and construction in many developing nations can leave Chinese state-owned firms with dominant market shares of these industries in developing countries as varied as Myanmar and Ghana, making Chinese state companies the main providers of essential infrastructure including electricity lines, cell phone towers, hydropower plants, railroad tracks, roads, and power plants. The Chinese state-owned companies thus enjoy monopoly power, potentially enhancing their unaccountability and making nations dependent on Chinese firms for their infrastructure. This dependence worries leaders of some countries that have become dependent on Chinese providers of infrastructure, from Myanmar to Kyrgyzstan. These leaders often wonder what might happen to their infrastructure projects should their bilateral relationships with Beijing deteriorate. "If we have Chinese companies build all of our roads, the new railway [line proposed through Myanmar], our ports, and we also had them build the phone systems, what would happen if we had any problem with China?" asked one senior Myanmar government official. "They could just shut down Myanmar, like that, and what could we do about it?"[23]

Still, developing nations need infrastructure, and Chinese firms are often able to provide it at the lowest costs. In November 2013, China's leading bankers announced that SOEs would increase their investments in infrastructure in Africa and other parts of the developing world, declaring that China would spend some $1 trillion on investments in Africa, loans to companies operating in Africa, and other types of financing between 2014 and 2025. Much of this financing and direct investment, said Zhao Changhui of China's Export-Import Bank, would go into infrastructure across sub-Saharan Africa.[24] In addition, in October 2014, China launched the Asian Infrastructure Investment Bank, a new Beijing-based lender designed to fund investment throughout developing Asia. The bank, in many ways a competitor to the existing Asian Development Bank, was launched with an initial capitalization of $100 billion and with over fifty countries that pledged to become members of it. China pledged to provide most of the proposed initial capital.

State companies from Brazil, Thailand, Indonesia, Qatar, Brazil, India, the United Arab Emirates, and several other prominent state capitalists have also been accused of using unfair subsidies and supports, although few employ as much state subsidization as China or Russia. China and Russia provide more state subsidies because they are able to get away with it, thanks to their power in regional and international organizations and their immense capital reserves, and because they have less transparency than most other violators excepting the Persian Gulf states. Still, India and Brazil have over the past five years faced a growing annual number of WTO cases launched against them for alleged illegal subsidies of industries ranging from large-scale agriculture to supermarkets. Even though India and Brazil have relatively close relationships with the United States—India more so than Brazil—and the White House is not eager to file WTO cases against these countries, pressure from US agriculture and other sectors has led to a sharp rise in WTO disputes with these large developing nations.[25]

In addition, in several of these countries, the government has written legislation that makes it almost impossible for citizens to investigate or criticize the doings of state companies. These laws make it far easier for the government to subsidize state companies without any complaints from private companies or investigations by nosy reporters or opposition politicians.

Although many Western governments have begun to understand the wide range of subsidies and protections used to assist *some* state companies, they have had little success in combating these tactics. It is extremely difficult to use normal remedies to force state-owned companies, especially from a country as powerful as China, to comply with international trade norms. There are several reasons why the typical measures used by states against companies from countries believed to be violating trade agreements are hard to apply to the giant SOEs from places like China. Punitive tariffs are extremely hard to calculate for state-owned companies that combine aspects of market-oriented competition and subsidized competition or dumping of products below cost. In private, the Obama administration and many congressional officials admit that existing countermeasures do not work well with state enterprises, and that the United States and other Western nations need to develop retaliatory measures better tailored to state-owned companies. Yet in public, both Congress and the White House continue to call for punishing state-owned firms from China and other countries that violate trade rules with the same tactics used in the past, that is, WTO cases and punitive tariffs like these used in the past against private multinationals that violate trade rules or against entire industries from one country that violate trade rules.

OR PERHAPS FAIR IS FAIR

Yet examples already exist of state firms, from China and elsewhere, which have matched the profitability and governance of Western multinationals; state companies *can* be accountable and transparent and profitable, without the crutch of massive state subsidies or illegal tariffs to protect them from real foreign competition. State companies can be accountable to the public through elections, as occurs in democratic state capitalists. Even in authoritarian states like China, some state enterprises can be relatively accountable, if the government forces executives of state enterprises to meet targets of profitability, innovation, and lack of corruption, and removes executives who do not meet these targets, and if the government enjoys a high degree of legitimacy due to widespread public support. (This is not to say that a Chinese style of accountability is the same as elections; real elections are a better way of holding a government and its state companies accountable.) Executives of state enterprises and government officials in a state capitalist system can be transparent by putting their full financial results and minutes of major executive meetings online, appointing independent directors to their boards, hiring independent auditors, and setting clear benchmarks for success.

Some state firms have already taken some of these steps. For example, Emirates, the flagship airline of Dubai, one of the emirates within the United Arab Emirates, has used both state support and transparent, foresighted management by executives recruited from all over the airline industry to build itself into the largest long-haul carrier in the world, and a byword for service and luxurious flying. After reporting a profit in 2013, Emirates had been profitable for twenty-six straight years, and in late 2013 it placed one of the largest orders of planes from Boeing in the aircraft manufacturer's history.[26] From a minor player in the global air market twenty years ago, Emirates could by the end of the 2010s surpass the biggest American carriers as the largest airline in the world by available seat miles, a common standard for judging the size of airlines. Already, Emirates has won a large share of the market for flights from Europe to

Asia from some of the big European carriers that once dominated these routes, like Lufthansa, Air France/KLM, and British Airways. As the airline has grown, Dubai International Airport, Emirates's home base, has mushroomed from a small regional airfield to the busiest international airport in the world, in terms of passengers served.[27]

In fact, as we have seen, the most successful state capitalist nations do boast *some* state companies that are leaders in new technology and do find ways, other than relying on domestic monopolies and state supports, to compete globally with private-sector multinationals. These firms have become competitive around the world by building new technologies, finding niches, exploiting economies of scale, using cheaper labor, working harder, and making investments that pay off.

And despite the common, mistaken idea that Beijing controls every move of state firms, Chinese state oil and gas companies have become globally competitive in part because they are willing, as China resources specialists Elizabeth Economy and Michael Levi note, "to take large political and security risks, particularly when Western companies will not."[28] Chinese firms were willing to gamble on drilling in Angola, plagued by years of civil strife, horrific infrastructure, and a predatory regime, well before Western multinationals would venture into the country. Now, many Western multinationals are setting up shop in Angola, whose civil war has ended, whose political system has become more stable, and whose economy is projected by the World Bank to be one of the fastest growing in the world over the next twenty-five years.[29]

Economy and Levi also note that some of the loans and other types of support for Chinese firms investing abroad are not so different from schemes that Western companies have long used.[30] Although many Western multinationals have complained that state companies from China, Russia, and other states frequently win contracts to build infrastructure or provide goods in developing countries because they offer off-the-books sweeteners to these nations' governments, a recent study by the *Financial Times* found that the twelve biggest Western defense companies all do the same thing, a practice known in the defense industry as "offsetting."[31] In "offsetting," major defense firms like Lockheed Martin, Raytheon, Europe's EADS, and Sweden's Saab agree to pay governments side sweetener deals if those governments agree to buy their fighter jets, ships, missile technology, or other products. To take one example that the *Financial Times* uncovered, the

British defense company BAE Systems agreed to pay Oman to upgrade the country's fishing industry if Oman, in turn, would buy from it. Lockheed Martin has amassed so many "offset" obligations that it owes its arms customers some $27 billion, the paper found, ten times what Lockheed Martin actually makes in annual profits.[32] These offsets, often done in an extremely opaque manner, have been harshly criticized by the WTO and other free-trade groups.

LABOR, ENVIRONMENTAL, AND TRANSPARENCY IMPACTS

Another significant threat from state-owned companies from Russia and China and to a lesser extent other authoritarian state capitalists is that they have few incentives to uphold international norms of environmental protection, corporate transparency, or labor rights. Indeed, many critics focus on the path of destruction to forests, rivers, air, and workers wrought by these state companies as they expand around the globe. As we have seen in Myanmar, many Chinese state companies have low labor, environmental, and safety standards, particularly when operating overseas. These companies' opaque corporate structures, histories of graft and bribery, and unresponsiveness to shareholders can makes it easy for them to evade punishments for bribing officials in countries where they invest. Globally, there are many documented instances of Chinese and Russian firms committing environmental and labor violations. There is reason to believe that, at least in the short run, as Chinese and Russian state companies expand further overseas, these types of abuses are going to increase dramatically.

One of the most extensive examinations of Chinese state companies' overseas investments, and the environmental and labor catastrophes they have caused, is in a long, heavily reported book on Chinese companies' activities in Africa, *China's Silent Army: The Pioneers, Traders, Fixers and Workers Who Are Remaking the World in Beijing's Image*, by Spanish journalists Juan Pablo Cardenal and Heriberto Araujo.[33] Working from extensive on-the-ground research, Cardenal and Araujo argue that Chinese investment overseas is likely to have massively negative effects on labor rights, corporate governance, and environmental protection throughout the developing world.

The two Spanish journalists also illustrate how ignoring basic environmental, transparency, and labor standards gives some Chinese state enterprises enormous advantages over multinational competitors. These Chinese state enterprises can pay lower wages, influence government officials aggressively by handing out cash, and spend little money on environmental impact surveys or modifying projects to reduce the impact on local environments. However, the journalists also reveal that, at times, private Chinese companies operating in Africa and other developing regions follow as bad or worse labor and environmental standards as the state firms. In contrast to Chinese companies, American multinationals are subject to the Foreign Corrupt Practices Act, US federal legislation passed in 1977 that made it illegal for American companies and individuals to pay foreign officials to win business. Most developed democracies have similar legislation on the books that prevents companies from their countries from bribing foreign officials to win business. To be sure, many Western multinationals in the natural resources industry have been accused of environmental destruction and ignoring local labor rights. Yet at least these Western multinationals can be held accountable in some ways, in addition to facing possible sanction under laws like the Foreign Corrupt Practices Act. US companies that commit environmental and labor abuses abroad not only face significant media and NGO investigations into their operations but they can potentially be sued, in American courts, by plaintiffs from the countries where they committed abuses. These suits are filed under a US law called the Alien Tort Claims Act. Many other leading democracies also have laws that allow plaintiffs from foreign countries to sue, back in a company's home country, for damages from environmental and labor abuses committed in the plaintiffs' nations. In fact, Unocal, a major US oil company that was eventually bought by Chevron, faced such a suit in the 1990s and 2000s by Burmese villagers. The villagers alleged that Unocal, in cooperation with the Myanmar military, had overseen massive rights abuses—including summary executions, forced labor, and torture—alongside Unocal's Yadana gas pipeline. Facing the possibility of substantial losses after a federal appeals court allowed the Burmese villagers' suit to go forward, Unocal reached a private settlement in 2005 that apparently included direct compensation payments to the plaintiffs.

One well-known example of the destructive impact of Chinese investment has taken place in Sudan. Most Western oil and gas firms were barred by sanctions from doing business with the brutal Sudanese regime, accused of abetting massacres in Darfur and southern Sudan. Chinese state firms have come to dominate the oil industry in Sudan. Chinese investment in Sudan, the two Spanish journalists found, appears to not only have helped the government of long-time Sudanese dictator Omar Bashir survive—for which China was criticized widely by other nations—but also to have resulted in large-scale displacement of people near oil and gas facilities in Sudan, as well as severe impacts on the environment alongside the pipeline built by Chinese firms through Sudan. One of the big Chinese state oil companies operating in Sudan, CNPC, allegedly spilled large amounts of crude oil on several occasions, with little effective cleanup. The company refused to meet with local Sudanese angry about CNPC's investments, and refused engagement with most international NGOs that tried to meet with CNPC in Sudan or in Beijing.

CNPC's actions in Sudan were hardly unique; they were consistent with the company's actions in many of the roughly thirty countries around the world where it has major investments. In a broad assessment of CNPC's environmental, labor, and transparency policies around the world, global environmental NGO Friends of the Earth concluded:

> The company has made broad statements that reflect the belief that the environment and society are important factors in the company's continued development, both at home and abroad. But as yet CNPC has not developed policies or designated personnel at the corporate level to specifically govern the environmental and social conduct of its overseas subsidiaries . . . A recent survey of 44 leading oil companies by Transparency International and Revenue Watch Institute found that CNPC scored below average in terms of its disclosure of anti-corruption initiatives and policies, company-level organizational and financial information and payments at the country level; all of which present corruption risks to the company. Indeed, CNPC and its subsidiaries have been accused of corrupt business practices.[34]

Other examples of these negative impacts on labor rights, the environment, and government transparency are more obscure than the abuses that took place in Sudan, which were covered by many international media outlets. Chinese state-owned enterprises have been linked to environmental disasters, graft, and labor abuses from Peru to the Philippines to Papua New Guinea to Myanmar, where I found anger at Chinese state companies in 2013 and 2014 the highest I had seen in fifteen years of reporting in Myanmar. Burmese anger was cresting at CNPC's Shwe gas pipeline project, a 1,700-mile overland pipeline that brings gas from offshore Burmese fields through the country and into southwestern China. (CNPC is one of several companies involved in the Shwe gas pipeline, but CNPC is believed to be the biggest investor in the project, though the overall amounts invested by each company remain opaque.) The pipeline project allegedly has resulted in massive deforestation, dumping of waste directly into rivers, eviction of thousands of Myanmar farmers from land traversed by the pipeline with minimal or no compensation, abuses of locals living by the pipeline route by the Myanmar security forces and forces working for CNPC, and many other serious labor and environmental problems.[35] Although several Myanmar and foreign NGOs have extensively reported on the problems caused by the Shwe gas pipeline project and have tried to bring their concerns to CNPC representatives in Yangon and in Beijing, they have gotten little direct response from CNPC.

In Papua New Guinea, meanwhile, the Metallurgical Corporation of China, a state-owned company involved in everything from mining to manufacturing metal-working equipment, paid $1.4 billion to buy the rights to develop the Ramu nickel mine in 2005, at that time the largest investment in natural resources in resource-rich Papua New Guinea. Although the mine proved enormously rich—by 2013, when it had started running at full capacity, the Ramu mine produced over thirty thousand tons of nickel per year—the Chinese operator soon angered local landholders and the Papua New Guinea government in Port Moresby.[36] The Chinese firm dumped toxic by-products of the mine into a nearby bay, with little analysis of how these toxins would affect marine life or the health of people living around the bay. The Papua New Guinea government became so angry that it forced the mine to shut down for a time. Yet the government, one of the most corrupt in the world, was receiving so much revenue from the Ramu mine that it let the mine reopen, and the mine continued to dump toxins into the bay. By the middle of 2014, local environmental groups again were reporting widespread deaths of marine life in areas surrounding the mine, though the company continued to deny that dumping had anything to do with problems in the bay.[37]

Western multinationals have also been guilty of serious labor and environmental abuses in Papua New Guinea. Anglo-Australian mining giant

BHP Billiton for years operated the Ok Tedi Mine in the country's western highlands, mining for copper and gold and causing massive environmental destruction, including leveling forests, dumping mining waste into nearby rivers, and eroding watersheds. However, in contrast to the Chinese companies now operating in Papua New Guinea, BHP Billiton could be influenced by shareholders, media accounts, NGOs, and lawsuits filed under Australian law. After years of media reports of the destruction caused by the Ok Tedi Mine, by the 1990s BHP Billiton was coming under increasing pressure from Australian NGOs and politicians to divest from Ok Tedi, and also faced a lawsuit by villagers living near the mine. The company eventually settled with the villagers out of court, admitted it had made huge environmental mistakes at Ok Tedi, and allowed the Papua New Guinea government to take control of the mine operations and use the proceeds for local development and environmental cleanup.

STATE COMPANIES VERSUS PRIVATE COMPANIES IN AUTHORITARIAN STATE CAPITALISTS

It remains unclear however, whether privately owned companies from China or other authoritarian state capitalists have better records of labor rights and environmental protection than state enterprises from authoritarian countries. Council on Foreign Relations senior fellows Elizabeth Economy and Michael Levi studied China's global quest for resources and found that about two-thirds of mining firms in China, for example, are small, privately owned companies, many of which are now investing in mining operations outside of China.[38] In one country that Economy and Levi studied in depth, Ghana, they found that much of the new Chinese investment coming into the country's mining sector was from small, privately owned, and mostly unregulated Chinese companies.[39] Most of these small, privately owned mining operations had no knowledge of the local environment or how to conduct a basic environmental impact assessment. Ghana's minister for lands and natural resources, Alhaji Inusah Fuseini, warned Chinese officials visiting Ghana that these investors were causing extensive environmental destruction and, not coincidentally, badly damaging the overall image of China in Ghana.

Indeed, through my own research I have found that many of the Chinese companies allegedly involved in land-grabbing; bribing local officials;

working with abusive security forces; and destroying pristine forests in Laos, Cambodia, and Myanmar are small, privately owned companies, not state behemoths.[40] Small Chinese firms, sometimes no more than just one family company, have played a central role in the new rubber industry that has emerged in Laos, for example, over the past two decades. These Chinese companies often make deals with local Lao officials in border regions to take control of land in Laos, where land tenure and land rights remain hard to establish for local people. Several aid workers in Laos who had studied the rubber industry told me that Chinese firms had bribed most of the senior officials in northern Laos to allow the Chinese companies to obtain land tenure and set up rubber plantations; if locals protested, Lao security forces would arrest or evict them.

The small Chinese companies operating in northern Laos have no stockholders, no global image to protect, and often not even a real name and mailing address. They export the grown rubber back to China but are totally obscure in the global rubber supply chain. Yet these small companies have had a devastating effect on northern Laos, which only twenty or thirty years ago was home to some of the richest virgin forest in Southeast Asia. Much of the forest of northern Laos has since the mid-2000s been cut down to build rubber plantations owned by these Chinese firms, leaving the land near the Chinese border denuded, arid, badly eroded, and pocked with stumps of trees and deep holes in the ground.[41]

State companies from relatively democratic nations, like Brazil or South Africa, generally have better records on labor rights and environmental protection than state firms or private companies from authoritarian states. These state companies from democratic nations often are held to higher standards of governance by shareholders and their own publics, and in these nations government officials rotate regularly and do not necessarily—or simply cannot—seek to control state-owned firms with an iron hand. These state companies cannot make profitable investments overseas forever if they adhere to such low labor, environmental, and safety standards that they wind up alienating workers, consumers, and government in foreign nations where they are operating. Unlike state companies from authoritarian states, these state-owned companies from countries like Brazil or South Africa or Norway cannot count on endless government support or protection from claims of labor or environmental abuses. They also potentially can be sued back at home for abuses committed abroad.

In addition, because many of these countries have strong domestic civil societies, state-owned companies from these democracies face regular criticism from NGOs and media outlets at home about their conduct of business around the world—criticism that Russian, Chinese, and Vietnamese state-owned companies rarely have to face. In countries like Vietnam and China, groups that have tried to act as watchdogs of large domestic infrastructure projects, monitoring graft, land-grabbing, and environmental destruction at sites like the Three Gorges Dam, have had their members arrested or simply disappeared.

Overall, the most important factor in the behavior of state companies outside their borders on labor and environmental issues is the type of political environment they come from at home, not whether their home country has a more or less economically interventionist government. In many ways, the overseas investments of state-owned companies from democratic state capitalists more closely resemble those of Western multinationals than they do those of state-owned enterprises from authoritarian nations.

11

Prescriptions for the Future

Responding to the implications of the growth of state capitalism will be critical for all the actors affected by the rebirth of statist economics. Yet at the same time, countries, multinational corporations, and other actors should not overreact to the emergence of this modern type of state capitalism, and should not assume that governments utilizing state-capitalist strategies are threats to democracy, free trade, and international security. All of these actors must recognize the different varieties of state capitalists, comprehend what makes state capitalists threatening—and what does not—and develop policies that differentiate between and respond to the multiple types of state capitalism. In addition, all of these actors must understand the five major potential threats of state capitalism and should respond appropriately to each one's challenge to economic freedom, international institutions, global security, and democracy and human rights.

MULTINATIONALS

First, Accept the Shift

For private multinationals, the first implication of the continued growth of state capitalists is one that many corporate executives have been in denial about for years already: state companies are not going away.

As we have seen, some fears about state companies' unfair advantages are real. But the portrayal of all state companies as inherently dangerous, both to multinationals' profits and to Western nations' security, is common among executives of multinationals, in part because they (and many politicians, analysts, and academics) often see the rise of state capitalism as a phenomenon primarily about China and China's state companies rather than understanding the differences among state capitalists. Of course, as we have seen, China is a major part of the growth of state capitalism, and some of these complaints about Chinese state companies certainly ring true. But China is not the whole story, and many of the democratic state capitalists and their state companies are no more threatening than private multinationals.

See the Differences in State Capitalism and Exploit Them

Indeed, focusing exclusively on Chinese state companies and viewing them primarily as a monolithic threat is committing several mistakes at once. For one, state capitalism is growing in China, in other authoritarian developing nations, and also in many boisterous democracies like Brazil and Indonesia. Second, the world of state companies—even state companies from one state—is hardly monolithic. There is a vast diversity of state companies even within a single country. If Western multinationals cannot learn to look beyond China, and make distinctions among state companies even from the same country, then these multinationals will miss out on major business opportunities and will not be able to compete effectively with state companies. On the other hand, multinationals that are able to differentiate between the many types of state companies, to understand which state companies are well-governed, profitable, and innovative, will be better able to compete with state companies—and to partner with state firms that could make powerful allies in certain situations.

Rebuild Your Strengths

Western multinationals still have huge competitive advantages over state companies from most nations. Western multinationals should, however, understand the areas where they still retain advantages over most state firms and ignore the idea of trying to beat state capitalists at their own games.

For one, most developed nations have a wealth of mature, large venture capital firms, while many state capitalists do not have much of a venture capital sector at all. Western venture capital giants can help small and innovative firms like Facebook grow, while in emerging markets such innovative companies, once they get large enough to leave the state's embrace, often have nowhere to turn. And in a world where the emerging market giants are learning to innovate, while also deploying their large and inexpensive workforces, and sizable savings, any advantage will be critical. In addition, most Western multinationals still enjoy edges over state company competitors in high-end innovation. State companies from Brazil, China, India, Singapore, and others have increased the number of patents applied for since the early 2000s, but most of these patents still remain inventions in lower-value-added technology, services, and processing, and not as valuable in the long term as the patents taken by most Western multinationals. Similarly, while the Chinese state's funding of science and technology research is impressive, and continues to grow while state funding for science in Western countries declines, some analysts have questioned whether Beijing's science funding really encourages much innovation. Timothy Beardsen, a veteran investment banker in Asia and author of a recent book questioning China's long-term economic strategy, argues that about 80 percent of government and private-sector Chinese funding of research and development goes into product development, with only about 5 percent of the money going toward basic science research. "This is an important point, as basic research promotes real inventiveness," he writes, though he also notes that Beijing has realized this and is beginning to increase funding for basic research.[1] By contrast, in Japan and the United States, about 13 to 19 percent of all government and private-sector funding for research and development in science and technology goes into basic science research.[2]

In addition, many state companies have little idea how to develop and brand the innovations and products they do put out. In a 2015 ranking by Interbrand, a consulting agency, of the hundred most valuable global brands in terms of success at getting consumers to buy that product, *none* of the brands came from state companies, a telling indicator of state firms' long way to go in consumer-oriented industries.[3]

Yet when investing in developing countries, many multinationals all but give away their high-end technology by partnering with domestic state companies and not imposing tough enough restrictions on technology transfer. They thus allow domestic "partners" to copy high-end technology. "Everyone gets their stuff [technology] stolen by their Chinese partners, but no big company is going to make too big a stink about it because they don't want to get cut out of the China market," says one longtime legal advisor to foreign companies in Shanghai. Foreign investors are likewise unwilling to alienate the host country government in Thailand, Malaysia, and many other developing countries with valuable domestic consumer markets.

Without facing the threat of losing consumer markets, multinationals will never be able to retain their technology. In the few instances—in Malaysia, Thailand, Vietnam, China, and other countries—where multinationals have refused to engage in joint ventures that they feared would lead to intellectual property theft, they were not railroaded out of the country, since their investment dollars, their global brand name, and their cachet were too important to lose. Indeed, the threat of pulling out of a country can prove a tool with enormous leverage, provided a multinational is willing to use that tool.

Instead of focusing on their advantages, some multinationals have tried to adopt the techniques and strategies of their state-capitalist competitors. Some Western and Asian private multinationals, concerned about state capitalists' abilities to offer low-interest loans or even bribes to government officials, have urged their home country governments to relax policies designed to promote transparency in corporate governance, or they have pushed their governments to reduce or eliminate restrictions on where companies can invest. For example, Western companies, and some Western political leaders, argued throughout the 2000s against sanctions on Myanmar imposed by many democratic nations because of the Myanmar military regime's atrocious human rights record. While Western companies sat on the sidelines, they argued, Chinese, Thai, Singaporean, and Indian firms exploited Myanmar's oil and gas and other natural resources.

But as Myanmar shows, Western multinationals that try to compete by taking on the same political risks as state companies, matching state companies' wallets, or ignoring human rights usually do not succeed. When sanctions were relaxed or lifted in Myanmar in the early and mid-2010s, many Western companies entered the country and began assessing offshore oil and gas deposits, potential copper mines, and an untapped consumer market for nearly every item. Most Western companies found that, though they had pressured their home governments to engage

Myanmar, and though some top Myanmar officials eagerly courted Western investment, these multinationals still could not—or did not want to—compete with Chinese, Indian, Thai, Malaysian, and Singaporean state companies operating in Myanmar. The Western multinationals did not have home country government officials who would hand out money to senior Myanmar leaders, as several Thai politicians allegedly did, or home country state banks who would subsidize investments in Myanmar that, because of the country's horrid physical infrastructure and tangled political environment, could take thirty years to make money. Despite Myanmar's changes, many Western governments' leaders remained reticent to appear too cozy with top Myanmar politicians, for fear of being blasted by a still-active Myanmar human rights lobby that held sway in Western capitals.

Western multinationals faced other hurdles in Myanmar that some of their state-capitalist competitors from China, Thailand, India, or Malaysia did not, such as shareholders who frown on the kind of bribe-paying that had become the norm in Myanmar and laws like the US Foreign Corrupt Practices Act or similar legislation in most European nations.

So, despite Myanmar's potential, most of the Western executives that had visited the country when sanctions were lifted had, by the mid-2010s, decided to wait to make significant investments in Myanmar.[4] Only Myanmar's offshore gas deposits, potentially some of the richest in the world, and isolated from many of the developing country's challenges, continued to hold the same allure to investors. As the *Wall Street Journal* reported, despite the relaxation of US sanctions on Myanmar, by 2015 US companies had committed just $2 million in official investments in the country of fifty million people.[5] In contrast, US companies had invested over ten times as much in Luxembourg, a country of roughly 500,000 people.

Curb SOEs by Enlisting Private Companies
in State-Capitalist Nations

Ultimately, it is private companies in state-capitalist nations, particularly in China, that could possibly play the biggest role in reducing the advantages given to state enterprises. In China, for example, although many middle-class, urban Chinese are proud of the ability of large Chinese state enterprises' ability to compete in the world, Chinese employed in the private sector also are frequently furious at the advantages offered by Beijing to state companies. These domestic private companies could be enlisted by multinationals to help push their governments to dismantle state enterprises and to promote more competition in many industries.

Nearly every Chinese private company, for example, has a story of having to contend with state enterprises' enormous clout. In one common case, highlighted across China by microblogs—China's version of Twitter—and the foreign press, a prominent, privately owned Chinese biotechnology company, Cathay Industrial Biotech, developed a new process to make types of nylon critical to drugs and other industrial applications and then applied for multiple patents. Cathay received major orders from Dupont Chemical and several rounds of investment from foreign private equity investors. Yet a state-controlled company called Hilead Biotech allegedly stole Cathay's secret process and ingredients and then used them to produce almost identical types of nylon; when Cathay sued Hilead for patent infringement, the government backed Hilead.[6] Cathay won a first round of the suit, showing that Chinese courts were gaining independence, at least when dealing with commercial matters, but as of 2015 the case continued to drag on, holding back Cathay's development of its products and inhibiting the company's growth.

CITIZENS OF STATE-CAPITALIST NATIONS

Make Governments Balance Efficiency with Job Creation

More than any other actors, citizens of countries where state intervention in the economy is growing will be affected by this new economic model. For citizens and leaders of state-capitalist nations, creating a balance in state companies between profitability and delivering some broader social goods will be critical. Even in an undemocratic system, the public often has ways to influence the government, and citizens can push for the government to create incentives for officials and state company executives to promote broad-based development and to meet profitability targets.

Sometimes, this state intervention may inhibit corporate profitability, making it less efficient than allowing the market to rule, yet pure economic efficiency is not always desirable or popular. For example, Norway's willingness to tolerate lower profits in exchange for state companies promoting some social good is exactly the type of "double bottom line" that analysts of state firms fear will make these companies unfocused and unable to compete with companies whose sole aim is to be profitable. Yet many Norwegian state firms have remained profitable while also investing money back into Norwegian social welfare programs.

Make State Capitalism Public Capitalism

If governments are going to intervene in economies, they cannot do so successfully—if success is measured by broad-based growth—over the long term without high degrees of public legitimacy. Without referendums on and monitoring of a state's economic performance, there are no metrics to assess whether economic interventions are beneficial to publics or only to a few government insiders.

People living in state-capitalist nations, then, must struggle to make state capitalism beneficial to the public in general; if it is not beneficial, they must work to change their economic systems and possibly their political systems. In democracies like Brazil or Indonesia, changing the political system may not mean tearing down the whole system but rather tinkering with it by amending constitutions and passing new legislation, or simply by voting in a new government. It is clear that the best way to obtain legitimacy for state intervention is, of course, through elections and other tools of democratic governance.

But several authoritarian or semi-authoritarian governments like China, Singapore in the past, and Malaysia have obtained some degree of legitimacy for their economic programs without holding truly free elections. Citizens of these nations where the government is authoritarian yet still somewhat responsive to public opinion must utilize the avenues for input that their governments currently have provided to hold regimes accountable, while also steadily applying pressure for greater political freedom. (The ways in which citizens could push for greater political freedom vary widely, and could take a whole book to describe, but some methods include public protest, promoting a freer print and online media, and taking advantage of periods of leadership transition to prod regimes to promote political reforms.) For example, Malaysia and Singapore have achieved a degree of legitimacy, at times, through regular town hall meetings and online conversations with their populations. These town halls and online forums are possible in small states like Singapore and Malaysia but unfeasible in a country with a sizable population and land area. Citizens could utilize these town hall meetings and online conversations to aggressively push for transparency in government policies and to publicly shame government officials who are unwilling to release information about state spending, state companies, and state funds.

Sometimes, as in China today or Singapore during its authoritarian past, undemocratic but responsive regimes have achieved some degree of legitimacy because the dominant political party consults regularly with opinion leaders and responds relatively effectively to public opinion, even if the party does not use elections to obtain public input. Opinion leaders in these nations can utilize these consultations, such as Chinese political leaders' closed-door Party school sessions with prominent academics, to convince politicians that embracing transparency in state spending, state companies, and state funds will improve economic efficiency and will be popular with the public.

Foster Selective Intervention

If citizens of state-capitalist nations are to make their economic systems work for them, they must also ensure that governments are only intervening selectively in the economy. State capitalists that are open, responsive, and innovative also tend to be selective in their interventions, as we have seen. Beijing does not dominate the economy as in the old Soviet Union or in today's crushingly statist economies like North Korea or Eritrea. Beijing allows private companies to flourish in many industries. Though the Chinese banking sector is still too focused on SOEs, private entrepreneurs have more avenues to raise capital now than they did two decades ago, including informal local urban lenders, foreign private equity investors including investors from Taiwan and Hong Kong, and seed capital from larger, established private companies in their industries.[7] In 2014, China had roughly forty-one million private companies, up from only five million private companies in China in 2006.[8]

In China, the central government also tries to force state companies to compete with each other, which they often do. The largest state-owned telecommunications, resources, and construction firms have challenged each other to win contracts in China and in developing nations around the world. To take one example, in bidding for a dominant stake in a pipeline across Sudan in 2005—a pipe across what was already one of China's leading sources of oil—state enterprises CNPC and Sinopec competed directly against each other for the contract.[9]

Prevent Government Mismanagement

What's more, successful state capitalists like Singapore and Norway create significant checks on the state's ability to mismanage the economy and try to blend the best elements of state capitalism with the best elements of global competition. Citizens of state-capitalist nations must insist that their governments operate with these real checks on the state's power. State-capitalist nations could set caps on the percentage of state companies that the state is allowed to own, reducing the possibility that leaders will use state companies and SWFs for political aims. For instance, Norway's government can only own up to 62.5 percent of the biggest Norwegian state firms, like oil giant Statoil.[10] State-capitalist nations also could recruit widely for leadership positions for state companies and SWFs, bringing in better talent and reducing the possibility that these companies and funds will be captured by one political party. Singapore and Norway, for example, search wide pools of talent to find leaders for their state companies and state funds. They put independent directors on the boards of their SWFs and biggest state companies, and they create term limits for executives of their funds and state companies.

Even China, for all its flaws, has put into place some mechanisms for drawing upon a broad range of talent to lead state firms. The influx of private-sector businesspeople into the Communist Party has exposed senior Party leaders to a much wider group of businesspeople and has created a larger talent pool for executive positions at SOEs. Indeed, many SOEs have poached top executives from truly private Chinese companies, and some have begun to add foreign directors to their boards as well.

The economically successful state capitalists utilize other measures as well to improve transparency and prevent mismanagement at state companies and state funds. Successful state capitalists usually offer open, real-time reports on the investments on their SWFs, such as by posting these reports on the funds' and companies' websites. They also sign up to international standards for governance of SWFs, standards known as the Santiago Principles.

GOVERNMENTS

Prioritize the Threats

Governments, particularly that of the United States, must prioritize the five major challenges posed by state capitalism. To review, the first threat is the possibility that state capitalism will foster democratic regression, and the second challenge is that this regression will undermine political stability in countries that are strategically important to the United States and the world. As we have seen, state capitalism's threat to undermine democracy is unlikely in established democracies—Norway is not going to become an autocratic state. The United States should worry about state capitalism's impact on democracy only in a handful of strategically important developing nations that have weak or failed democracies and that also have embraced state capitalism. State capitalism's impact on democracy in strategically irrelevant nations like Timor-Leste should remain a low priority for the United States and other leading democratic powers. The United States and other leading nations also should be relatively unconcerned about state capitalism's impact on political freedom in developing countries like Indonesia where, despite growing economic nationalism, democracy is thoroughly entrenched.

As state capitalism potentially undermines political freedom in strategically important nations where democracy is not entrenched, state capitalism also potentially contributes to political instability in these countries. This instability endangers these nations' relations with the United States. These countries of concern include Thailand, Malaysia, South Africa, and Egypt, among others (see figure 11.1).

Already, as we have seen, political regression and state capitalism in Thailand and Malaysia have impaired these nations' abilities to partner with the United States on a range of economic and security issues.

Thailand	Venezuela
Malaysia	Myanmar
South Africa	Argentina
Ukraine	Egypt

FIGURE 11.1. Countries of Concern.

As a result, the United States and other leading democracies should employ several strategies to solidify democracy in these countries of concern. These strategies would include, most importantly, making US aid less contingent on countries embracing free-market economic reforms. Assistance should focus on politics, and not on economics, separating democracy promotion from promoting economic liberalization. Right now, US government aid, as well as aid from many other countries and private foundations, tends to link promoting democracy with promoting economic freedom. Indeed, both US government donors and many private donors that finance democracy promotion and civil society in developing Asia, Africa, and Latin America now automatically assume that a state that is curtailing economic freedoms would be a poor choice to receive democracy promotion assistance. Yet we have seen that countries can be democratizing while also becoming less free economically.

Making a shift to funding democracy promotion programs in countries regardless of how they manage their economies would be a major break from recent trends in American foreign aid. It might be challenging to get such a shift approved by congresspeople who also link promoting economic and political freedom. But showing private donors, US government aid agencies, academic specialists in democracy promotion, and congresspeople and Congressional staff examples of successful democratization in varied economic environments can help foster this delinking of democracy promotion and promoting market reforms. (However, this delinking does not mean that donors should not push for the basics of good governance in developing countries; good governance can exist in state capitalists, as seen by Norway, Singapore, and other examples.) To take one example, several congressional delegations that visited Indonesia in the late 2000s and early 2010s, comprised of congresspeople from both American political parties and their staffers, came home impressed by Indonesia's democratization. Many of these congresspeople and their staffers returned home supportive of greater US democracy promotion assistance for Indonesia, even though they also saw that the economic climate in Indonesia had become increasingly nationalistic and statist. They saw that, in Indonesia, the two types of freedoms were not necessarily linked, and that the two types of aid to Indonesia need not be linked either.

Prepare for Autocratic State Capitalists' Meltdowns

Responding to the growth of state capitalism at times requires making preparations and taking actions that could seem contradictory. But because the challenges posed by state capitalism are so varied, the responses must be varied as well. So, even as the United States and other democracies treat some aspects of state capitalism as a threat because of its strength, they must also prepare for the implications of some state capitalists' weaknesses, the third challenge posed by the growth of state capitalism.

This preparation includes developing a better understanding of whether or not some state capitalists' economic weaknesses would be in the United States and other democracies' strategic interests. The United States and other leading economies should consider, now, which of the major state capitalists are likely to suffer drastic economic slowdowns in the next ten years, and whether—and why—the United States and other countries might organize economic bailouts for these nations. In some cases, the strategic gains that came from these countries' economic downturns would be large enough to offset the harm to the world economy, and so the United States might quietly celebrate the economic slowdown. In other cases, the strategic gains would not outweigh the potential negative impact to the world economy of a state capitalist's economic weakness, and the United States and other leading nations might help these state-capitalist economies to recover.

For example, although Russia's economy is important to the world economy, there could be a strategic upside to a Russian economic slowdown. A severe slowdown could undermine Vladimir Putin, reduce Russia's ability to threaten its neighbors, and possibly precipitate political change in Russia. Of course, a Russian economic slowdown also could lead an authoritarian Kremlin to become more aggressive in its foreign policy, as a means of uniting the Russian public and defusing dissent. Still, in the long run, economic weakness would make it difficult for the Kremlin to sustain an aggressive foreign policy, if that foreign policy required significant outlays of money for military actions.

A Russian economic slowdown, even a severe one, thus might lead to no response from the United States and Europe. Having already discussed in detail—now, before any Russian collapse—Russian contingencies with major partners like the European Union and Japan, the United States would be prepared to quickly understand how severe a Russian economic downturn might be, how much this slowdown might impact the world economy, and how the slowdown might affect Kremlin's behavior abroad and at home. Similarly, a long-term economic slowdown in Iran, or in several Central Asian autocracies, might create significant strategic benefits for the United States and other democracies; the United States should examine Iranian and Central Asian economic contingencies in much greater detail.

In contrast to the Russian example, the United States and other democracies probably would not celebrate severe economic slowdowns in autocratic state capitalists like the United Arab Emirates or Vietnam that pose little threat to their neighbors and that are largely responsible members of international institutions. Many of these nations, like Vietnam or the UAE, also are close strategic partners of the United States. A severe economic slowdown in one of these countries thus would be of little benefit and would have potentially significant effects on the world economy. The United States and its major economic partners thus should be prepared to assist these autocratic state capitalists in the event of severe economic downturns, by offering the types of credit and aid packages provided to other countries in times of economic distress, like Thailand in 1997.

How does China fit into this puzzle? Would a severe Chinese economic slowdown be an event that the United States and other Western nations would (quietly) celebrate, since a Chinese economic slowdown—far beyond the reduction in growth that could be expected from a reduction in state spending and an end to China's debt bubble—could have strategic benefits for the United States and could foster political reform in China? Lacking the legitimacy provided by strong economic growth, Beijing might have to seek other means of gaining legitimacy, like holding real elections—at least, according to one theory. In addition, an economically weaker China would have little ability to promote its model of development to other nations, and might have to significantly curtail its military spending, which has risen from roughly $15 billion in 2001 to over $130 billion in 2014, according to China's own published statistics. Reduced military spending would impact China's ability to threaten its neighbors in Asia, to build up its navy in a possible effort to force US ships out of many Pacific waters, and to achieve other military goals. A weaker China might allow other East Asian nations to cut their military budgets as well, stopping a regional arms race. All of these changes would, on balance, be positive strategically for the United States and for its partners in Asia.

Still, should the United States and other leading democracies sit back and do nothing if China's economy goes into a deep and dangerous recession, which has not happened in China in over thirty years? No. The United States and other leading democracies should take steps to try to defuse the appeal of China's economic model, and to stop China from using state companies as weapons. However, reducing the threat, or even encouraging Chinese leaders to manage a slowdown in growth and an end to China's bubbles, does not mean wishing for a Chinese economic collapse. China's economy is too large, too important to the world economy, and too important to the United States for Washington and other leading democracies to desire a serious Chinese economic slowdown, which easily could push the world economy back into a long-term recession. In other words, while the strategic gains of a Russian economic slide might well be worth the costs to the world economy, the strategic gains from a severe Chinese downturn would not outweigh the serious potential impact to the world economy. The United States, other developed nations, and international financial institutions should have discussions, now, about how they would help Beijing handle a severe Chinese economic slowdown, and whether the United States, Germany, other rich countries, and the international financial institutions even have the means to assist Beijing if China's economy ever slowed down dramatically.

Understand, But Don't Hype the China Model

The fourth challenge is that state capitalists, principally China, may be successful enough economically that they will be able to promote a model of authoritarian state capitalism to other countries, undermining democracy and economic freedom in other nations. Yet American officials and others interested in China's model need a more nuanced understanding of what is most threatening about the so-called Beijing Consensus. Although China's continued economic success rests in part on its state-capitalist strategy, and although that economic success is important to China's influence over foreign officials through training programs and aid, it is the anti-democratic elements of this training and aid, not the pro-economic interventionist elements, which should primarily worry the United States and other democracies. The anti-democratic elements should be more worrying because we have seen no clear evidence that state intervention in economies, whether promoted by China or not, necessarily makes countries less free politically, or more challenging to US strategic interests. So, even if other countries adopt some of China's economic strategies, this shift would not necessarily make these countries more challenging to US strategic interests or to democratic rights and freedoms. However, adopting China's political strategies—particularly at a time when the Xi Jinping government has repressed dissent, minority rights, artistic freedom, and media freedom more harshly than any Chinese government in two decades—could potentially make other countries both more authoritarian and more challenging to US strategic interests.

Most importantly, speaking more openly and in a more nuanced way about the rise of state capitalism would help defuse the idea that China's success, the success of the so-called China model, necessarily depends on authoritarian rule. In fact, if American officials and scholars, and officials and opinion leaders from other democracies, more openly acknowledged that state capitalism is a trend occurring not only in authoritarian states like China but also in several prominent democracies—democracies that have enjoyed some economic success with state capitalism—they would, by speaking about this phenomenon, actually undermine the appeal of authoritarianism. It is, I think, impossible to overstate this point, since the idea of the China model now is completely intertwined with China's authoritarian rule, and since many leaders from developing nations automatically—and wrongly—assume that China's authoritarianism is what has prompted its massive development, without looking closely at the real details of China's economic strategy.

Recognize When State Companies are Used as Weapons

The most serious threat from state capitalism is that the two big state-capitalist authoritarian powers, China and Russia, will use their state companies as weapons in conflicts with other countries, as vehicles to control certain types of natural resources, as vehicles for obtaining and stealing sensitive technology from other nations, or as tools for undermining environmental and labor norms in countries where their state companies invest.

Combating this threat requires taking a multitude of approaches simultaneously. Democracies first must be better prepared to distinguish which investments by authoritarian state capitalists are potentially threatening and which pose no more risk than any other type of foreign direct investment. What types of investments by authoritarian state capitalists are potential threats? How should governments distinguish potential threats? Few leading democracies are even prepared to make these decisions in an informed manner. Although the United States has a specific committee tasked with analyzing the national security implications of foreign investment into the United States, most other leading democracies do not have such commissions, and even the United States' commission is underfunded and understaffed.

Leading democracies should provide specific training in assessing SOEs to diplomats focused on economic issues, while also creating incentives in their diplomatic corps for economic officers to focus on one country or region throughout their careers. Similarly, the US Commerce Department and, potentially, the National Institutes of Health (NIH), should create positions for science and technology specialists who would be based in China, Brazil, India, Singapore, and other leading state capitalists to examine their government-backed science research programs and state corporations' research and development programs.[11]

Right now, although the US State Department supposedly has committed to fostering regional and country-specific knowledge, the reality is that State still provides few incentives for foreign service officers to focus on a region or country, so those who choose to do so do it because they are personally interested in that area.[12] Although State's economic officers may research and file cables on state companies while in their posts, they almost never receive training in how to analyze state corporations, even when they are going to serve in Russia or China for five years or more.

In addition, both the United States and other leading democracies should, through securities legislation, require far greater disclosure by foreign state companies that are listing subsidiaries on foreign stock exchanges. Furthermore, leading Western nations need to create consistent statistical systems to track direct investment and bond purchases by all foreign entities; right now, the European Union and many other leading democracies have no real system for tracking direct investments and bond purchases.

When countries clearly are using state-owned companies as weapons, the way Gazprom or China's state oil companies have been used, the threat is not a narrow one and must be addressed like any serious, coercive threat. Countries should prepare for these threats by reducing their reliance on state companies, like Gazprom, that have a history of being used as weapons in international disputes. And if state companies are used as weapons in international conflicts, they should be treated as instruments of war, not as economic entities. Moscow's use of Gazprom to cut off gas supplies to Ukraine and threaten other European nations, for instance, should be treated with the same tough response as if Moscow used traditional types of military coercion to bully its neighbors.

Since many of the state companies that could be used as weapons are natural resources companies, construction companies, and telecommunications firms, countries that could be threatened by these firms need to find alternative sources of resources and providers of roads, rails, ports, fiber optic cables, and other types of infrastructure. European nations, particularly those in eastern Europe, must reduce their reliance on energy from Gazprom and other Russian firms by developing a pan-European strategy for energy security. Such an energy security strategy could include gradually boosting imports from other gas suppliers like Norway and Qatar and (in the future) the United States, creating incentives to improve energy efficiency in residential and commercial buildings, storing more natural gas (Europe currently only stores about half the natural gas it has the capacity to store), and building a more connected European grid of natural gas pipelines, so that countries within Europe could more easily lend or sell each other gas, among other measures.[13] (Currently, many eastern European nations only have gas pipelines running to Russia.) In the long term, this strategy would make it much harder for Gazprom to threaten customers. The European Commission has produced a plan for increasing Europe's energy security—a plan that includes boosting production of renewable energy and working toward creating a single, connected energy market within the European Union, but so far Europe has taken few steps to implement the commission's proposals.[14]

The same logic about long-term preparation holds for countries in Asia, Africa, Latin America, and other parts of the world that have become heavily reliant on Chinese state companies to build their infrastructure. In so doing, they have potentially given Beijing too much control over critical physical and telecommunications infrastructure. Such countries need to diversify their suppliers of infrastructure over the long term. They also need to find a broader range of sources of capital for infrastructure funding. To accomplish these two goals, they can take several steps. They can make tenders for infrastructure more competitive and more transparent, to attract bids from a wider range of construction and telecommunications companies—South Korean, Japanese, Indian, and German companies, for a start. Many Japanese and German construction companies, for example, which have much experience building physical infrastructure around the world, have declined to bid on projects tendered by governments in countries from South Africa to Sri Lanka because the bidding process is opaque and the winning bids are often chosen with minimal public input. With more open bidding processes for roads, rails, ports, and other infrastructure, countries that have relied on Chinese construction companies would probably get bids from a wide range of firms. More bids, from more companies, would make the tendering process more competitive and likely would result in higher-quality roads, rails, ports, or other projects.

In addition, countries in places like Africa could pool capital to fund infrastructure projects that cross borders. This strategy, proposed by several prominent South African businesspeople, though politically challenging, would make African countries less reliant on Beijing to not only build infrastructure but also provide soft loans or grants to fund the construction—loans and grants that give China significant strategic influence. Pooling capital would allow African nations to take bids for tenders that were not necessarily the lowest bids. Being able to choose bids based on bidding companies' history, transparency, and quality of past work instead of on cost alone would lead to better quality infrastructure projects.

The next step in addressing the use of state companies as weapons of war would be to make clear to Russia, China, and any other countries that take such actions that the United States and other democracies view these tactics as security challenges, not merely economic issues. Clearly demonstrating that the use of state companies as weapons is a security challenge requires involving the Pentagon immediately in any response to actions like those taken by Gazprom in Eastern Europe, and publicly showing states like China and Russia that Washington will treat such actions as possible military matters.

The specific responses to using state companies as weapons could vary along a spectrum from rhetorical pressure by the US president and other leaders on these state firms to targeted sanctions on the leaders of a state company to broader economic sanctions against the state firm and its home country government to, in the most extreme cases, military action against the country using the state company as a weapon. Whatever the level of response they ultimately choose, the United States and other democracies must demonstrate that they do not distinguish between state companies that are serving aggressive ends and the governments taking those aggressive decisions.

To stop state firms from being used as weapons, the United States and other democracies also must better protect themselves from technology theft by state companies from authoritarian nations. The Federal Bureau of Investigation lists Russian and Chinese firms as the largest violators of intellectual property and the most likely to be involved in cybersecurity breaches. For one, the United States should encourage China to have its state companies join trade associations in countries where these state firms operate, so that the state companies have more interaction with Western multinationals, and so the US government and multinational companies can get a better understanding of how Chinese firms copy or innovate. To take one example, several Chinese state companies belong to the trade association of foreign oil companies operating in Jakarta, Indonesia. The fact that Chinese state companies belong to the Jakarta trade group has allowed other, non-Chinese oil firms working in Indonesia to gain greater understanding of the Chinese companies' operations.[15] Chinese oil companies in Indonesia joined the trade association because they, like any firm that joins, stand to benefit from the trade group's efforts to improve the local business climate for foreign oil and gas companies. Second, all US government employees should increasingly adopt the high-security practices now utilized by intelligence organizations, some companies, and some US government agencies when working in or traveling to China, Russia, and other authoritarian state capitalists known for intellectual property theft and cyber espionage.

On a broader level, both the US government and major companies operating in authoritarian state capitalists like China and Russia should make clearer that there will be severe consequences for cybersecurity breaches and/or intellectual property theft. I have already argued that, for major companies operating in countries like China, the threat of pulling out of joint ventures if intellectual property is stolen must be perceived to be a real possibility by the host government. The US government must convince countries like Russia and China that there will be real consequences for technology theft as well.

Encourage Innovation

Although protecting intellectual property is important, leading democracies cannot merely assume that authoritarian state capitalists' companies pose a challenge and prosper only through theft of intellectual property and cheap outlays of state capital. Some state companies do survive only on cheap state capital and intellectual property theft. Yet many of the state capitalists are also lavishing money on innovation. As we have seen, China has moved up to become the world's second largest spender on research and development, according to statistics compiled by the Global Innovation Index, which is co-produced by Cornell University researchers, INSEAD business school researchers, and the World Intellectual Property Organization. (These figures include spending both by governments and by companies in a country.[16]) China and other state capitalists still lack big-name brands and breakthrough innovations, but the gap is closing. China likely will become the world's largest spender on research and development within a decade.[17] At the same time, US government sources of research, including the prestigious NIH, are slashing their budgets dramatically, while many of the largest American companies are cutting research and development budgets as well.

According to Council on Foreign Relations public health expert Yangzhong Huang:

> Between 2003 and 2013, the number of applications increased from nearly 35,000 to more than 51,000, while NIH appropriations shrunk from $21 billion to $16 billion (in 1995 dollars). As a consequence, it has become increasingly difficult for our [US] scientists to garner an NIH grant. Overall application success rates fell from 32 percent in 2000 to 18 percent in 2012. This is particularly bad news for the new applicants, most of whom are young scientists who are at their most productive age and are most in need of grant support: not only have the number of research project grants dropped in absolute numbers, but the success rates for first-time award recipients has dropped from 22 percent to 13 percent.[18]

For leading wealthy democracies, then, an effective approach to innovation and technology would be one that recognizes that state capitalists are copying and innovating at the same time, and that wealthy nations cannot simply ignore the state's role in promoting innovation. Reinvesting in basic and advanced science would not break the US budget. Boosting congressional appropriations for NIH back to $21 billion annually would consume a fraction of the United States' national budget, just as small increases in government spending on basic science research would have little impact on the overall annual budgets of other rich nations like France, Britain, or Japan.

Punish the Most Extreme Violators of Trade, Labor, Environmental, and Intellectual Property Norms

The United States and other democracies cannot punish every state company that violates basic trade rules. As it is, pursuing WTO cases against alleged violators is time-consuming and often result in negotiated solutions with weak remedies; the organization is hardly equipped to handle even more cases, as it currently faces an enormous backlog. And applying unilateral sanctions against an entire industry or range of companies—or against an entire country—is feasible but even harder to implement.

Still, it will be important for the United States and other leading free-market nations to develop a more consistent and effective strategy of punishing companies from state-capitalist nations that are the most extreme violators of trade, labor, and environmental norms. Selecting the most extreme violators helps defuse the charge that rich nations are punishing entire developing countries and makes it easier to pursue effective remedies against this small number of violating firms. And picking out only the most extreme violators as examples creates incentives for other state companies to follow these norms on environmental protection, labor rights, bribery, and intellectual property protection.

The specific elements of these punishments are less important than nations working together to implement them and selecting only the most extreme rules violators. Some of the elements of punishment could include retaliatory sanctions on a small number of companies, restricting government procurement, and banning procurement from certain foreign firms.

While meting out punishments to state capitalists who violate trade norms, wealthy democracies also need to gain other points of leverage over state capitalists. The best way to gain this leverage would be to push forward with an aggressive free-trade agenda, including finalizing the Trans-Pacific Partnership (TPP) trade deal on the Pacific Rim, completing a free-trade deal between the United States and the European Union, and potentially pursuing a deal that expands on the North American Free Trade Agreement to include other countries in the Western Hemisphere. All of these deals would give the United States, and other countries that signed the agreements, greater leverage over state capitalists, by cutting trade barriers all around the state capitalists and thus pushing state capitalists to join these trade deals and to adhere to the trade rules contained in them, or else be left out of this wave of trade liberalization. Successful completion of the TPP, which was nearing completion at the time this book was published, would show participants in other trade negotiations that the United States can deliver on a free-trade deal.

Keep the Right Focus

In the end, responding to modern state capitalism requires keeping alarmism in check and understanding which state capitalists are worrisome and which are not. As we have seen, the political natures of state-capitalist governments matter most to the economic and national security implications of their state capitalism. If policymakers understand only one thing about modern-day state capitalism, they should know to focus on how state capitalists are governed. This is why aid programs should focus on political freedom and not on economic freedom. Few Western leaders should be up at night worrying about the national security implications of the growth of Brazilian, Indonesian, or Norwegian state companies. Although it is theoretically possible that Indonesia's PT Pertamina or Norway's Statoil could be used as weapons against other countries, there is no evidence that the democratic state capitalists have taken this tack in the past, and no evidence their governments have considered doing so in the future.

The most powerful authoritarian state capitalists—primarily China, Russia, Venezuela, Saudi Arabia, and Iran—do raise legitimate national security concerns for the United States and for other leading democracies. Yet even in these cases of real threats, the United States and other leading democracies must understand how the threats of state capitalism fit into authoritarian state capitalists' broader attempts at power projection. China and Russia pose serious national security challenges to the United States and its partners, but for now those challenges mostly come from traditional threats, like China's naval buildup, increasingly aggressive naval patrolling in Japanese waters, or growing dominance of the military balance across the Taiwan Strait. Russian and Chinese state companies serve as additional levers of influence, and ones that could become more powerful hammers for Moscow and Beijing in the future. So, the United States and its partners must address these traditional national security challenges effectively at the same time as Washington and its partners take steps to blunt the threats of state capitalism.

One could write an entire book on how the United States should respond to Russian and Chinese military might and China's soft power. This is not that book; the point is simply to emphasize that addressing these traditional threats must go hand in hand with facing the challenges posed by state capitalism. Still, to say the least, Washington should respond to Asian partners' desire for a guarantor of stability in the Pacific, at a time of increasingly aggressive Chinese behavior, by following through on the United States' commitment to Asian nations like Singapore, the Philippines, Indonesia, and Vietnam to upgrade their naval, air, coast guard, and missile capacities. The United States also should consider signing a formal treaty alliance with Singapore and, in the future, with Vietnam, and should increase the interoperability of US forces in the Pacific with Singaporean, Philipino, Vietnamese, South Korean, Japanese, and Indonesian forces, among others. Furthermore, the United States should take a clearer public position on the growing disputes over contested waters in Asia, delineating how the United States hopes these disputes will be resolved and how the United States might act if one of the parties to these disputes tries to use military force to stake its claim to contested areas. I will leave the specific recommendations for how to address Russia's traditional threats in the former Soviet Union to Russia experts, having made the broader point that Russia's challenge stems from a combination of traditional power projection and state capitalism.

Still, since the nature of state capitalists' government is critical, the best way for the United States and other democracies to ensure that state capitalism proves no long-term threat is to revive aggressive advocacy for democracy and human rights. Yet wealthy democracies have not been aggressive advocates for democratization.

The United States in particular has failed to effectively promote democracy over the past decade. The George W. Bush administration, though rhetorically touting the United States' commitment to democracy around the world, in fact badly undermined American democracy promotion efforts by linking the idea of democratization to the US invasion in Iraq, suggesting that democracy promotion is somehow tied to force. Then, the Barack Obama administration, seeking to distance itself from the policies of its predecessor, downplayed democracy and human rights in the president's foreign visits and cut government funding for a range of democracy promotion programs. The Obama White House slashed funding for democracy promotion programs in nearly every region of the world and consolidated democracy promotion programming with governance programming in many countries.

On foreign trips, President Obama routinely declined to meet with prominent human rights activists in authoritarian states, sending a very public signal that he was focused on strategic and economic interests and had little interest in pushing issues of democracy and rights. To take one example, during a visit to Malaysia in the spring of 2014, the president chose not to meet with leading rights activist and opposition politician Anwar Ibrahim, even though Anwar faced a long jail term for sodomy charges that would have been thrown out by any impartial court. Instead of having a short meeting with Anwar, Obama spent his trip to Malaysia praising the increasingly authoritarian Malaysian prime minister, Najib tun Razak, and held a brief meeting with a group of Malaysian civil society activists, who got about five minutes of conversation with Obama and then a photo opportunity.[19] (Months after the president's visit to Malaysia, Vice President Joseph Biden used several tweets to cautiously chide the Malaysian government for Anwar's trial, though the White House was relatively quiet when Anwar was found guilty and sentenced to jail in 2015.) The Obama White House has tried to eliminate the Brownback amendment, a provision passed in 2005 that bars any American administration from requesting foreign governments' approval to allocate democracy promotion aid to embassies, NGOs, and consultants working in those countries. The amendment was designed to ensure that authoritarian governments could not simply block American aid projects.[20]

The United States is not alone in de-emphasizing democracy promotion. Other leading democracies also have ignored the growing climates of repression in developing nations. In its 2015 report on the state of freedom in the world, Freedom House declared that global freedom had declined for the ninth year in a row, the longest streak of democratic regression in four decades.[21] "Nearly twice as many countries suffered declines [in freedom in 2014] as registered gains—61 to 33—and the number of countries with improvements [in political freedom in 2014] hit its lowest point since the nine-year erosion began," Freedom House noted.[22] Yet even as democracy has regressed around the world, democracy promotion assistance budgets have been cut since the late 2000s not only in the United States but also in nearly every other rich democracy. Meanwhile, many of the democratic emerging powers that could have helped fill this void in democracy promotion left by Europe, the United States, and other rich countries have been extremely cautious in promoting democracy in other countries, even though at home they have vibrant democratic cultures and strong institutions. India, for instance, has shied away from rhetorically prodding other countries in South Asia, such as Bangladesh, to uphold democratic norms, and India has allocated only a miniscule fraction of its overseas aid monies toward programs that could help build democratic institutions and culture.[23]

In Asia, the world's economic engine and the home of many countries stuck between authoritarianism and democracy, the Obama White House not only ignored democracy promotion but also actively pursued strategic relations with some of the region's most autocratic states. The Obama administration focused much of its policy making in Asia on rapprochement with the countries of Southeast Asia, including authoritarian regimes like Myanmar, Thailand, Malaysia, and Vietnam, among others. Although the White House insisted that this rapprochement was contingent on political reforms in these countries, the process of rapprochement continued, into the Obama administration's second term, even though there was no sign that these countries were headed toward democracy. Several of these states, such as Thailand, Vietnam, and Malaysia, actually have become more repressive since the 2000s, with Thailand suffering a military coup in May 2014 and Malaysia's governing party allegedly committing massive fraud in the 2013 national elections.[24] In 2015, amid a massive potential scandal involving Malaysian state fund 1MDB, the Malaysian government shuttered one of the country's finest financial publications, sacked the country's attorney general, and jailed tens of activists who led street rallies calling for cleaner government.

This global democratic regression has been sharp, but a wave of democratization could be launched once again; such a wave would help minimize any potential threats posed by state capitalism. The world could return to the democratic progress that it had embarked upon in the 1990s and early 2000s; in many nations where democracy has regressed, there is still intense public demand for democratic change, despite recent setbacks. Young generations in many developing countries, though angered by the disappointing performances of many elected governments and frustrated with the lack of progress on fundamental rights even under elected leaders, generally remain committed to the idea of democracy, according to polling data amassed by the regional *Barometer* series of democracy studies.

Whether or not democracy succeeds in developing nations will be determined, first and foremost, by the people and leaders of these countries themselves. Yet the United States, though challenged by other powers and weaker at home than it once was, still will play a critical role in the world's political trajectory. But the United States can only play a proactive role in fostering democratic change if leaders in Washington recognize that democracies around the world will, over time, prove the best strategic partners, even if in the short term democracy can create populist pressures that sometimes complicate bilateral relationships. This mindset shift will require understanding that the United States still has more leverage to foster democracy than some in Washington currently believe. Utilizing that leverage will help endear the United States to rising generations in developing nations around the world, ensure that America's partnerships last well into the twenty-first century, and minimize the potential threats of modern-day state capitalism.

Acknowledgments

This book could not have been written without the generous assistance and wise advice of many people.

At the Council on Foreign Relations (CFR), Richard N. Haass and James M. Lindsay read drafts of the work and offered critical and insightful comments. Elizabeth Leader, Hunter Marston, Michael Levi, Darcie Draudt, Ariella Rotenberg, James West, and Paul Stares contributed important research and analysis and editorial advice. The CFR library offered essential abilities to find nearly anything, and Patricia Dorff and the CFR publications staff worked to bring it to publication. Amy Baker, Janine Hill, and Dominic Bocci helped me in every possible way to raise the funds necessary to research and write this book. Elizabeth Economy and Samantha Ravich offered essential guidance and mentorship.

Generous grants from the Henry Luce Foundation, Starr Foundation, Open Society Foundations, and Smith Richardson Foundation allowed me to do the research and writing of the book; without their help, it would not have happened. At Smith Richardson, I am specifically grateful to Allan Song, while at Luce I am grateful to Helena Kolenda and Li Ling. At the Open Society Foundations I am grateful to Maureen Aung-Thwin and Michael Paller.

At Oxford University Press, I am grateful to editor David McBride for his guidance and thoughts in shaping the book.

Shira provided not only counsel and advice throughout but also love. Throughout it all, Caleb and Jonah remained the joy in my life.

Notes

CHAPTER 1

1. Peggy Sito, "Energy Projects Opened up to Private Investors," *South China Morning Post*, April 24, 2014, B1.

2. "China Issues Guidelines to Deepen SOE Reforms," *Xinhua*, September 13, 2015, news.xinhuanet.com+c_134620039.htm.

3. Michael Wines, "China Fortifies State Businesses to Fuel Growth," *New York Times*, August 29, 2010, B1.

4. John Lee, "China's Corporate Leninism," *The American Interest*, May/June 2012, 36–45.

5. "The State Advances," *The Economist*, October 6, 2012, 53.

6. For more on this point, see Howie Fraser and Carl Walter, *Red Capitalism: The Fragile Financial Foundation of China's Extraordinary Rise* (Hoboken, NJ: John Wiley, 2012).

7. Vijay Vaitheeswaran, "Back to Business," *The Economist Special Report*, September 12, 2015, 4.

8. Minxin Pei, *China's Trapped Transition: The Limits of Developmental Autocracy* (Cambridge, MA: Harvard University Press, 2008), 23–28.

9. Vijay Vaitheeswaran, "Back to Business," *The Economist Special Report*, September 12, 2015, 18.

10. "China's State Capitalism: Not just Tilting at Windmills," *The Economist*, October 6, 2012.

11. G. E. Anderson, "Is China Re-Nationalizing?," *ChinaBizGov Blog*, April 12, 2010, http://chinabizgov.blogspot.com/2010/04/is-china-re-nationalizing-iii.html.

12. Vaitheeswaran, "Back to Business," 4.

13. Wines, "China Fortifies State Businesses to Fuel Growth," B1.

14. "Untameable Market," *The Economist*, July 3, 2015, http://www.economist.com/news/business-and-finance/21656867-bad-week-chinas-stockmarkets-could-be-felt-years-untameable-market.

15. "The State Versus the Stockmarket," *The Economist*, September 2, 2015, http://www.economist.com/blogs/freeexchange/2015/09/state-v-stockmarket.

16. Ibid.

17. "United States," in *Index of Economic Freedom 2014* (Washington, DC: Heritage Foundation, 2014), http://www.heritage.org/index/explore?view=by-variables.

18. Sergio Lazzarini and Aldo Musacchio, "Leviathan as a Minority Shareholder: A Study of Equity Purchases by the Brazilian National Development Bank, 1995–2003," Harvard Business School working paper 11-073, December 2010, 12–13.

19. James Gwartney, Joshua Hall, and Robert Lawson, *Economic Freedom of the World 2012* (Vancouver: Fraser Institute Press, 2013), 1–8.

20. Ibid.

21. "Executive Summary," *Index of Economic Freedom 2015* (Washington, DC: Heritage Foundation Press, 2015), 1–8.

22. Ibid.

23. "Brazil," in *Index of Economic Freedom 2013* (Washington, DC: Heritage Foundation, 2013).

24. "Indonesia," in *Index of Economic Freedom 2013* (Washington, DC: Heritage Foundation, 2013).

25. Author interviews with mining executives, Jakarta, January 2008, Washington, DC, March 2013.

26. To take just a few examples, Chuan Leekpai of Thailand and Anwar Ibrahim of Malaysia.

27. "Economic System Seen as Unfair: Global Poll," *GlobeScan/BBC global poll*, April 25, 2012, http://www.globescan.com/images/images/pressreleases/bbc2012_economics/BBC12_Economics.pdf.

28. Vinod Sreeharsha, "Brazilian Senator and a Banker are Arrested as Petrobras Scandal Widens," *New York Times*, http://www.nytimes.com/2015/11/26/world/americas/brazil-corruption-petrobas.html?_r=0, 26 Nov 2015.

29. "Asia Pacific to take 1,500 Regional Jets over 20 Years—Embraer," *Reuters*, February 12, 2014.

30. Giovanna Maria Dora Dore, "Democracy is Not the Only Game in Town: Democratic and Authoritarian Attitudes in Indonesia, the Philippines, South Korea and Thailand," in Giovanna Maria Dore, Karl Jackson, and Jae Ku, eds., *Incomplete Democracies in the Asia-Pacific: Evidence from Indonesia, Korea, the Philippines and Thailand* (New York: Palgrave Macmillan, 2014), 47.

31. For more on this theory, see Chris Anderson, *The Long Tail: Why the Future of Business Is Selling Less of More* (New York: Hyperion, 2006).

32. *World Economic Outlook 2012* (Washington, DC: International Monetary Fund, 2013), 1–13.

33. "The Super-Cycle Lives: Emerging Markets Growth Is Key," *Standard Chartered Global Research Special Report*, November 6, 2013, https://www.sc.com/en/news-and-media/news/global/2013-11-06-super-cycle-EM-growth-is-key.html.

34. Author interview with Singapore ambassador to the United States, Chan Heng Chee, Washington, DC, November 2011. Author interview with Chinese official, Singapore, January 2012. Author interview with Li Mingjiang, Singapore, August 2007.

35. Cole Kyle and Andrew Szamosszegi, "An Analysis of State-Owned Enterprises and State Capitalism in China," report for U.S.–China Economic and Security Review Commission, October 26, 2011, 89.

36. Ibid.

37. "Gazprom Today," http://www.gazprom.com/about/today/.

38. Peter Finn, "Gazprom Warns Ukraine of Gas Reduction," *Washington Post*, October 3, 2007, A1.

CHAPTER 2

1. "Saudi Arabia," in *Freedom in the World 2015* (New York: Freedom House, 2015).

2. Michael S. Lewis-Beck, Nicholas Martini, and Wenfang Tung, "Government for the People in China?," *The Diplomat*, June 17, 2013, http://thediplomat.com/2013/06/17/government-for-the-people-in-china/.

3. Ibid.

4. Tucker van Aken, "China's Secret? Performance Targets," *The Diplomat*, June 27, 2013, http://thediplomat.com/2013/06/27/chinas-secret-performance-targets/.

5. Lynette Ong, "Fiscal Federalism and Soft Budget Constraints: The Case of China," *International Political Science Review*, November 2011, 465.

6. See, for example, Transparency International, *Global Corruption Barometer 2013* (Berlin: Transparency International, 2013) and *Global Corruption Barometer 2012* (Berlin: Transparency International, 2012).

7. James Ang and David Ding, "Government Ownership and the Performance of Government-Linked Companies: The Case of Singapore," *Journal of Multinational Financial Management*, August 2005, 64.

8. "The Scope of Corruption in Nigerian Oil is Truly Horrifying," *The Economist*, October 19, 2012.

9. Carmen M. Reinhart and M. Belen Sbrancia, "The Liquidation of Government Debt," Bank for International Settlements Working Paper no. 363, November 2011.

10. "Banks in China: Too Big to Hail," *The Economist*, August 31, 2013, http://www.economist.com/news/leaders/21584342-chinas-banking-behemoths-are-too-beholden-state-it-time-set-finance-free-too-big.

11. Bo Hu, "Financial Repression and Interest Rate Liberalization in China," Indiana University Department of Economics working paper, April 2014, https://economics.indiana.edu/home/conferences/2014-jordan-river-economics-conference/files/2014-05-02-05.pdf.

12. Izabella Kaminska, "China as Post-Capital Economy," *Financial Times* (Alphaville, blog), July 12, 2012, http://ftalphaville.ft.com//2012/07/12/1080091/china-as-a-post-capital-economy/?ftcamp=crm/email/2012712/nbe/AlphavilleNewYork/product.

13. Francisco Flores-Macias and Aldo Musacchio, "The Return of State-Owned Enterprises: Should We Be Afraid?," *Harvard International Review*, July 31, 2009, http://www.stwr.org/multinational-corporations/the-return-of-state-owned-enterprises-should-we-be-afraid.html.

14. World Economic Forum, *Global Competitiveness Report 2013–2014* (Davos: World Economic Forum, 2014); World Economic Forum, *Global Competitiveness Report 2012–2013* (Davos: World Economic Forum, 2013).

15. "China's Xi Says Fiscal Reform Urgent but Needs Planning," *Reuters*, June 6, 2014, http://www.reuters.com/article/2014/06/06/china-economy-reforms-idUSL3N0ON3DF20140606.

16. Anders Aslund, "Putin's State Capitalism Means Falling Growth," *Moscow Times*, May 22, 2013, http://www.themoscowtimes.com/opinion/article/putins-state-capitalism-means-falling-growth/480301.html.

17. Michael Kelley, "Russia's Underground Economy is Massive," *Business Insider*, February 15, 2013, http://www.businessinsider.com/russia-largest-underground-economy-in-the-world-2013-2.

18. For example, Charles Clover, "Russia's Missing Billions Revealed," *Financial Times*, February 20, 2013, A1.

19. "Most Expensive Olympics in History: Sochi 2014 Games to Cost Over $50 Billion," *RT*, February 4, 2013, http://rt.com/business/sochi-cost-record-history-404/.

20. Ibid.

21. "Castles in the Sand," *The Economist*, July 13, 2013, 58.

22. Ibid.

23. Ibid.

24. Andrew E. Kramer, "Russian Site Aims to Expose State Corruption," *New York Times*, March 27, 2011, B1.

25. Jack A. Goldstone and Adriana Kocornik-Mina, "Democracy and Development: New Insights from Dynagraphs," George Mason University Center for Global Policy working paper no. 1, August 25, 2005, http://globalpolicy.gmu.edu/documents/papers/DemocracyandDevelopment_rev.pdf.

26. Seymour Martin Lipset, "Some Social Requisites of Democracy," *American Political Science Review* 53, no. 1 (1959): 69–105. See also Samuel P. Huntington, *Political Order in Changing Societies* (New Haven, CT: Yale University Press, 1968).

27. Joshua Kurlantzick, *Democracy in Retreat: The Revolt of the Middle Class and the Worldwide Decline in Representative Government* (New Haven, CT: Yale University Press, 2013).

28. Serhat Unaldi, "The Tyranny of Southeast Asia's Establishment," *The Diplomat*, November 8, 2014, http://thediplomat.com/2014/11/the-tyranny-of-se-asias-establishment/.

CHAPTER 3

1. Minxin Pei, *China's Trapped Transition: The Limits of Developmental Autocracy* (Cambridge, MA: Harvard University Press, 2008), 58–82.

2. "Landesa 6th 17-Province China Survey," *Landesa*, April 2012, 14.

3. Ian Williamson and Roberto Zagha, "From the Hindu Rate of Growth to the Hindu Rate of Reform," Stanford Institute for Economic Policy Research Working Paper 144, July 1, 2012.

4. See, for example, David Rosnick and Mark Weisbrot, "Another Lost Decade? Latin America's Debt Failure Continues into the 21st Century," Center for Economic and Policy Research Working Paper, November 13, 2013.

5. Francis Fukuyama, "The End of History?," *The National Interest*, Summer 1989, 5–30.

6. John Williamson, "What Washington Means by Policy Reform," in John Williamson, ed., *Latin American Readjustment: How Much Has Happened* (Washington, DC: Institute for International Economics Press, 1989).

7. Dani Rodrik, "Goodbye Washington Consensus, Hello Washington Confusion? A Review of the World Bank's *Economic Growth in the 1990s: Learning from a Decade of Reform*," *Journal of Economic Literature* 44, no. 4 (2006): 973–975.

8. "World Bank Aims to Cut Poverty, Hunger in Half," *Associated Press*, November 30, 1993.

9. World Bank Group, *Economic Growth in the 1990s: Learning from a Decade of Reform* (Washington, DC: World Bank Group, 2005).

10. Joseph Stiglitz, *Globalization and its Discontents* (New York: Norton, 2003).

11. Eamonn Fingleton, "The Myth of Japan's Failure," *New York Times*, January 6, 2012, http://www.nytimes.com/2012/01/08/opinion/sunday/the-true-story-of-japans-economic-success.html?pagewanted=all.

12. Randall Peerenboom, *China Modernizes: Threat to the West or Model for the Rest?* (New York: Oxford University Press, 2007), 133.

13. Peerenboom, *China Modernizes*, 3–8.

14. John Minns, "Of Miracles and Models: The Rise and Decline of the Developmental State in South Korea," *Third World Quarterly*, December 2001, 1025–1029.

15. Minns, "Of Miracles and Models," 1029–1031.

16. "Table and Rankings," *Transparency International Corruption Perceptions Index 2013*, http://cpi.transparency.org/cpi2013/results/.

17. Peter Hatcher, "Singapore a Model for Chinese Democracy," *Sydney Morning Herald*, October 30, 2012, http://www.smh.com.au/federal-politics/political-opinion/singapore-a-model-for-chinese-democracy-20121029-28fkc.html.

18. Author interviews with Singaporean academics, Singapore, January 2012.

19. Kor Kien Beng and Peh Shing Huei, "CCTV Goes Big on Singapore with 10-Parter," *Straits Times* (Singapore), October 28, 2012, http://www.asiaone.com/News/Latest%2BNews/Singapore/Story/A1Story20121026-379862.html.

20. Ibid.

21. The World Bank, *The East Asian Miracle: Economic Growth and Public Policy* (Washington, DC: World Bank, 1993), 83.

22. Thomas Fuller, "Disputed Election Sends Malaysian Politician Back to Fight on the Streets," *New York Times*, May 18, 2013, A5.

23. Kevin Brown, "Singapore Opposition Makes Historic Gains," *Financial Times*, May 8, 2011, A1.

24. See, for example, Kishore Mahbubani, "The Pacific Way," *Foreign Affairs*, January/February 1995, http://www.foreignaffairs.com/articles/50565/kishore-mahbubani/the-pacific-way.

CHAPTER 4

1. "Thaksin is Puea Thai's Election Slogan," *Bangkok Post*, April 12, 2011, http://www.bangkokpost.com/most-recent/231653/somchai-unveils-puea-thai-slogan.

2. Author interview with Chiang Mai resident, Chiang Mai, December 2012.

3. Author interview with Sukhamband Paribatra, Bangkok, December 2000; author interview with Panitan Watanigayorn, Washington, DC, March 2011.

4. John Dempsey, "Thailand's Privatization of State-Owned Enterprises During the Economic Downturn," *Georgetown Journal of International Law*, Winter 2000, 374.

5. Author interview with Finance Minister Tarrin Nimmanhaeminda, Bangkok, December 1998.

6. James Kelly, "We Can Count on Thailand," speech to Asia Foundation, Bangkok, March 13, 2002.

7. Michael Montesano, "The End of the Thai Fairy Tale," *Wall Street Journal*, April 9, 2010, http://online.wsj.com/article/SB10001424052702304198004575171724075109414.html.

8. Author interviews with Assembly of the Poor members, Bangkok, January 1999.

9. "A Casualty of Independence," *The Nation* (Thailand), May 30, 2001, A1.

10. "Boonsong Fails to Reveal Rice Data," *Bangkok Post*, June 8, 2013, A1.

11. "Thailand Plans $70 Billion Infrastructure Investment," *Agence France-Presse*, March 24, 2012.

12. Sarun Kijvasin and Supannee Puthapisuth, "Ex-Finance Ministers Warn about Public Debt," *The Nation* (Thailand), January 24, 2013, A1.

13. Shawn Crispin, "In Thailand, Economic Recovery is Driven by Consumer Spending," *The Wall Street Journal*, June 11, 2002, http://online.wsj.com/news/articles/SB1023730258157963960. See also Duncan McCargo and Ukrist Pathmanand, *The Thaksinization of Thailand* (Copenhagen: Nordic Institute of Asian Studies, 2004).

14. Joshua Kurlantzick, *Democracy in Retreat: The Revolt of the Middle Class and the Worldwide Decline of Representative Government* (New Haven, CT: Yale University Press, 2013), 1–19.

15. Ibid., 2–28.

16. Ibid., 3–28.

17. "Global Findings," Bertelsmann Transformation Index 2014, http://www.bti-project.org/reports/global-findings/.

18. Joshua Kurlantzick, "Southeast Asia's Regression from Democracy and its Implications," Council on Foreign Relations Working Paper, May 2004, 5–8.

19. "What Will Professional Organization Constituencies Mean for Thailand?," *Bangkok Pundit*, June 5, 2014, http://asiancorrespondent.com/123475/analysis-of-professional-organization-constituencies-in-hong-kong/.

20. "Thailand: Two Months Under Military Rule," Human Rights Watch report, July 21, 2014, http://www.hrw.org/news/2014/07/21/thailand-two-months-under-military-rule.

21. Patrick Kingsley, "Divided Egypt Disputes Strength of Sisi's Mandate," *The Guardian*, May 29, 2014, http://www.theguardian.com/world/2014/may/29/divided-egypt-dispute-mandate-sisi.

22. Dani Rodrik, "The Future of Economic Convergence," National Bureau for Economic Research Working Paper No. 17400, September 2001, 46.

23. "World Development Indicators," World Bank, http://data.worldbank.org/indicator/NY.GDP.MKTP.KD.ZG.

24. "Indignant, Undignified," *The Economist*, May 25, 2013, http://www.economist.com/news/europe/21578415-it-young-who-suffer-most-high-unemployment-indignant-undignified.

25. Roger C. Altman, "The Great Crash, 2008," *Foreign Affairs*, January/February 2009, http://www.foreignaffairs.com/articles/63714/roger-c-altman/the-great-crash-2008.

26. Thomas Friedman, "Our One Party Democracy," *New York Times*, September 8, 2009, http://www.nytimes.com/2009/09/09/opinion/09friedman.html.

27. John Williamson, "Is the Beijing Consensus Now Dominant?" *Asia Policy* 13 (January 2012): 1–16.

28. Stewart Patrick, "Irresponsible Stakeholders?," *Foreign Affairs*, November/December 2010, 44–52.

29. Lidia Kelly and Alessandra Prentice, "BRICS to Commit $100 Billion to FX Fund, Completion a Way Off," *Reuters*, September 5, 2013.

30. C. Raja Mohan, "Balancing Interests and Values: India's Struggle with Democracy Promotion," *Washington Quarterly*, Summer 2007, 101.

31. Geoff Dyer and Amy Kazmin, "U.S. Urges Delhi to Ease Curbs on Foreign Investment and Trade," *Financial Times*, June 24, 2013, A7.

32. Charles Freeman III and Wen Jin Wuan, "The Influence and Illusion of China's New Left," *Washington Quarterly*, Winter 2012, 66–79.

33. Ibid., 69.

34. Ibid., 66.

35. Hannah Beech, "Lessons from the Fall of Party Boss Bo Xilai," *Time*, March 19, 2012, http://world.time.com/2012/03/19/the-fall-of-bo-xilai-lessons-from-one-of-chinas-biggest-political-scandals/.

36. Charles Freeman III and Wen Jin Yuan, "China's New Leftists and the China Model Debate after the Financial Crisis," Center for Strategic and International Studies Freeman Chair in China Studies report, July 2011, http://csis.org/files/publication/110728_Freeman_ChinaNewLeftists_Web.pdf, 3–12.

37. Author interview with Chinese official, Washington, DC, April 2013.

38. Freeman III and Jin Yuan, "China's New Leftists," 1–23.

39. Lucy Hornby, "China's Anti-Corruption Drive Focuses on Energy Industry," *Financial Times*, May 28, 2014, A1. Author interviews with Chinese state company officials, Hong Kong, December 2013.

40. Elizabeth Economy, "China's Imperial President," *Foreign Affairs*, November/December 2014, http://www.foreignaffairs.com/articles/142201/elizabeth-c-economy/chinas-imperial-president.

41. Simon Denyer, "In China, No Reforms on the Horizon," *Washington Post*, October 3, 2013, A13.

42. Chris Buckley, "China Takes Aim at Western Ideas," *New York Times*, August 19, 2013, A1.

43. Ibid.

44. Buckley, "China Takes Aim at Western Ideas," and author interviews with Chinese academics, Washington, June 2013.

45. Cheng Li and Ryan McElveen, "Can Xi's Governing Strategy Succeed?," *Current History*, September 2013, 208.

46. "Chasing the Chinese Dream," *The Economist*, May 4, 2013, http://www.economist.com/news/briefing/21577063-chinas-new-leader-has-been-quick-consolidate-his-power-what-does-he-now-want-his.

47. Dennis Blasko and M. Taylor Fravel, "Xi Jinping and the PLA," *The Diplomat*, March 19, 2013, http://thediplomat.com/china-power/xi-jinping-and-the-pla/2/?print=yes.

48. Jamil Anderlini, "China: Red Restoration," *Financial Times*, November 4, 2013, A7.

49. Jamil Anderlini, "China Clamps Down on U.S. Consulting Groups," *Financial Times*, May 25, 2014, http://www.ft.com/intl/cms/s/0/310d29ea-e263-11e3-89fd-00144feabdco.html.

50. Haroon Bhorat, "Economic Inequality is a Major Obstacle to Growth in South Africa," *New York Times*, December 6, 2013, http://www.nytimes.com/roomfordebate/2013/07/28/the-future-of-south-africa/economic-inequality-is-a-major-obstacle-to-growth-in-south-africa

51. "Cyril Ramaphosa; Africa's 50 Richest," *Forbes*, November 13, 2013, http://www.forbes.com/profile/cyril-ramaphosa/.

52. Bill Keller, "Could Cyril Ramaphosa Be the Best Leader South Africa Has Not Yet Had?," *New York Times Magazine*, January 23, 2013, http://www.nytimes.com/2013/

01/27/magazine/could-cyril-ramaphosa-be-the-best-leader-south-africa-has-not-yet-had.html?pagewanted=all.

53. Ibid.

54. Sergio G. Lazzarini and Aldo Musacchio, *Reinventing State Capitalism: Leviathan in Business, Brazil and Beyond* (Cambridge, MA: Harvard University Press, 2014), 98–100.

55. Author interview with leading Thai politician, Bangkok, January 2012.

56. "Capital Gain, Asset Loss: European Bank Deleveraging," Deloitte bank survey 2012, October 2012.

57. Viktor Shvets, "Who is Vulnerable to a Decline in Bank Liquidity?," Credit Suisse research note, May 23, 2012.

58. Lazzarini and Musacchio, *Reinventing State Capitalism*, 98–100.

59. "Falling in Love Again with the State," *The Economist*, March 31, 2010, http://www.economist.com/node/15816646.

60. Lazzarini and Musacchio, *Reinventing State Capitalism*, 17.

61. "Fund Rankings," Sovereign Wealth Funds Institute, http://www.swfinstitute.org/fund-rankings/.

62. Stefano Curto, "Sovereign Wealth Funds in the Next Decade," World Bank Economic Premise paper no. 8, April 2010, 1–2.

63. Chris Anderson, *The Long Tail: Why the Future of Business is Selling Less of More* (New York: Hyperion, 2006).

64. "Despite Boom, Oil Companies Struggling," *Associated Press*, August 1, 2013, http://www.foxnews.com/world/2013/08/01/despite-boom-oil-companies-struggling/.

65. Daniel Gilbert and Justin Scheck, "Big Oil Companies Struggle to Justyify Soaring Project Costs," *The Wall Street Journal*, January 28, 2014, http://www.wsj.com/articles/SB10001424052702303277704579348332283819314.

66. "Huawei's $30 Billion China Credit Opens Doors in Brazil, Mexico," *Bloomberg News*, April 25, 2011, http://www.bloomberg.com/news/2011-04-25/huawei-counts-on-30-billion-china-credit-to-open-doors-in-brazil-mexico.html.

67. Kathrin Hille and Andrew Parker, "Upwardly Mobile—Huawei," *Financial Times*, March 20, 2009, http://www.ft.com/intl/cms/s/0/328c6656-0f9a-11de-a8ae-0000779fd2ac.html#axzz34HHUgA6F.

68. "Huawei CFO Announces 2012 Financial Results," January 21, 2013, http://www.huawei.com/en/about-huawei/newsroom/press-release/hw-202000-cfo.htm.

69. Paul Carsten, "Huawei Profit Jumps on Smartphones," *Reuters*, January 15, 2014 http://www.reuters.com/article/2014/01/15/us-huawei-results-idUSBREA0E02P20140115.

70. China Global Investment Tracker, Heritage Foundation, http://www.heritage.org/research/projects/china-global-investment-tracker-interactive-map.

CHAPTER 5

1. Author interview with Alex Feldman of the U.S.-Asian Business Council, Washington, DC, September 2013.

2. "Forbes Columnist Gordon Chang Predicts Chinese Economy's Catastrophic Failure," *Benzinga.com*, June 24, 2013, http://www.benzinga.com/media/cnbc/13/06/3699472/forbes-columnist-gordon-chang-predicts-chinese-economys-catastrophic-failur#ixzz2XXT3Pd6F.

3. "The Debt to the Penny and Who Holds It," US Department of the Treasury, http://www.treasurydirect.gov/NP/debt/current.

4. Don Weinland, "NPLs Overwhelm Chinese Lenders but State Bad Banks Look the Other Way," *South China Morning Post*, January 12, 2015, http://www.scmp.com/business/economy/article/1678398/npls-overwhelm-chinese-lenders-state-bad-banks-look-other-way.

5. See Gordon Chang, *The Coming Collapse of China* (New York: Random House, 2001).

6. Gao Zitan, "China's Manufacturing to Collapse by 2015, Says Economist," *Epoch Times*, May 30, 2012, http://www.theepochtimes.com/n2/china-news/chinas-manufacturing-to-collapse-by-2015-says-economist-244905.html.

7. Jamal Anderlini, "How Long Can the Communist Party Survive in China?," *Financial Times*, September 20, 2013, A7.

8. Andrew Nathan, "China at the Tipping Point? Foreseeing the Unforeseeable," *Journal of Democracy*, January 2013, 20–21.

9. Chang, *The Coming Collapse of China*, 55.

10. "Fortune Global 500 2013," *Fortune*, July 8, 2013, http://fortune.com/global500/royal-dutch-shell-plc-1/.

11. Panos Mourdoukoutas, "World's 500 Largest Companies in 2013: The Chinese are Rising," *Fortune*, July 17, 2013, http://www.forbes.com/sites/panosmourdoukoutas/2013/07/17/worlds-500-largest-corporations-in-2013-the-chinese-are-rising/.

12. This rise was determined by examining the *Global Competitiveness Index* rankings going back to 2008. See *Global Competitiveness Index* (Davos: World Economic Forum, 2013), and previous years of the Index's data.

13. Robert J. Samuelson, "Will China Crash?," *The Washington Post*, September 7, 2015, A17.

14. Ibid.

15. Nicholas Lardy, "False Alarm on a Crisis in China," *The Business Standard* (India), August 26, 2015, http://www.business-standard.com/article/opinion/nicholas-r-lardy-false-alarm-on-a-crisis-in-china-115082601375_1.html.

16. George Magnus, "The Chinese Model is Nearing its End," *Financial Times*, August 21, 2015, http://www.ft.com/intl/cms/s/0/388bf2ca-475a-11e5-af2f-4d6e0e5eda22.html#axzz3l5ZC70YG.

17. Ibid.

18. Ian Taley, "What if the China Panic Is All Wrong?" *The Wall Street Journal*, September 2, 2015, http://blogs.wsj.com/economics/2015/09/03/what-if-the-china-panic-is-all-wrong/.

19. For example, Gao Xu, "Rebalancing China through SOE Reform," paper for 3rd Annual New York University Conference on Chinese Capital Markets, December 6, 2013.

20. "China Vows to Tackle Local Government Debt Amid Reform Push," *Bloomberg Businessweek*, December 14, 2013, http://www.businessweek.com/news/2013-12-13/china-pledges-to-tackle-local-government-debt-amid-reform-push.

21. James Parker, "Is China Getting Ready to Clean Up its Debt?" *The Diplomat*, September 27, 2013, http://thediplomat.com/2013/09/27/is-china-getting-ready-to-clean-up-its-debt/.

22. Joshua Kurlantzick, "The End of Asia's Boom Is No Cause for Panic," *Bloomberg Businessweek*, August 27, 2013, http://www.businessweek.com/articles/2013-08-27/the-end-of-asia-s-boom-is-no-cause-for-panic.

23. Nicholas Lardy, "Writing China: Nicholas Lardy, 'Markets Over Mao,'" *China Real Time* (blog), *Wall Street Journal*, September 2, 2014, http://blogs.wsj.com/chinarealtime/2014/09/02/writing-china-nick-lardy-combats-conventional-wisdom-in-markets-over-mao/.

24. Ibid.

25. Simon Rabinovich, "March of the State Presses Private Companies," *Financial Times*, November 12, 2012, A6.

26. Cole Kyle and Andrew Szamosszegi, "An Analysis of State-Owned Enterprises and State Capitalism in China," report for U.S.–China Economic and Security Review Commission, October 26, 2011, 90.

27. Michael Pettis, "Forget the Minsky Moment, Could It Be a Minsky Century?," *Global Economic Intersection*, July 7, 2012, http://econintersect.com/b2evolution/blog2.php/2012/07/21/forget-the-minsky-moment-could-it-be-a-minsky-century-1. See also Kyle and Szamosszegi, "An Analysis of State-Owned Enterprises and State Capitalism in China," 47.

28. "Chinese Multinationals Gain Further Momentum," Vale Columbia Center and Fudan University survey, December 9, 2010, http://www.vcc.columbia.edu/files/vale/documents/EMGP-China-Report-2010-Final-07_Dec_10_0.pdf, 1.

29. Francoise Nicolas, "China and Foreign Investors: The End of a Beautiful Friendship?," *Institut Français des Relations Internationales*, April 2008, 1–22.

30. Kyle and Szamosszegi, "An Analysis of State-Owned Enterprises and State Capitalism in China," 46.

31. Mikael Mattlin, "The Chinese Government's New Approach to Ownership and Financial Control of Strategic State-Owned Enterprises," Bank of Finland occasional paper, June 19, 2007, 2–3.

32. "2013 Annual Report and 10-K; The New York Times Company," http://investors.nytco.com/files/doc_financials/annual/2013/2013%20Annual%20Report.pdf.

33. "China Global Investment Tracker," The Heritage Foundation, http://www.heritage.org/research/projects/china-global-investment-tracker-interactive-map.

34. Mattlin, "The Chinese Government's New Approach," 2–8.

35. Kyle and Szamosszegi, "An Analysis of State-Owned Enterprises and State Capitalism in China," 45.

36. Sebastian Heilmann, "Authoritarian Upgrading and Innovative Potential," in Joseph Fewsmith, ed., *China Today, China Tomorrow: Domestic Politics, Economics, and Society* (Lanham, MD: Rowman and Littlefield, 2010), 109.

37. James MacGregor, "China's Drive for 'Indigenous Innovation': A Web of Industrial Policies," United States Chamber of Commerce/Global Intellectual Property Center Report, 2009, http://www.uschamber.com/sites/default/files/reports/100728chinareport_0.pdf, accessed January 2013, 3–9.

38. George Haley and Usha Haley, *Subsidies to Chinese Industry: State Capitalism, Business Strategy, and Trade Policy* (Oxford: Oxford University Press, 2013), 175.

39. Bill Vlasic, "Quietly, Chinese Automakers Build Their Presence in Detroit," *New York Times*, May 13, 2013, B1.

40. Bill Vlasic, "Chinese Firm Wins Bid for Auto Battery Maker," *New York Times*, December 9, 2012, http://www.nytimes.com/2012/12/10/business/global/auction-for-a123-systems-won-by-wanxiang-group-of-china.html.

41. Dani Rodrik, "Making Room for China in the World Economy," paper prepared for the American Economic Association meeting, December 2009, 1–10.

42. "Is China Catching the U.S. in R and D?," *Asia Sentinel*, July 12, 2012, http://www.asiasentinel.com/econ-business/is-china-catching-the-us-in-rd/.

43. Chris Nuttall, "Chinese Supercomputer Gains Title of World's Fastest," *Financial Times*, http://www.ft.com/intl/cms/s/0/8a3dfobe-d75e-11e2-8279-00144feab7de.html#axzz34HHUgA6F, accessed February 2014.

44. *Global Competitiveness Reports 2013, Global Competitiveness Report 2012, Global Competitiveness Report 2011* (Geneva: World Economic Forum, 2013, 2012, 2011).

45. Lucy Hornby and Tom Mitchell, "China Pledge of Big Reforms Cements Era of Market Forces," *Financial Times*, November 13, 2013, A1.

46. William Pesek, "No, China Isn't Really Rebalancing," *Bloomberg View*, May 30, 2014, http://www.bloombergview.com/articles/2014-05-30/no-china-isn-t-really-rebalancing.

47. Ibid.

48. Dinny McMahon, "Chinese Industrial Subsidies Grow 23%," *The Wall Street Journal*, June 23, 2013, http://online.wsj.com/news/articles/SB10001424127887323836504578551474072138676.

49. Ibid.

50. Mattlin, "The Chinese Government's New Approach," 1–23. See also James MacGregor, *No Ancient Wisdom, No Followers: The Challenges of Chinese Authoritarian Capitalism* (Connecticut: Prospecta Press, 2012), 3.

51. Michael Forsythe and Henry Sanderson, *China's Superbank: Debt, Oil and Influence—How China Development Bank is Rewriting the Rules of Finance* (New York: Bloomberg Press, 2013), 3–22.

52. Victoria Ruan, "Rates Reform," *South China Morning Post*, March 24, 2014, B8.

53. Kishore Mahbubani, "The Pacific Way," *Foreign Affairs*, January/February 1995, http://www.foreignaffairs.com/articles/50565/kishore-mahbubani/the-pacific-way.

54. Author interviews with Singapore officials, Singapore, January 2011.

55. Zhongying Pang, "China's Soft Power Dilemma: The Beijing Consensus Revisited," in Li Mingjiang, ed., *Soft Power: China's Emerging Strategy in International Politics* (Lanham, MD: Lexington Books, 2009), 134.

56. See, for example, Joshua Kurlantzick, "South China Sea: From Bad to Worse?," Council on Foreign Relations Expert Brief, July 24, 2012, http://www.cfr.org/china/south-china-sea-bad-worse/p28739.

57. Author interviews with Vietnamese diplomats, Washington, DC, March 2013.

58. Thomas Fuller, "Vietnam Confronts Economic Quagmire," *New York Times*, January 10, 2011, B1.

59. Zhao Huanxin, Sun Shangwu, and Tang Yue, "The Nation's Top Calling Card," *China Watch/China Daily*, September 25, 2013, A1.

60. Michael Green and Nicholas Szechenyi, "Power and Order in Asia: A Survey of Regional Expectations," Center for Strategic and International Studies Asia Program report, July 2014, http://csis.org/files/publication/140605_Green_PowerandOrder_WEB.pdf.

CHAPTER 6

1. "FDI in Brief: Brazil," United Nations Conference on Trade and Development World Investment Directory Online, 2012, http://unctad.org/sections/dite_fdistat/docs/wid_ib_br_en.pdf; "FDI in Figures," Organization for Economic Cooperation and Development, April 2013, http://www.oecd.org/daf/inv/FDI%20in%20figures.pdf.

2. Jenny Barchfield, Bradley Brooks, and Marco Sibaja, "One Million Brazilians Hit the Streets," *Associated Press*, June 21, 2013.

3. Author interview with Democratic Party official, Jakarta, December 2012.

4. Pankaj Mishra, "Indonesia's New Economic Model," *Bloomberg News*, November 4, 2012, http://www.bloomberg.com/news/2012-11-04/indonesia-s-new-economic-model.html. Also, author interview with Elina Noor, Washington, DC, September 2012; author interview with Indonesian minister, New York, March 2013.

5. Sita Dewi, "Jokowi Hands over his Metallica Guitar to KPK," *Jakarta Post*, May 6, 2013, A1.

6. Pierre van der Eng, "All Lies? Famines in Sukarno's Indonesia, 1950s–1960s," paper prepared for Indonesia Project, Australian National University.

7. Neil Chatterjee, "Widodo Shows Protectionist Side as Indonesian Vote Looms," *Bloomberg News*, June 6, 2014, http://www.bloomberg.com/news/articles/2014-06-05/indonesia-frontrunner-adopts-protectionist-views-as-vote-nears.

8. Welian Wiranto, "Indonesia is Missing a Modi," *Beyond Brics Financial Times* (blog), June 6, 2014, http://blogs.ft.com/beyond-brics/2014/06/06/L.

9. Raymond Zhong, "How Financial Repression Protects India from Capital Flight," *Wall Street Journal*, January 9, 2014, http://blogs.wsj.com/economics/2014/01/09/how-financial-repression-protects-india-from-capital-flight/.

10. Victor Mallet, "India Launches Chinese-Style Economic Revival Plan," *Financial Times*, June 9, 2014, http://www.ft.com/intl/cms/s/0/bc33983c-efa7-11e3-bee7-00144feabdc0.html#axzz34e7rbmRX.

11. Author interview with Narendra Modi advisor, Washington, DC, May 2014.

12. Frank Nxumalo, "South Africa Inequality Widening: Institute for Justice and Reconciliation," *South African Broadcasting Corporation online*, February 24, 2012, http://www.sabc.co.za/news/a/0631c2804a4828388f6dbf316e9aa538/SA-Inequality-Widening:-Institute-for-Justice-and-Reconciliation.

13. Mike Cohen and Andres R. Martinez, "Labor Laws Cut Hiring as South Africa Unemployed Swell," *Bloomberg*, August 8, 2012, http://www.bloomberg.com/news/2012-08-08/labor-laws-chill-hiring-as-south-africa-s-unemployed-swell-jobs.html.

14. Author interviews with South African officials, Beijing, September 2012.

15. Eve Fairbanks, "You Have All the Reasons to be Angry," *The New Republic*, March 4, 2013, http://www.newrepublic.com/article/112499/julius-malema-anc-and-fight-south-africas-future.

16. Matuma Letsaolo, Charles Molele, and Shara Naidoo, "State of the Nation: Zuma Adopts Chinese Model," *The Mail and Guardian* (South Africa), February 3, 2012, A1.

17. "South Africa: State Capitalism," American Insurance Group outlook report, July 3, 2012, http://www.aig.com/South-Africa-State-Capitalism_2590_434539.html.

18. Jay Naidoo, "A Giant Stumbling through the Minefield of Political Division—My Appeal to the Cosatu Workers," *The Daily Maverick*, March 24, 2014, http://www.daily-maverick.co.za/article/2014-03-23-op-ed-a-giant-stumbling-through-the-minefield-of-political-division-my-appeal-to-the-cosatu-workers/#.Vl4Lf4006YY.

19. For more on this thesis, see Dani Rodrik, *One Economics, Many Recipes: Globalization, Institutions, and Economic Growth* (Princeton, NJ: Princeton University Press, 2008).

20. United Nations Human Development Program, "Human Divided: Confronting Inequality in Developing Countries," UNHDP report, January 2014, chap. 3, 1–56.

21. For more on this point, see Joshua Kurlantzick, "Indonesia," in Isobel Coleman and Lawson-Remer, eds., Terra, *Pathways to Freedom: Political and Economic Lessons from Democratic Transitions* (New York: Council on Foreign Relations Press, 2013), 131–156.

22. Laldinkima Sailo, "Protectionism in Indonesia's Mining Sector," *East Asia Forum*, June 19, 2013, http://www.eastasiaforum.org/2013/06/20/protectionism-in-indonesias-mining-sector/.

23. *Economic Freedom of the World 2012* (Vancouver: Fraser Institute Press, 2013), 1–8.

24. Simon Romero, "As Growth Ebbs, Brazil Powers Up its Bulldozers," *New York Times*, June 21, 2012, http://www.nytimes.com/2012/06/22/world/americas/brazil-combats-slowdown-with-even-more-stimulus.html.

25. Matthias Ebenau and Victorial Liberatore, "Neodevelopmentalist State Capitalism in Brazil and Argentina: Chances, Limits, and Contradictions," *DMS -Der Moderne Staat* 6, no. 1 (2013): 118.

26. Brian Ellsworth and Denise Luna, "Brazil's Lula Moves to Boost State Control over New Oil Wealth," *Reuters*, August 31, 2009.

27. Vivianne Rodrigues, "Petrobras $11 Billion Bond Sale Breaks Record," *Financial Times*, May 14, 2013, B1.

28. Kenneth Rapoza, "Petrobras Puts Brazil President Dilma in Hot Seat," *Forbes*, March 23, 2014, http://www.forbes.com/sites/kenrapoza/2014/03/23/petrobras-puts-brazil-president-dilma-in-hot-seat/.

29. Mario Schapiro, "Rediscovering the Developmental Path? Development Bank, Law, and Innovation Financing in the Brazilian Economy," Sao Paolo Law School working paper, January 2012, http://ssrn.com/abstract=1986915 or http://dx.doi.org/10.2139/ssrn.1986915?, 2.

30. "Falling in Love Again with the State," *The Economist*, March 30, 2010, http://www.economist.com/node/15816646.

31. Glauco Arbix and Scott Martin, "Beyond Developmentalism and Market Fundamentalism in Brazil: Inclusionary State Activism without Statism," paper presented at the Workshop on States, Development and Global Governance, University of Wisconsin-Madison, March 12–13, 2010, 2–4.

32. Ibid.

33. Simon Romero, "As Growth Ebbs, Brazil Powers up it Bulldozers," *New York Times*, June 21, 2012, http://www.nytimes.com/2012/06/22/world/americas/brazil-combats-slowdown-with-even-more-stimulus.html.

34. "A Fall from Grace," *The Economist*, June 8, 2013, http://www.economist.com/news/leaders/21579007-how-squander-inheritanceand-how-easily-it-could-be-restored-fall-grace.

35. Joe Leahy, "BNDES: Lender of First Resort for Brazil's Tycoons," *Financial Times*, January 11, 2015, A6.

36. Ibid.

37. Julia Leite, "Petrobras Probe Making Brazil Stocks World's Most Volatile," *Bloomberg News*, December 30, 2014, http://www.theglobeandmail.com/report-on-business/international-business/latin-american-business/petrobras-probe-making-brazil-equities-worlds-most-volatile/article22240734/.

CHAPTER 7

1. Michael Montesano, "Southeast Asia's New Strongman," *Foreign Policy*, November 1, 2003, http://www.foreignpolicy.com/articles/2003/11/01/southeast_asias_new_strongman. See also Joshua Kurlantzick, "Thailand," in Isobel Coleman and

Terra Lawson-Remer, eds., *Pathways to Freedom: Political and Economic Lessons from Democratic Transitions* (New York: Council on Foreign Relations, 2013), 157–180.

2. Author interview with Songpol Kaoputumtip, Bangkok, August 2007.

3. Author interviews with Thai civil servants, Bangkok, January 2006. Author phone interview with Thaksin Shinawatra, January 2010.

4. "Thailand," in *Freedom in the World 2010* (New York: Freedom House, 2011), http://www.freedomhouse.org/report/freedom-world/2010/thailand?page=22&year=2010&country=7932. The author has served as a consultant for Freedom House reports on Thailand.

5. Pattsara Jikkham and Phusadee Arunmas, "Rotten Rice Came from Old Pledge Scheme," *Bangkok Post*, September 16, 2013, A1. Also, Thanong Khantong, "Bad Credit Rating or Not, the Outlook Doesn't Look Good," *The Nation* (Thailand), June 7, 2013, A6.

6. "Press Freedom Index 2013," Reporters without Borders, http://fr.rsf.org/IMG/pdf/classement_2013_gb-bd.pdf, accessed September 2013.

7. "Thailand," in *Freedom on the Net 2012* (New York: Freedom House, 2013), http://www.freedomhouse.org/report/freedom-net/2012/thailand. The author has served as a consultant for Freedom House reports on Thailand.

8. Yingluck Shinawatra, "Speech to the Seventh Ministerial Conference of the Community of Democracies," Ulan Bator, Mongolia, April 29, 2013.

9. Aekarach Sattaburuth, "Yingluck Sues Cartoonist for Evil Woman Jibe," *Bangkok Post*, May 4, 2013, A1.

10. Joshua Kurlantzick, "Rise of the False Reformers," *Bloomberg Businessweek*, September 4, 2014, http://www.businessweek.com/articles/2014-09-04/false-reformers-like-xi-modi-rise- in-emerging-markets.

11. Ron Corben, "Thai Economy Shows Signs of Improvement after Coup," *Voice of America*, July 3, 2014, http://www.voanews.com/content/thai-economy-shows-signs-of-improvement-after-coup/1950034.html.

12. "The World's Richest Royals," *Forbes*, April 29, 2011, http://www.forbes.com/sites/investopedia/2011/04/29/the-worlds-richest-royals/.

13. Julie Wernau, "Argentine Creditors Can't Seize Assets of Central Bank, Court Rules," *Wall Street Journal*, August 31, 2015, http://www.wsj.com/articles/argentina-creditors-cant-seize-assets-of-central-bank-court-rules-1441040165.

14. "Argentina," in *Freedom in the World 2013* (New York: Freedom House, 2013).

15. "Twenty Years of South African Democracy," Freedom House report, December 17, 2013, https://freedomhouse.org/report/special-reports/twenty-years-south-african-democracy.

16. Author interview with Nurul Izzah Anwar, Washington, DC, September 2013.

17. Author interview with UMNO politician, Kuala Lumpur, December 2013.

18. Political and Economic Risk Consultancy, *Annual Report 2013* (Hong Kong: PERC, 2013), 23–25.

19. Nicholas Confessore, Eric Lipton, and Brooke Williams, "Foreign Powers buy Influence at Think-Tanks," *New York Times*, September 6, 2014, A1.

20. "Corporate Governance," Statoil, http://www.statoil.com/en/about/corporategovernance/corporategovernance/pages/corporateassemblyboardofdirectors.aspx, accessed Sept 2013.

21. "Timor-Leste," Aid Effectiveness Portal, http://www.aideffectiveness.org/index.html, accessed June 2014.

22. "Petroleum Fund of Timor-Leste," Timor-Leste Ministry of Finance, http://www.mof.gov.tl/budget-spending/petroleum-fund/, accessed October 2013.

23. *Freedom in the World 2014* (Washington, DC: Heritage Foundation, 2014).

24. Joshua Kurlantzick, *Democracy in Retreat: The Revolt of the Middle Class and the Worldwide Decline in Representative Government* (New Haven/Council on Foreign Relations: Yale University Press, 2013).

25. Trevor Cohen, "The Softer Superpower: Brazil on the International Stage," *Fair Observer*, October 1, 2012, http://www.fairobserver.com/region/latin_america/softer-superpower-brazil-international-stage/.

26. Paul Krugman, "What's the Matter with France?," *New York Times*, August 27, 2014, http://krugman.blogs.nytimes.com/2014/08/27/whats-the-matter-with-france/.

27. Ted Piccone, "Do New Democracies Support Democracy? The Multilateral Dimension," *Journal of Democracy*, October 2011, 139–152.

28. "Opinion of the United States; Global Indicators Database," Pew Global Attitudes Project, Spring 2014, http://www.pewglobal.org/database/indicator/1/.

CHAPTER 8

1. "The Super-Cycle Lives: EM Growth is Key," Standard Chartered Global Research report, November 6, 2013, 1–8.

2. Edmund Terence Gomez and Johan Saravanamuttu, eds., *The New Economic Policy in Malaysia: Affirmative Action, Ethnic Inequalities and Social Justice* (Singapore: National University of Singapore Press, 2012).

3. "Malaysia," *Central Intelligence Agency Factbook*, https://www.cia.gov/library/publications/the-world-factbook/geos/my.html, accessed June 2014.

4. Syarina Hyzah Zakaria, "Petronas and the Bumi Agenda," *The Edge Malaysia*, October 7, 2013.

5. Joshua Kurlantzick, "Why Malaysia Will Say Almost Nothing about the Missing Plane," *Bloomberg News*, March 12, 2014, http://www.businessweek.com/articles/2014-03-12/why-malaysia-will-say-almost-nothing-about-the-missing-flight. Also, "Flight's Disappearance Knocks Malaysia Airlines," *Reuters*, May 15, 2014, http://www.nytimes.com/2014/05/16/business/international/flights-disappearance-knocks-malaysia-airlines.html.

6. Morton Halperin, Joseph Siegle, and Michael Weinstein, *The Democracy Advantage: How Democracies Promote Prosperity and Peace* (New York: Routledge/Council on Foreign Relations, 2005), 33.

7. Ibid., 51.

8. See Amartya Sen, *Poverty and Famines: An Essay on Entitlements and Deprivation* (Oxford: Oxford University Press, 1982).

9. Neil Robinson, "The Contexts of Russia's Political Economy," in Neil Robinson, ed., *The Political Economy of Russia* (Lanham, MD: Rowman and Littlefield, 2013), 35.

10. Gerald Easter, "Revenue Imperatives: State over Market in Postcommunist Russia," in Neil Robinson, ed., *The Political Economy of Russia* (Lanham, MD: Rowman and Littlefield, 2013), 65.

11. William Partlett, "State Capitalism and Russia's Energy Strategy in the Far East," Brookings Institution memo, January 4, 2012, http://www.brookings.edu/research/opinions/2012/01/04-russia-energy-strategy-partlett.

12. "A Choice of Models: Theme and Variation," *The Economist*, January 21, 2012, http://www.economist.com/node/21542924.

13. "Russia," U.S. Energy Information Agency country report, http://www.eia.gov/countries/country-data.cfm, March 2013.

14. Ellen Barry and Michael Schwirtz, "After Election, Putin Faces Challenges to Legitimacy," *New York Times*, March 5, 2012, A1.

15. "Rating World Leaders," Pew Global Attitudes Project report, June 13, 2012, http://www.pewglobal.org/2012/06/13/chapter-5-rating-world-leaders/.

16. Peter Zeihan, "Russia's Far East Turning Chinese," *ABC News*, July 14, 2013, http://abcnews.go.com/International/story?id=82969&page=1.

17. "Tipping the Scales," *The Economist*, May 1, 2014, http://www.economist.com/news/finance-and-economics/21601536-crisis-ukraine-hurting-already-weakening-economy-tipping-scales.

18. Nicholas Eberstadt, "Drunken Nation: Russia's Depopulation Bomb," *World Affairs Journal*, Spring 2009, 51–52.

19. "World Development Indicators," World Bank, http://data.worldbank.org/data-catalog/world-development-indicators, accessed August 2013.

20. Ibid.

21. Ed Crooks, "U.S. Shale Gas Hits Gazprom Exports," *Financial Times*, September 21, 2014, http://www.ft.com/intl/cms/s/0/34c90b6c-419f-11e4-b98f-00144feabdc0.html#axzz3E5xJqiaN.

22. Global Financial Integrity, *Global Illicit Financial Flows Report: 2013*, December 2013, http://www.gfintegrity.org/report/2013-global-report-illicit-financial-flows-from-developing-countries-2002-2011/.

23. Konstantin Borovoy, "Russia's Collapse is Inevitable," *The Interpreter* (Institute of Modern Russia), October 23, 2013, http://www.interpretermag.com/russias-collapse-is-inevitable/.

24. "Gazprom: Russia's Wounded Giant," *The Economist*, March 23, 2013, 59.

25. Jack Farchy, Kathrin Hille, and Courtney Weaver, "Yevtushenkov Loses Favor as New Moscow Order Emerges," *Financial Times*, September 17, 2014, http://www.ft.com/intl/cms/s/0/66a2a474-3e7d-11e4-a620-00144feabdc0.html#axzz3DhbZ29jl.

26. Ibid.

27. "ExxonMobil Corp," *Bloomberg News*, September 11, 2013, http://www.bloomberg.com/quote/XOM:US.

28. All data from *CIA World Factbook 2014* (Washington: GPO, 2014)

29. Landon Thomas Jr., "As Prime Russian Trading Partner, Germany Appears Crucial to Ending Crisis," *New York Times*, March 4, 2014, http://www.nytimes.com/2014/03/04/business/international/as-prime-russian-trading-partner-germany-appears-crucial-to-ending-crisis.html.

30. Elena Mazneva, "Gazprom Said to Face Biggest Decline in EU Revenue in Five Years," *Bloomberg News*, September 10, 2014, http://www.bloomberg.com/news/2014-09-10/gazprom-said-to-face-biggest-decline-in-eu-revenue-in-5-years.html.

31. Robert Peston, "Who Loses from Punishing Russia?," March 4, 2014, *British Broadcasting Corporation*, http://www.bbc.co.uk/news/business-26431849.

32. Author interviews with British diplomats, Washington, DC, July 2014.

33. Shuli Ren, "Russia Roils Emerging Markets," *Barron's*, August 9, 2014, http://online.barrons.com/news/articles/SB50001424053111904329504580071531968746 308.

34. Andrew Ross Sorkin, "High Hopes for Russia Are Fading on Wall Street," *New York Times*, September 22, 2014, http://dealbook.nytimes.com/2014/09/22/high-hopes-for-russia-are-fading-on-wall-st/?_php=true&_type=blogs&_r=0.

35. United Nations Economic Commission for Latin America and the Caribbean, "Summary of Current Conditions and Outlook. Economic Survey of Latin America and the Caribbean, 2001–2002," August 1, 2002, http://www.cepal.org/cgi-bin/getProd. asp?xml=/prensa/noticias/comunicados/9/10739/P10739.xml&xsl=/prensa/tpl-i/p6f. xsl&base=/prensa/tpl/top-bottom.xslt.

36. John Paul Rathbone and Andres Schipani, "Venezuela Bond Struggle Raises Specter of Default," *Financial Times*, September 12, 2014, A3.

37. Ibid.

38. James Hookway, "Vinashin Casts a Shadow," *Wall Street Journal*, May 16, 2011, http://online.wsj.com/article/SB30001424052748703864204576321241877911856.html.

39. "Vietnam's Incredible Shrinking Currency," *The Economist*, February 14, 2011, http://www.economist.com/blogs/banyan/2011/02/vietnams_incredible_shrinking_currency.

40. John Boudreau and Mai Ngoc Chau, "Samsung's Vietnam Leap Has Farmhand Living Dream," *Bloomberg News*, September 11, 2014, http://www.bloomberg.com/news/2014-09-10/samsung-vietnam-phone-leap-has-farmhand-living-a-dream.html.

41. "Steady as She Staggers," *The Economist*, January 6, 2011, http://www.economist.com/node/17859425.

CHAPTER 9

1. World Bank Group, "Executive Summary," *Ease of Doing Business 2013* (Washington, DC: World Bank publications, 2013), 2–10.

2. Sergio G. Lazzarini and Aldo Musacchio, *Reinventing State Capitalism: Leviathan in Business, Brazil and Beyond* (Cambridge, MA: Harvard University Press, 2014), 178–200.

3. William Megginson and Jeffry Netter, "From State to Market: A Survey of Empirical Studies of Privatization," *Journal of Economic Literature* 39, no. 2 (2001): 321–389.

4. Howard Pack and Kamal Saggi, "Is There a Case for Industrial Policy? A Critical Survey," *World Bank Research Observer*, Fall 2006, 290–292.

5. Ibid.

6. Ibid.

7. "E.U. to Accuse Apple of Taking Illegal Tax Aid from Ireland," *Agence France Presse*, September 28, 2014, http://www.theguardian.com/technology/2014/sep/29/eu-accuse-apple-illegal-tax-aid-ireland-reports.

8. Jonathan Anderson, "Beijing's Exceptionalism," *The National Interest*, March/April 2009, 23.

9. "The World Bank and Poverty in Indonesia," World Bank Group, http://web.world-bank.org/WBSITE/EXTERNAL/COUNTRIES/EASTASIAPACIFICEXT/0,,contentM DK:23191612~pagePK:146736~piPK:146830~theSitePK:226301,00.html. Also, Menno Pradhan, Lant Pritchett, Sudarno Sumarto, and Asep Suryahardi, "Measurements of Poverty in Indonesia—1996, 1999, and Beyond," World Bank Group Policy Research Working Paper, September 2000, http://documents.worldbank.org/curated/en/2000/09/693280/measurements-poverty-indonesia-1996-1999-beyond, 1–8.

10. Minxin Pei, "Corruption Threatens China's Future," Carnegie Endowment for International Peace Policy Outlook, October 9, 2007, http://carnegieendowment.org/2007/10/09/corrupt ion-threatens-china-s-future/1m68.

11. Chris Buckley, "China Arrests Ex-Chief of Security in Graft Case," *The New York Times*, December 5, 2014, http://www.nytimes.com/2014/12/06/world/asia/zhou-yongkang-china-arrests-former-security-chief.html?_r=0.

12. Transparency International, "Corruption Perceptions Index 2013," http://www.transparency.org/cpi2013/results.

13. Thalif Deen, "UN Hails China on Poverty Cuts," *Asia Times*, July 2, 2013, http://www.atimes.com/atimes/China_Business/CBIZ-01-020713.html.

14. Zachary Keck, "Japan's Debt about Three Times Larger than ASEAN's GDP," *The Diplomat*, August 10, 2013, http://thediplomat.com/pacific-money/2013/08/10/japans-debt-about-3-times-larger-than-aseans-gdp/.

15. "Public Debt," *The World Factbook 2013–14* (Washington, DC: Central Intelligence Agency, 2013), https://www.cia.gov/library/publications/the-world-factbook/ran-korder/2186rank.html.

16. Ibid.

17. Ibid.

18. Edward Wong, "In New China, 'Hostile' West is Still Derided," *New York Times*, November 12, 2014, http://www.nytimes.com/2014/11/12/world/asia/china-turns-up-the-rhetoric-against-the-west.html?hp&action=click&pgtype=Homepage&module=first-column-region&region=top-news&WT.nav=top-news.

19. Jane Perlez, "China's Plan for Regional Development Bank Runs into U.S. Opposition," *New York Times*, October 9, 2014, A1.

20. Neil Chatterjee and Rieka Rahadiana, "Indonesia's Decade of Direct Local Elections Threatened," *Bloomberg News*, September 16, 2014, http://www.bloomberg.com/news/2014-09-16/indonesia-s-decade-of-direct-local-elections-threatened.html.

21. Minxin Pei, "Five Ways China Could Become a Democracy," *The Diplomat*, February 13, 2013, http://thediplomat.com/2013/02/13/5-ways-china-could-become-a-democracy/.

22. Chris Buckley and Andrew Jacobs, "Chinese Activists Test New Leader and Are Crushed," *New York Times*, January 16, 2014, http://www.nytimes.com/2014/01/16/world/asia/chinese-activists-test-new-leader-and-are-crushed.html?hp&_r=0.

23. Patrick Boehler, "Timeline: Activist's List of Chinese Political Arrests Shows Crackdown is Gathering Pace," *South China Morning Post*, August 21, 2013, http://www.scmp.com/news/china-insider/article/1298316/infographic-activists-list-chinese-political-arrests-shows.

24. Simon Denyer, "In China, No Reforms on the Horizon," *Washington Post*, October 3, 2013, A13.

25. Kellee Tsai, *Capitalism without Democracy: The Private Sector in Contemporary China* (Ithaca, NY: Cornell University Press, 2007), 2–18.

26. Hou Liqiang, "Report Identifies Sources of Mass Protest," *China Daily*, April 9, 2014, http://www.chinadaily.com.cn/china/2014-04/09/content_17415767.htm.

27. Joseph Fewsmith, "The Political Implications of China's Growing Middle Class," *China Leadership Monitor* 21, Summer 2007.

28. "Olivia Lum: Group CEO and President," Hyflux Group staff bios, http://www.hyflux.com/abt_mgm.html, accessed March 2012.

29. See Bechtel, "Bechtel Annual Report 2012," http://www.bechtel.com/annual-report-2012.html, accessed March 2013.

30. Dax Chong and Andy Chor, "Can Hyflux's Tap Continue to Flow Beyond the Home Turf?," *Shares Investment Newsletter*, March 2, 2012, http://www.sharesinv.com/articles/2012/03/02/can-hyflux%E2%80%99s-tap-continue-to-flow-beyond-the-home-turf/.

31. Author interviews with Bilahari Kausikan, Simon Tay, and Chan Heng Chee, Singapore, November 2011, and Washington, DC, March 2012.

32. Fiona Chen, "Singapore's Hyflux Signs Agreement for Development of Sichuan Project," *Straits Times* (Singapore), August 2013, http://www.straitstimes.com/business/singapores-hyflux-signs-agreement-for-development-of-sichuan-project.

33. "Singapore's External Trade," Statistics Singapore, July 2013, http://www.news.gov.sg/public/sgpc/en/media_releases/agencies/ie%20singapore/press_release/P-20130816-1/AttachmentPar/0/file/MR02413_Monthly%20Trade%20Report%20-%20July%20 2013_2013%2008%2016.pdf.

34. "Membrane Innovations," Hyflux Ltd, http://www.hyflux.com/membrane_inno.html, accessed January 2013.

35. "Annual Report 2012," Hyflux Ltd, http://hyflux.listedcompany.com/ar.html, accessed September 2013.

36. Author interviews with officials at the Singapore Economic Development Board, Singapore, December 2012.

37. Data from Singapore Stock Exchange, http://www.sgx.com, accessed September 2013.

38. *World Development Report 2013* (Washington: World Bank Group, 2013)

39. Fang Feng, Qian Sun, and Wilson H. S. Tong, "Do Government-Linked Companies Underperform?," *Journal of Banking and Finance* 28 (2004): 2461–2492.

40. Ibid.

41. For more on the People's Action Party's overall strategy, see Cherian George, *Singapore: The Air-Conditioned Nation. Essays on the Politics of Comfort and Control* (Singapore: Landmark Books, 2000).

42. "Strategic Research Programs," Prime Minister's Office, Republic of Singapore, http://www.nrf.gov.sg/nrf/strategic.aspx?id=152, accessed June 2013. Also, Lim Chuan Poh, "Singapore: Betting on Biomedical Science," *Issues in Science and Technology*, Spring 2010, http://www.issues.org/26.3/poh.html.

43. Alexius A. Pereira, "Whither the Developmental State? Explaining Singapore's Continued Developmentalism," *Third World Quarterly*, November 2008, 1197–1200.

44. Author interview with Thai businessman, Chiang Mai, Thailand, December 2013.

45. Carlos Ramirez and Ling Hui Tan, "Singapore Inc. Versus the Private Sector: Are Government-Linked Companies Different?," International Monetary Fund Working Paper, July 2003, 1–13.

46. "Singapore Airlines Looks to Ride Out the Storm as Profits Continue to Slide," Center for Aviation report, February 9, 2013, http://centreforaviation.com/analysis/singapore-airlines-looks-to-ride-out-the-storm-as-profits-continue-to-slide-96949.

47. DBS Group, "Historical Financial Performance," http://www.dbs.com/investor/historicalperformance/default.aspx, accessed September 2013.

48. Wilson Ng, "The Evolution of Sovereign Wealth Funds: Singapore's Temasek Holdings," *Journal of Financial Regulation and Compliance* 1 (2010): 6–9.

49. "Group Financials," Temasek Holdings Annual Report, July 2013, http://www.temasek.com.sg/investorrelations/financialhighlights/groupfinancials.

50. Henri Ghesquiere, *Singapore's Success: Engineering Economic Growth* (Singapore: Thomson Learning Press, 2007), 78–79.

51. Andrew Jacobs, "In Singapore, Vitriol Against Chinese Newcomers," *New York Times*, July 26, 2012, http://www.nytimes.com/2012/07/27/world/asia/in-singapore-vitriol-against-newcomers-from-mainland-china.html?pagewanted=all.

52. "China's Program for Science and Technology Modernization: Implications for American Competitiveness," Centra Technology report prepared for the U.S.–China Economic and Security Review Commission, January 2011, 1.

53. "Science and Engineering Indicators 2014: Overview," National Science Foundation Report, http://www.nsf.gov/statistics/seind14/, accessed June 2015.

54. Ibid.

55. Author interviews with Singaporean technology executives, Singapore, January 2011.

56. Jeremy Grant, "Singapore Loosens Switzerland's Grip on Wealth Management," *Financial Times*, July 23, 2013, A7.

57. "Number of Financial Institutions and Relevant Organizations in Singapore," Monetary Authority of Singapore, https://secure.mas.gov.sg/fid/, accessed August 2013.

58. "Corporate Income Tax," Singapore Ministry of Finance, http://app.mof.gov.sg/TemSub.aspx?pagesid=20090918965913283168&pagemode=live&&AspxAutoDetectCookieSupport=1, accessed August 2013.

59. "Our Singapore Conversation," Government of Singapore, http://www.reach.gov.sg/Microsite/osc/index.html, accessed June 2014.

60. Author interview with Singapore Ambassador Chan Heng Chee, Washington, DC, May 2012.

61. See, for example, Korin Davis and William A. Galston, "Setting Priorities, Meeting Needs: The Case for a National Infrastructure Bank," Brookings Institution paper, December 13, 2012, http://www.brookings.edu/research/papers/2012/12/13-infrastructure-bank-galston-davis,.

62. Peter Baker and Mark Schwartz, "Obama Pushes Plan to Build Roads and Bridges," *New York Times*, March 29, 2013, A1.

63. Ibid.

64. Mike Cohen and Franz Wild, "South Africa's ANC Rejects Mine Nationalization for Taxes," *Bloomberg News*, December 20, 2012, http://www.bloomberg.com/news/2012-12-20/south-africa-s-anc-rejects-mine-nationalization-proposals.html. Also, William Wallis and James Wilson, "South Africa Open to Mine Bill Moves," *Financial Times*, September 18, 2013, A4.

65. Thomas Fuller, "In Thailand, Rubber Price Plunge has Political Cost," *New York Times*, August 30, 2013, A6.

66. Fergus Hanson, "Shattering Stereotypes: Public Opinion and Foreign Policy/Indonesia Poll 2012," Lowy Institute for International Policy (Australia) report, http://www.lowyinstitute.org/files/lowy_indonesia_poll_2012.pdf, accessed June 2013.

CHAPTER 10

1. Neil Buckley, "Gazprom Raises Supply Pressure on Ukraine," *Financial Times*, October 30, 2013, A3.

2. Shaun Walker, "Russia and Ukraine Edge Closer to Gas War," *The Guardian*, October 29, 2013, http://www.theguardian.com/world/2013/oct/29/russia-ukraine-gazprom-gas-war.

3. "Putin Signs Bills Completing Russia's Annexation of Crimea," *Reuters*, March 21, 2014, http://www.cnbc.com/id/101488951.

4. Steven Erlanger, "Russia Ratchets Up Ukraine's Gas Bills in Shift to an Economic Battlefield," *New York Times*, May 10, 2014, A1.

5. Neil MacFarquhar, "Gazprom Cuts Russia's Natural Gas Supply to Ukraine," *New York Times*, June 16, 2014, A1.

6. Andrew Kramer, "Gazprom of Russia to Double Prices for Georgia," *International Herald Tribune*, December 22, 2006, http://www.nytimes.com/2006/12/22/business/worldbusiness/22iht-gazprom.3992669.html?_r=0.

7. John Lee, "China's Economic Engagement with Southeast Asia: Thailand," Institute of Southeast Asian Studies (Singapore) Trends in Southeast Asia Paper no. 1, 2013, 6.

8. Ibid.

9. Author phone interviews with Western oil executives, May–June 2014.

10. Nguyen Phoung Linh and Manuel Mogato, "Philippine, Vietnamese Troops Drink Beer, Play Volleyball on Disputed Isle," *Reuters*, June 8, 2014, http://www.reuters.com/article/2014/06/08/us-philippines-vietnam-idUSKBN0EJ06820140608.

11. Dexter Roberts, "China's State Enterprises Told to Stop Investing in Vietnam," *Bloomberg Businessweek*, June 9, 2014, http://www.businessweek.com/articles/2014-06-09/chinas-state-enterprises-told-to-stop-investing-in-vietnam.

12. Zhang Jianhua and Nguyen Thi Hang Ngan, "More Chinese Investment Boosts China-Vietnam Trade Ties," *Xinhua*, January 16, 2014, http://news.xinhuanet.com/english/indepth/2014-01/16/c_133050466.htm.

13. "Military Expenditure Project Database," Stockholm Peace Research Institute, http://www.sipri.org/research/armaments/milex/milex_database/milex_database, accessed May 2014.

14. Andreas Fuchs and Neils-Hendrik Klann, "Paying a Visit: The Dalai Lama Effect on International Trade," University of Goettingen Center for European, Governance and Economic Development paper no. 113, 2011, 1–7.

15. Ibid.

16. "China Global Investment Tracker," The Heritage Foundation, http://www.heritage.org/research/projects/china-global-investment-tracker-interactive-map, accessed October 2013.

17. "Issues: U.S.A Engage," http://usaengage.org/Issues/Sanctions-Programs/Iran/, accessed June 2013. Also, author interview with Sean Turnell, Washington, DC, March 2012. Also, "Profile," National Foreign Trade Council, http://archives.usaengage.org/archives/background/nftc.html, accessed September 2013.

18. See, for example, Peter Maass, "A Touch of Crude," *Mother Jones*, January/February 2005, http://www.motherjones.com/politics/2005/01/obiang-equatorial-guinea-oil-riggs. Also, "Map of Freedom 2013," in *Freedom in the World 2013* (New York: Freedom House, 2013), http://www.freedomhouse.org/report/freedom-world-2013/map-freedom-2013.

19. Ewa Krukowska and Jonathan Stearns, "EU Says Probe Finds Chinese Solar-Panel Makers Got Aid," *Bloomberg News*, August 28, 2013, http://www.bloomberg.com/news/2013-08-28/eu-says-probe-finds-chinese-solar-panel-makers-got-subsidies.html.

20. Jim Brunsden and Jonathan Stearns, "China-EU Solar Panel Deal Avoids Tariffs with Import Cuts," *Bloomberg News*, July 28, 2013, http://www.bloomberg.com/news/2013-07-27/european-union-china-agree-on-solar-panel-shipment-deal.html.

21. Francois Godement, Jonas Parello-Plesner, and Alice Richard, "The Scramble for Europe," European Council on Foreign Relations Policy Brief, 2012, 6, http://www.ecfr.eu/page/-/ECFR37_Scramble_For_Europe_AW_v4.pdf.

22. "China's Economy: Perverse Advantage," *The Economist*, April 27, 2013, http://www.economist.com/news/finance-and-economics/21576680-new-book-lays-out-scale-chinas-industrial-subsidies-perverse-advantage.

23. Author interview with Myanmar official, Naypyidaw, January 2014.

24. Toh Han Shih, "China to Provide Africa with $1 Trillion Financing," *South China Morning Post*, November 18, 2013, http://www.scmp.com/business/banking-finance/article/1358902/china-provide-africa-us1tr-financing.

25. Author interview with United States Trade Representative officials, January 2013.

26. Aya Batrawy, "Boeing: Record 777X order placed in Dubai," *Associated Press*, November 17, 2013.

27. "United Ends 2012 as World's Biggest Airline, Emirates Third. Turkish and Lion Air the Biggest Movers," Center for Aviation 2012 final report, December 31, 2012, http://centreforaviation.com/analysis/united-ends-2012-as-worlds-biggest-airline-emirates-third-turkish-and-lion-air-the-biggest-movers-93047.

28. Elizabeth Economy and Michael Levi, *By All Means Necessary: How China's Resource Quest is Changing the World* (New York: Oxford University Press, 2014), 81.

29. "Angola Economic Update," The World Bank, June 2013, http://www.worldbank.org/content/dam/Worldbank/document/Africa/Angola/angola-economic-update-june-2013.pdf.

30. Ibid.

31. Carola Hoyos, "Defense Groups Agree $75 Billion of Sweeteners to Win Big Contracts," *Financial Times*, October 10, 2013, A1.

32. Ibid.

33. Heribierto Araujo and Juan Pable Cardenal, *China's Silent Army: The Pioneers, Traders, Fixers and Workers Who Are Remaking the World in Beijing's Image* (New York: Crown, 2013).

34. Friends of the Earth, "Crude Beginnings: The Environmental Footprint of China National Petroleum Corporation around the World," February 2012, http://www.foe.org/news/archives/2012-02-crude-beginnings-the-environmental-footprint-of-chin.

35. For more on the Shwe pipeline and Chinese firms' involvement, see Shwe Gas Movement, http://www.shwegas.org.

36. Economy and Levi, *By All Means Necessary*, 173–177.

37. "Incident Not Our Fault," *Papua New Guinea Mine Watch*, June 5, 2014, https://ramumine.wordpress.com/tag/ramu-nickel-mine/.

38. Economy and Levi, *By All Means Necessary*, 173–177.

39. Ibid.

40. Author interview with Masao Imamura, Chiang Mai, Thailand, August 2007. Author interview with Aung Naing Oo, Chiang Mai, Thailand, December 2012. Author interview with official from Ministry of Foreign Affairs, Vietnam, Washington, DC, October 2012.

41. Author research in northern Laos. Also, "A Bleak Landscape," *The Economist*, October 26, 2013, http://www.economist.com/news/asia/21588421-secretive-ruling-clique-and-murky-land-grabs-spell-trouble-poor-country-bleak-landscape.

CHAPTER 11

1. Timothy Beardson, *Stumbling Giant: The Threats to China's Future* (New Haven, CT: Yale University Press, 2014), 90.

2. Ibid.

3. Italics added by the author. "Best Global Brands 2013," Interbrand, http://www.interbrand.com/en/best-global-brands/2013/Best-Global-Brands-2013-Brand-View.aspx, accessed June 2014.

4. Author interviews with Western executives, Washington, DC, and Yangon, December 2013.

5. Shibani Mahtani, "Buzz Over Post-Sanctions Myanmar Fades for Most U.S. Investors," *Wall Street Journal*, August 31, 2015, http://www.wsj.com/articles/buzz-over-post-sanctions-myanmar-fades-for-many-u-s-investors-1440796685.

6. David Barboza, "Entrepreneur's Rival in China: The State," *New York Times*, December 7, 2011, B1.

7. Kellee S. Tsai, *Back-Alley Banking: Private Entrepreneurs in China* (Ithaca, NY: Cornell University Press, 2004), 1–32.

8. "Private Companies Playing a Bigger Role," *People's Daily*, January 29, 2008, http://english.peopledaily.com.cn/90001/90776/90884/6346769.html. Also, Patrick Foulis, "Business in Asia: How to Keep Roaring," *The Economist*, May 29, 2014, http://www.economist.com/blogs/schumpeter/2014/05/special-report-business-asia.

9. Carola Hoyas, "Burning Ambition," *Financial Times*, November 4, 2009, A7.

10. "Norway, the Rich Cousin," *The Economist*, February 1, 2013, http://www.economist.com/news/special-report/21570842-oil-makes-norway-different-rest-region-only-up-point-rich.

11. I am indebted to Adam Segal for this point. Adam Segal, *Advantage: How American Innovation Can Overcome the Asian Challenge* (New York: W. W. Norton and Co., 2011), 186–187.

12. Author interview with senior US Foreign Service official, Washington, DC, September 14, 2013.

13. "Conscious Uncoupling," *The Economist*, April 5, 2014, http://www.economist.com/news/briefing/21600111-reducing-europes-dependence-russian-gas-possiblebut-it-will-take-time-money-and-sustained.

14. "Energy Strategy," The European Commission, http://ec.europa.eu/energy/en/energy-strategy/, accessed December 2014.

15. Author interviews with Chinese businesspeople, Jakarta, August 2007. Author interview with Alex Feldman, Washington, DC, September 2012.

16. Soumitra Dutta and Bruno Lanvin, eds., *The Global Innovation Index 2013: The Local Dynamics of Innovation* (Geneva: WIPO, 2013).

17. Patrick Thibadeou, "U.S. Could Fall behind China in R&D Spending by 2023?," *Computer World*, January 14, 2013, http://www.computerworld.com/s/article/9235573/U.S._could_fall_behind_China_in_R_D_spending_by_2023.

18. Yangzhong Huang, "The United States Is Quietly Losing its Innovation Edge to China," *Asia Unbound* (blog), Council on Foreign Relations, October 22, 2013, http://blogs.cfr.org/asia/2013/10/22/the-united-states-is-quietly-losing-its-innovation-edge-to-china/.

19. Joshua Kurlantzick, "The Pivot in Southeast Asia: Balancing Interests and Values," CFR Working Paper, January 2015, http://www.cfr.org/asia-and-pacific/pivot-southeast-asia-balancing-interests-values/p35925.

20. "The Obama Administration Is Trying to Remove a Key Tool in Democracy Promotion," *Washington Post* editorial, June 17, 2014, http://www.washingtonpost.com/opinions/the-obama-administration-is-trying-to-remove-a-key-tool-in-democracy-promotion/2014/06/17/d4feccd2-f57f-11e3-a3a5-42be35962a52_story.html.

21. Freedom House, *Freedom in the World 2015* (New York: Freedom House, 2015). The author has worked as a consultant for Freedom in the World's chapters on Southeast Asia.

22. Ibid.

23. Lorenzo Piccio, "India's Foreign Aid Program Catches up with its Global Ambitions," devex.com, May 10, 2013, https://www.devex.com/news/india-s-foreign-aid-program-catches-up-with-its-global-ambitions-80919.

24. Joshua Kurlantzick, "The Pivot in Southeast Asia: Balancing Interests and Values," Council on Foreign Relations working paper, January 2015, http://www.cfr.org/asia-and-pacific/pivot-southeast-asia-balancing-interests-values/p35925.

Index

AFK Sistema, 168–69
African National Congress (ANC),
    123, 124–25, 145
al-Sisi, Abdel Fattah, 74
Altman, Roger, 77
ANC youth league, 201
Anderson, Chris, 21
Anderson, Jonathan, 178
Angola, 217
Anwar, Nurul, 146
Aquino, Corazon, 138
Araujo, Heriberto, 218–19
Arbix, Glauco, 133
Asian Development Bank, 185
Asian financial crisis
    state intervention
        following, 75–77
    Thailand following, 66–67, 68
Asian Infrastructure Investment
    Bank, 214
Asian Values, 62, 109
Aslund, Anders, 42
Association of Southeast Asian
    Nations, 152
autocrats
    in bilateral relations, 153–54
    versus democrats, 27–32
    and long-term future of state
        capitalism, 162–69
    rise of elected, 71–74
    and spread of state
        capitalism, 19–20

and state firms as weapons, 203–11
    and unfair advantages for state-
        owned enterprises, 211–16
automobile industry, 105–6, 212–13
Ayuldayej, Bhumibol, 142

Bangkok Post, 139
Bank of Thailand, 68
Barisan Nasional (BN), 145, 146
basic science research, 104, 227
Beardsen, Timothy, 227
Bernanke, Ben, 94
Bharatiya Janata Party (BJP), 80
BHP Billiton, 221–22
Biden, Joseph, 248
Biomedical Sciences Initiative
    (Singapore), 194
Black Economic
    Empowerment, 85–86
BlackRock, 5
Boao Forum for Asia, 113
Borovoy, Konstantin, 168
Bo Xilai, 82
Brazil
    calls for state intervention
        in, 116–17
    corruption in, 162
    criticism of Chinese orthodox
        economics, 84–85
    and democracy's reinforcement
        of state capitalism, 134–36
    democratization of, 128

Brazil (*Cont.*)
  development bank of, 36, 88
  economic freedom and free-market
    capitalism in, 16
  economic growth in, 115, 179
  economic inequality in, 127
  Indonesia studies state intervention
    model of, 129–31
  in international community, 152–53
  and long-term future of state
    capitalism, 160–61
  macroeconomic stability of, 40
  popular pressure in, 105
  privatization in, 85
  and promotion of China model, 186
  recession in, 23
  rise of state capitalism in, 24
  state bank of, 36–37
  state intervention in, 18–19, 45, 131–34
  state versus private companies in, 223
  stock markets of, 87
  unfair advantages for state-owned
    enterprises in, 215
Bremmer, Ian, 137–38
BRICS development bank, 185
BRICS nations, 78
Brownback amendment, 248
Brunei, 158
Bush, George W., 247

Cambodia
  Chinese influence on, 183
  and promotion of China model, 186
  ties between Chinese political parties
    and, 112
Cambodian People's Party, 112
Camdessus, Michel, 75
Canada, 10
Cardenal, Juan Pablo, 218–19
Cardoso, Fernando Henrique, 85
Cathay Industrial Biotech, 230
Central Bank of Brazil, 133
chaebols, 58–59, 70
Chan Heng Chee, 199–200
Chan-ocha, Prayuth, 73, 74
Chavez, Hugo, 19
Cheng Enfu, 110
China

checks on government
    mismanagement in, 233
competitiveness of state enterprises
    in, 217
corporate responsibility of state
    enterprises in, 218–21
countries studying state intervention
    model of, 128–29
critics of economic reforms in, 80–86
critics of state capitalism in, 94–96
currency of, 97
and economic crisis of June 2013,
    94, 98–99
economic rebound in, 96–98
economic reform in, 1–3
entrenchment of state companies in, 122
evidence for continued state
    capitalism, 99–103
financial repression in, 33–34, 35–36
government funding as seed capital in, 197
growth of, 17–18
Hyflux Limited and, 191
impact of economic collapse
    of, 237–38
as inspiration for developing
    nations, 24
legitimacy and trust of Communist
    Party in, 30–31
legitimacy of state intervention in, 232
macroeconomic stability of, 40–41
as national security challenge to
    United States, 246–47
possibility of economic collapse of, 174
predatory elites in, 39
promotion of state-capitalism model,
    78, 108–14, 182–89
recovery from Asian financial
    crisis, 75–77
research and development in, 244
and state firms as weapons, 203–5,
    207–11, 239
state intervention in, 51–52, 55, 58,
    59–60, 232–33
state versus private companies in, 222–23
subsidized state-owned enterprises in, 196
success at economic planning, 104–8
success of state capitalism in, 175, 178–82
survival of state capitalism in, 3–7

technology theft and, 243
ties with South Africa, 124
understanding and promotion of
    China model, 238–39
unfair advantages for state-owned
    enterprises in, 211–16, 229–30
China Development Bank, 108
China is Not Happy, 80, 81
China National Offshore Oil
    Corporation (CNOOC), 103
China National Petroleum Company
    (CNPC), 208, 220–21
Clinton, Bill, 126
CNOOC Limited, 103
colonial era, 49–50
communications technology, sparks
    skepticism of free-market model, 21–22
Communist Party
    Chinese executives as members of, 4
    conferences with United Russia, 111
    economic growth and legitimacy of
        Chinese, 186–87
    legitimacy and trust of Chinese, 30–31
    and recognition of income
        inequality, 82
Confucius Institutes, 113
corruption
    in Brazil, 162
    in China, 179–80
    in Indonesia, 162
    poverty and, 180–81
    in Russia, 43–44
    in Vietnamese SOEs, 173
    under Xi Jinping, 82–83, 180
Corruption Eradication Commission,
    147, 149–50
countries of concern, 234–35
Crimea, 206
Cuba, 169–70

Dalai Lama, 209–10
DBS, 195–96, 198
debt, 182
decentralization, political, 149–50
democracy/democracies. *See also*
    democratization; political freedom
    cooperation among, 153
    criticism in, 84–86

increased popularity of state
    capitalism in new, 121–25
and long-term future of state
    capitalism, 162–64
middle class and acceptance of, 46
and modernization theory, 45
possibilities for coexistence with state
    capitalism, 146–51
promotion of, 247–50
reinforcing state capitalism, 134–36
and rise of elected autocrats, 72–73
souring on, 20–21, 165
state capitalism and erosion of, 137–46,
    154–56, 234–35
state capitalism as threat to security
    in, 151–54
state intervention models in
    emerging, 128–34
tigers and tiger cubs as, 61
democratization. *See also* democracy/
    democracies; political freedom
    and Chinese economic collapse, 95
    efficient state capitalism and, 134
    mistaken links between economic
        growth and, 20, 126–28
    promoting, 235
Democrat Party (Thailand), 66–68
democrats
    versus autocrats, 27–32
    and state-capitalist efficiency, 38–39
Deng Xiaoping, 1–2, 109
developing nations
    Chinese foreign aid in, 113
    Chinese summits with, 113
    increased popularity of state
        capitalism in, 121–25
    locked out of global capital, 86–89
    and long-term future of state
        capitalism, 157
    market fall's impact on, 93
    and spread of state capitalism, 23–24
    state capitalism as viable strategy
        for, 177–78
    state companies in, 211, 213–14
    state intervention models in, 128–34
    success of state capitalism in, 175–76
    ties between Chinese political parties
        and, 111–12

Directorate of Special Operations, 147
"Document No. 9," 83
domestic manufacturing sectors, fostering Western, 200
dual classes of shares, 102–3

Ease of Doing Business reports (World Bank), 176–77
East Asian economies, state intervention in, 57–63. *See also* tigers and tiger cubs
East China Sea, 109, 185, 207
economic crisis. *See also* Asian financial crisis
    democracies' recovery from, 163–64
    of June 2013, 93–94, 98–99
    state support during, 10–11
economic freedom, 15–16, 45–47, 150, 187–88, 235. *See also* economic liberalization
economic growth
    in Brazil, 115, 179
    and financial repression, 35–36
    in Indonesia, 179
    and legitimacy of Chinese Communist Party, 186–87
    mistaken links between democratization and, 126–28
    and national debt, 182
    and political freedom, 45–46
    and satisfaction with Chinese regime, 188–89
    in Singapore, 193–94
economic liberalization. *See also* economic freedom
    and efficient versus inefficient state capitalists, 36–37
    embraced by state capitalists, 198, 200
    promoting democracy versus, 235
    under Xi Jinping, 82–83
economic planning, success at, 104–8
economies of scale, 89–92
economy
    increase in state intervention in, 15
    largest economies in world, 14*fig.*
    state intervention in, 9, 10–11
Economy, Elizabeth, 217, 222
efficient state capitalism

and autocrats versus democrats, 28, 162
    democratization and, 134
    economic planning and, 104
    versus inefficient state capitalism, 29*fig.*, 32–44
Egypt, 174–75
elections
    accountability of state enterprises through, 216
    in autocratic state capitalists, 29, 71–74
    confidence in government through, 163
    economic planning and, 105
    and legitimacy of state intervention, 231
    and state companies as vote banks, 145–46
Eletrobras, 133
Embraer, 18–19
emerging markets. *See* developing nations
Emirates, 216–17
energy security strategy, 241
entrepreneurship
    in China and Singapore, 197–98
    in Russia, 42–43
environmental protection, 218–24
equity markets, liberalization of, 5–6

Facebook, 102, 103
Feldman, Alex, 93
Fernandez de Kirchner, Cristina, 142–44
financial repression, 33–37
Flores-Macias, Francisco, 36
foreign aid programs
    Brazilian, 152–53
    Chinese, 113
foreign banks, stop lending in emerging markets, 86–88
Foreign Corrupt Practices Act (1977), 219
foreign investment
    Chinese restrictions on, 101
    as potential threat, 239–40
foreign officials, Chinese training programs for, 110–11
France

recovers from 2009 economic
    slowdown, 153
as state capitalist, 9–10
state intervention in, 50–51, 55–56
Freedom in the World index, 150
Freeman, Charles, 82
free-market capitalism
    financial repression in, 34–35
    skepticism of, 21–22
    stagnation of, 15, 16–17
    state capitalism as challenge to,
        22–24, 189
    weaknesses in, 74
Freeport McMoRan Copper and
    Gold, 131
free trade, mercantilist views on, 49–50
Friedman, Thomas, 77
fuel subsidies, 80, 120
Fukuyama, Francis, 54
Fuseini, Alhaji Inusah, 222

Gandhi, Rahul, 121
Gazprom, 167–70, 204, 205–7, 241
General Motors, 105–6
Georgia, 206–7
Ghana, 222
Gigaba, Malusi, 125
global capital
    developing nations locked out
        of, 86–89
    and impact of state economic
        collapse, 170–71
Global Competitiveness Index, 96
Global Competitiveness Report, 37–38
global economic freedom, 15–16
global financial markets, fall of,
    93–94, 99
globalization
    and re-emergence of state
        capitalism, 89–92
    sparks skepticism of free-market
        model, 21–22
Gordon Chang, 94, 95, 96
government debt, 182
governments, recommendations
    for, 234–50
gray economy, 42–43
Guo Jin min tui, 4

Haley, George, 105, 213
Haley, Usha, 105, 213
Halperin, Morton, 163
Hasina Wazid, Sheik, 121
Heilmann, Sebastien, 105
Heritage Foundation, 15–16
Hilead Biotech, 230
Hong Kong, 199–200. *See also* tigers and
    tiger cubs
Huawei, 91, 205
Hun Sen, 112, 183
hybrid state capitalists, 30
Hyflux Limited, 189–92

Ibrahim, Anwar, 154, 248
immigration, to Singapore, 196–97
import substitution, 53–54
income inequality. *See also* poverty
    as ammunition for New Leftists, 81–82
    in China, 181–82
Index of Economic Freedom (Heritage
    Foundation), 15–16, 150
India
    as critic of Western model, 79–80
    history of statism in, 121–23
    and promotion of China model, 186
    state intervention in, 53
    unfair advantages for state-owned
        enterprises in, 215
Indonesia. *See also* tigers and tiger cubs
    and coexistence of democracy and
        state capitalism, 147
    corruption in, 162
    democratization of, 128, 235–36
    economic freedom and free-market
        capitalism in, 16
    economic growth in, 179
    history of statism in, 121
    in international community, 152
    middle class and democratic change in, 46
    natural resources of, 158
    political decentralization in, 149–50
    and promotion of China model, 186
    recovery from Asian financial crisis, 75
    state capitalism in, 117–20
    state intervention in, 53–54, 201–2
    studies state intervention
        models, 129–31

inefficient state capitalism
  and autocrats versus democrats, 162
  economic planning and, 104
  versus efficient state capitalism,
    29*fig.*, 32–44
infrastructure investment
  in Brazil, 131
  of Chinese SOEs, 214, 241–42
  economic planning and, 104
  in India, 122–23
  in Indonesia, 120
  motivations for, 13
  in Thailand, 142
  in United States, 200
innovation. *See also* research and
    development; technology
  Chinese, 105–7
  in efficient state capitalists, 40
  encouraging, 244–45
  science funding and, 227
intellectual property, 227–28, 243
international capital, developing nations
    locked out of, 86–89
Ivanov, Sergei, 165

Japan
  financial repression in, 35
  as state capitalist, 9–10
  state intervention in, 51, 55–56
  tensions between China and, 207
job creation, 230–31
Jokowi, 117–18, 119–20, 129–30

Kaoputumptip, Songpol, 139
Kazakhstan, 174–75
Kelly, James, 68
Kirchner, Cristina Fernandez de, 142–44
Kirchner, Nestor, 142–44
Kwak, Donna, 96–97

labor rights, 218–24
Lang Xianping, 81
Laos, 223
Lardy, Nicholas, 97, 99–100
Larry Lang, 95
Lazzarini, Sergio, 87, 105, 177
Lee, John, 107
Levi, Michael, 217, 222

Lewis-Beck, Michael S., 30
License Raj, 79
Li Datong, 188, 190
Li Keqiang, 2, 31, 99, 107
Ling Jihua, 179–80
Li Yifei, 7
Lockheed Martin, 217–18
long-term economic future of state
    capitalism, 157–62. *See also*
    success of state capitalism
  and autocrats versus
    democrats, 162–64
  and impact of state economic
    collapse, 169–74
  Russian model, 164–69
Lula da Silva, Luiz Ignacio, 18, 129,
    131–33, 134–35

macroeconomic stability, 40–41
Mae On, Thailand, 64–65
Magnus, George, 97
Mahbubani, Kishore, 109
Malaysia. *See also* tigers and tiger cubs
  and corrosive impact of state
    capitalism on democracy, 144,
    145–46, 155
  as democracy, 61
  legitimacy of state intervention
    in, 231–32
  and long-term future of state
    capitalism, 158–60
  Obama's visit to, 248
  political freedom in, 45
  political scandal in, 249
  recovery from Asian financial
    crisis, 75–76
Malaysia Airlines, 160
Malema, Julius, 125
Mallet, Victor, 123
Mandela, Nelson, 85, 123
Manuel, Trevor, 123
manufacturing sectors, fostering
    Western, 200
Martin, Scott, 133
Martini, Nicholas, 30
Mbeki, Thabo, 85, 123
media
  and Chinese soft power, 112–13

openness of Russian, 165
megaprojects, undertaken in
    Thailand, 69, 70
mercantilism, 49–50
Metallurgical Corporation, 221
Mexico, 10
Ministry of International Trade and
    Industry (MITI), 51
Minxin Pei, 179, 187
modernization theory, 45–46
Modi, Narendra, 80, 121–23
Mohamad, Mahathir, 76
Mohan, C. Raja, 79
Mongolia, 111
Musacchio, Aldo, 36, 87, 105, 177
Myanmar, 211, 214, 219, 220–21, 228–29

Naidoo, Jay, 125
Nathan, Andrew, 95
National Bank for Social and Economic
    Development (BNDES), 131, 134
national debt, 182
national infrastructure banks, 200
National Manufacturing Plan (India), 80
natural resources
    in autocratic state capitalists, 41–42
    as insulation from political reform, 32
    of Malaysia, Brunei, and
        Indonesia, 158
    Russian, 165–69
    Russian control of, 205
natural resources extraction
    industry, 89–91
Navalny, Alexei, 44
Nehru, Jawaharlal, 53, 121
Nemtsov, Boris, 43
New Citizens Movement, 188
New Left (China), 80–82
Newmont Mining, 131
New York Times, 102, 103
Nigeria, 41
North Atlantic Treaty Organization
    (NATO), 153
Norway, 10, 147–49, 233

Obama, Barack, 56–57, 200, 247–48, 249
offsetting, 217–18
oil multinationals, 90–91

Ok Tedi Mine, 221–22
oligarchs, 164
Olympic Games (2014), 43–44

Papua New Guinea, 221–22
Patel, Ebrahim, 124
Peeremboom, Randall, 58, 110
People's Action Party (PAP), 62
People's Liberation Army (PLA), 205
performance targeting, 31
Petrobras, 18, 90, 132, 133, 134, 162
Petronas, 159, 160
PetroVietnam, 91–92
Philippines, 138, 208, 209
Political and Economic Risk
    Consultancy, 147
political decentralization, 149–50
political freedom. See also democracy/
    democracies; democratization
    in autocratic state capitalists, 29
    and economic growth, 45–46
    of tigers and tiger cubs, 61–62
    under Xi Jinping, 188–89
political parties, ties between Chinese
    and developing nations', 111–12
postcolonial period, 52–54
poverty. See also income inequality
    in Brazil and Indonesia, 179
    corruption and, 180–81
    in South Africa, 124
Prabowo Subianto, 46, 118–20, 129, 130
predation, 39–40, 43–44
private-sector companies and
    multinationals
    consolidation of, 90–91
    defined, 12
    recommendations for, 225–30
    SOE's advantages over, 211–13, 218–19
    state companies competitive with, 36,
        105, 217
    versus state companies
        in authoritarian state
            capitalists, 222–24
privatization
    critics of, 85
    in emerging democracies, 127
    in Russia, 164
profitability, 230–31

public sentiment, responsiveness
  to, 30–32
Puea Thai, 65
Putin, Vladimir, 42, 71, 165–66, 168,
  204–5, 206

Qatar, 41
quantitative easing, 94

Ramaphosa, Cyril, 86
Ramu nickel mine, 221
rare earth metals, 207
Razak, Najib tun, 19, 248
re-emergence of state capitalism
  Chinese critics, 80–86
  and developing nations locked out of
    global capital, 86–89
  economies of scale and, 89–92
  and emergence of new critics, 78–80
  and growing weaknesses in other
    models, 74–77
  promotion of state capitalism, 78
  rise of elected autocrats, 71–74
  in Thailand, 64–71
Reinhart, Carmen M., 33
renminbi, gradual liberalization of, 37
research and development. See also
    innovation
  Chinese spending on, 197–98, 227
  economic planning and, 104
  growing cost of, 91
responsiveness to public sentiment,
    30–32, 172
rice sector, Thai government's control
    of, 140
Rodrik, Dani, 74, 106, 126
Romas, Fidel, 138
Rosneft, 169
Rotenberg, Arkady, 43
Rousseff, Dilma, 115, 116, 129, 130,
    132–35, 152
Russia
  corporate responsibility of state
    enterprises in, 218
  corruption and cronyism in, 43–44
  entrepreneurship in, 42–43
  impact of economic collapse of,
    169–72, 236–37

and long-term future of state
    capitalism, 164–69
as national security challenge to
    United States, 246–47
and state firms as weapons, 203–7,
    209, 239
unfair advantages for state-owned
    enterprises in, 215
Russian National Wealth Fund, 166–67

Santiago Principles, 233
Saudi Arabia, 174–75
Sbrancia, M. Belen, 33
science and technology research,
    104, 227
security, state capitalism in democracies
    and threat to, 151–54
Sen, Amartya, 163
shadow banking system, 34
Shanghai Cooperation Organization,
    111, 185
Shinawatra, Thaksin, 65–66, 68–71, 74,
    121, 138–41
Shinawatra, Yingluck, 65, 70, 74, 140–41
Shwe gas pipeline project, 220–21
Siegle, Joseph, 163
Singapore. See also tigers and tiger cubs
  banking sector of, 198–99
  checks on government
    mismanagement in, 233
  and coexistence of democracy and
    state capitalism, 147
  compared to Hong Kong, 199–200
  as democracy, 61–62
  economic strategies of, 62–63
  efficiency and trade of, 37
  as efficient state capitalist, 33, 38
  in international community, 152
  legitimacy of state intervention
    in, 231–32
  new talent in, 40
  performance targeting in, 31
  political freedom in, 45
  promotes state capitalism
    model, 108–9
  state intervention in, 58, 59–60
  success of state capitalism in, 189–98
Singapore Airlines, 195–96

Singh, Manmohan, 79–80
Sochi, Russia, 43–44
social welfare programs, 178
soft power, Chinese, 112–14
solar industry, Chinese, 212
South Africa, 85–86, 123–25, 144–45,
    201, 223
South China Sea, 92, 109, 129, 152,
    185, 207–9
South Korea. *See also* tigers and
    tiger cubs
  financial repression in, 35
  reforms following Asian financial
    crisis, 75
  state intervention in, 58–59, 61
sovereign wealth funds (SWFs), 13, 88–
    89, 166–67, 195–96
Soviet Union, state intervention in, 51–
    52. *See also* Russia
State Assets Supervision and
    Administration Commission
    (SASAC), 3
state capitalism. *See also* long-term
    economic future of state capitalism;
    re-emergence of state capitalism;
    success of state capitalism; types of
    state capitalism
  as challenge to free-market
    economics, 22–24
  as continuum, 7–8
  growth of, 15–17
  increased popularity of, 121–25
  reasons for spread of, 19–22
  survival of, in China, 3–7
  understanding, 8–13
state capitalists
  defined, 9–12
  efficient versus inefficient, 32–44
  gaining leverage over, 245–46
  and largest economies in world, 14*fig.*
  preparing for meltdowns of
    autocratic, 236–38
  recommendations for citizens
    of, 230–33
  success or failure of, 17–19
state development banks, 88–89, 200
state intervention
  in Brazil, 116–17

in China, 3
  countries with histories of, 121–25
  in emerging democracies, 128–34
  following Asian financial crisis, 75–77
  history of, 49–63
  increase in, 15, 16
  in Indonesia, 53–54, 117, 201–2
  legitimacy for, 231–32
  promoting growth and innovation
    through, 18
  selective, 232–33
  in South Africa, 201
State-owned Assets Supervision and
    Administration Commission
    (SASAC), 101
state-owned enterprises (SOEs)
  accountability, profitability, and
    transparency of, 216–18
  and Chinese outward investment, 25,
    92, 101
  on Chinese stock markets, 103
  competition with, 167
  control of Chinese, listed on stock
    markets, 102
  co-opting leading talents into, 196–97
  corruption and understanding in
    Vietnamese, 173
  curbing, by enlisting private
    companies in state-capitalist
    nations, 229–30
  and economic reform under Xi, 107
  entrenchment of Chinese, 122
  expansion of Chinese, 108
  funding for, 196, 197
  governments as minority owners
    of, 177
  in Hong Kong, 199
  Indian, 122–23
  industrial output of Chinese, 4
  and labor, environmental, and
    transparency impacts, 218–22
  ownership of Chinese, 3
  performance targeting and Chinese, 31
  versus private companies
    in authoritarian state
    capitalists, 222–24
  profitability of Chinese, 83, 100
  shuttering of bankrupt Chinese, 100

state-owned enterprises (SOEs) (*Cont.*)
  in Singapore, 192–94, 199
  and social welfare programs, 178
  stimulus package given to Chinese, 100
  in Thailand, 195
  unfair advantages given to, 211–16
  as vote banks, 145–46
  as weapons, 151, 152, 203–11, 239–43
state spending, and defining state
    capitalist, 10
Statoil, 148
steel, 212–13
Stiglitz, Joseph, 55
stock markets
  capitalizations of, 87
  Chinese SOEs listed on, 102
  dual classes of shares, 102–3
success of state capitalism. *See also*
    long-term economic future of state
    capitalism
  in China, 178–82
  continuation of state-capitalist model,
    198–202
  long-term, 175–78
  promotion of China model, 182–89
  in Singapore, 189–98
Sudan, 219–20
Suharto, 75
Sukarno, 53–54, 119
Sukarnoputri, Megawati, 118
summits, between China and developing
    nations, 113

Tao Wang, 96–97
technology. *See also* innovation
  development of, 91, 105–6
  of private multinationals, 227–28
  protecting, against theft, 243
  and SOE competition with private-
    sector multinationals, 217
telecommunications, 91, 205, 241–42
Temasek Holdings, 196
Thailand. *See also* tigers and tiger cubs
  Chinese development model and soft
    power in, 113–14
  and corrosive impact of state
    capitalism on democracy,
    138–42, 154–55

efficiency and trade of, 37
locked out of global capital, 87
overthrow of elected autocrats in, 73–74
political freedom in, 62
predatory elites in, 39
and promotion of China model, 186
recovery from Asian financial
    crisis, 75
and re-emergence of state
    capitalism, 65–70
state-owned enterprises in, 195
support for democracy in, 20
Thaksinomics, 66–71
Tiananmen Spring, 52
tigers and tiger cubs, 57–63
Timor-Leste, 148–49
trade
  and efficient state capitalists, 37
  openness to international, 11–12
  punishing violations in, 245–46
  tariffs of tigers and tiger cubs, 60–61
training programs, Chinese, for foreign
    officials, 110–11
Transneft, 44
transparency
  in Indonesia, 120
  and maintaining macroeconomic
    stability, 40–41
  in Norway, 148
  and political decentralization, 149–50
  relaxing policies promoting, 228–29
  of state enterprises, 216, 218–24
Transparency International, 180
Tsai, Kellee, 189
types of state capitalism
  autocrats versus democrats, 27–32
  efficient versus inefficient, 32–44
  posing threats, 47–48
  significance of distinctions
    between, 44–47

Ukraine, 205–6, 241
Unaldi, Serhat, 45–46
United Arab Emirates, 237
United Russia, 111
United States
  call for national infrastructure bank
    in, 200

financial repression in, 34
income inequality in, 181
and promotion of democracy, 247–50
recommendations for, 234–38,
    242–43, 247
relations with, 153–54
security challenges to, 246–47
security presence in Pacific Rim, 184
state intervention in, 50, 56–57
Xi challenges strategic influence
    of, 184–85
Unocal, 219

Venezuela, 171–72
venture capital giants, 227
Vietnam
    desire for alliance with United
        States, 154
    impact of economic collapse of,
        172–74, 237
    PetroVietnam, 91–92
    tensions between China and, 208–9
    ties between Chinese political parties
        and, 111–12
Vinashin, 173

Wang Xiaolu, 7
Wanxiang Group, 106
Washington Consensus
    confidence in, during Asian financial
        crisis, 76, 77
    defined, 54–55
    disillusionment with, 20–21
    proponents of, 55
water treatment, 189–92
Weinstein, Michael, 163
welfare programs, 178

Wen Jiabao, 4–5
Wen Yunchao, 188
Wenfang Tung, 30
White, James, 35–36
Widodo, Joko. See Jokowi
Williamson, John, 54, 77
Winter Olympics (2014), 43–44
Workers Party, 40
World Bank, 176–77, 178
World Economic Forum's *Global
    Competitiveness Report*, 37–38
World Trade Organization (WTO), 84

Xi Jinping
    crackdown on corruption under, 180
    and economic crisis of June 2013, 99
    economic reform under, 1–3, 107
    fights against corruption, 82–83
    and liberalization of equity markets, 5
    and maintenance of Chinese state
        capitalism, 108
    and New Left, 82
    performance targeting and, 31
    political freedom under, 188–89
    and promotion of China model,
        184–85, 186–87
    state capitalism under, 84

Yangzhong Huang, 244
Yevtushenkov, Vladimir, 168–69
Yudhoyono, Susilo Bambang, 117,
    130, 147

Zhou Xiaohong, 189
Zhou Yongkang, 179
Zhu Rongji, 3, 100, 101
Zuma, Jacob, 19, 124–25